THE
RISE AND
OF A
REGENCY DANDY

THE
RISE AND FALL
OF A
REGENCY DANDY

The Life and Times of
Scrope Berdmore Davies

T.A.J. BURNETT

WITH A FOREWORD BY
BEVIS HILLIER

OXFORD UNIVERSITY PRESS
1983

Oxford University Press, Walton Street, Oxford OX2 6DP

London Glasgow New York Toronto
Delhi Bombay Calcutta Madras Karachi
Kuala Lumpur Singapore Hong Kong Tokyo
Nairobi Dar es Salaam Cape Town
Melbourne Auckland

and associated companies in
Beirut Berlin Ibadan Mexico City Nicosia

Oxford is a trade mark of Oxford University Press

First published 1981 by John Murray (Publishers) Ltd
First issued as an Oxford University Press paperback 1983

British Library Cataloguing in Publication Data

Burnett, T. A. J.
The rise and fall of a regency dandy.
—(Oxford paperbacks)
1. Davies, Scrope   2. Byron, George Gordon,
Baron—Friends and associates
I. Title
942.07'3'0924   CT788.D3/
ISBN 0-19-285124-1

Printed in Great Britain by
The Guernsey Press Co. Ltd.
Guernsey, Channel Islands

In memory of

WILLIAM RONALD CUTHBERT QUILTER

25 January 1937 — 22 March 1981

Quantum minus est cum reliquis versari quam tui meminisse

Contents

Acknowledgements   xi

Foreword by Bevis Hillier   1

1 Beginnings   11

2 The Friend of Byron   29

3 Among the Dandies   43

4 The Go-between: Piccadilly and Geneva   97

5 Radicalism and Flight   144

6 Exile   192

A Selection of Letters and Mss found
in the Scrope Davies Trunk   218

Sources   234

Catalogue of the Scrope Davies Papers   239

Index of Correspondents   244

General Index   247

Acknowledgements

The compilation of a list of acknowledgements is at best an invidious business, and it is rendered even more so when the author, as in the present case, has been the recipient of so much and so generous assistance. Someone, however, must be mentioned first, and the place of *primus inter pares* is clearly due to a collateral descendent of 'Scrope the Great', Mr Martin Davies. His idea it was that this book should be written, and he also offered to be a sponsor. Mr Davies has been interested since his schooldays in his illustrious forebear, and the fruits of his researches he has placed freely at my disposal. The other begetter of the book is Mr Christopher Norman-Butler, Local Director of Barclays Bank, who not only discovered Scrope Davies's trunk, but with great public spirit ensured that it should be placed on indefinite loan in the Department of Manuscripts at the British Library. Barclays Bank have also most kindly agreed to act as sponsors. My thanks are also due to Mr Donovan Richnell, sometime Director General of the Reference Division of the British Library, and to Dr Daniel Waley, Keeper of Manuscripts, who agreed that the book should be undertaken, in part at least, as an official assignment. Mr John Murray and Mr John Gibbins have been the most painstaking and encouraging of publishers and editors respectively, and have made many and most profitable suggestions. Dr Judith Chernaik gave me invaluable help in identifying the hands in, and understanding the significance of, the three poetical notebooks of Byron and Shelley. My colleague Mrs Ann Payne has been an unfailingly patient listener to my ramblings while in the agonies of composition, and her perceptive comments have helped to reveal whatever ore of sense was contained in an ever growing mountain of evidence. I am grateful too for the immaculate and incredibly speedy typing of Miss Linda Seale and Mrs Mandy Salvoni, and for the transcripts made by Mrs Megan Price, and to John Murray who has kindly given copyright permission to print a selection of the Byron letters recently found in the Scrope Davies trunk. The index has been prepared by Miss Linda Graham. My gratitude is due to my wife who must often have felt that Scrope Davies, to avoid being 'dodged', had moved into new chambers in her house. Last but by no means least my gratitude is due to Scrope Berdmore Davies himself thanks to whom I have made many new and loyal friends, and who has given us all as much amusement as in the days when Byron, Matthews and Hobhouse 'yielded to [his] dashing vivacity'.

T.A.J.B

Foreword
by Bevis Hillier

We had always known about Scrope Davies in the family — the enjoyably *un*-respectable relation. He had a glamorous pantomime wickedness, like that of Aladdin's uncle. He had been a friend of the most romantic of all poets, Byron, and of the most exquisite of all dandies, Beau Brummell. He was a scholar, a dandy, a womanizer, an ace tennis-player, a manic drinker and a reckless gambler. He squandered his fortune in the best traditions of Victorian melodrama, and met with the approved fate of such wastrels, fleeing abroad and ending his days in penury — though not, like Brummell, in an asylum. (Occasionally he feared he might go the same way: 'Babylon in all its desolation is a sight not so awful as that of the human mind in ruins', he wrote to Thomas Raikes in 1835.) A half-broken figure, he would sit on a bench in the Tuileries garden in Paris, reminiscing to anyone who would listen about the parties and bright lights of Regency London and boasting about the memoirs he claimed to be writing, which would surely be a best-seller.

It was hard to link this raffish character with my paternal grandmother, *née* Davies, who was a direct descendant of Scrope's younger brother Thomas, a Fellow of Merton College, Oxford. (Scrope died an unrepentant bachelor, in spite of Byron's punning suggestion that he should marry 'and beget some Scrooples'.) She was a hard-working, somewhat severe woman, who had brought up a family of six on little money. She was not in the slightest interested in her remote kinsman, beyond speculating sourly that, but for him, we might all have been a sight richer. But one of her sons, my uncle Kenneth Hillier, was interested and began researching into Scrope's ancestors, who seemed mainly to be reproachless parsons. Through a newspaper correspondence about Scrope, my uncle made contact with Mr Martin Davies, a direct descendant of Scrope's eldest brother, John. A Bristol solicitor and a member of the Society of Genealogists, Martin Davies carried my uncle's researches much further. He proved that Scrope's ancestors, and therefore ours, included not only eminent Protestant

1

theologians, such as Pierre du Moulin (1568–1658), the learned Samuel Bochart (1599–1667), and Jean-Maximilien de Baux, Seigneur de L'Angle (1590–1674) but, in one line, John of Gaunt, and hence the royal lineage stretching back through Edward III to William the Conqueror and Alfred the Great.

Martin Davies' family possesses miniatures of Scrope's dour-faced parents, also a painting of Scrope's youngest brother Samuel Decimus (1797–1824), one of the sailors who accompanied Napoleon on his last journey to St Helena in *HMS Northumberland* in 1815. Unfortunately no portrait of Scrope is known to exist, beyond a possible self-portrait sketch in a letter to Byron of June 1809 in John Murray's collection, though it is known that he and Byron exchanged miniatures of each other by James Holmes: that of Byron belongs to Mrs Doris Langley Moore; that of Scrope was last recorded in a Christie's sale of 5 December 1906 and is now lost to view.

It was in 1956 that my uncle and Martin Davies began corresponding. It was exactly twenty years later that the extraordinary discovery was made in the vaults of Barclays Bank, Pall Mall East, London, which was to tell us so much more than we already knew about Scrope, and to form the basis for the fascinating book which follows. I had the privilege and delight of breaking the news of this discovery, in a front page 'scoop' in *The Times*, London, of 20 December 1976. The task fell to me in a roundabout way. In 1971 I had visited Doris Langley Moore the Byron scholar and costume expert who herself had made a notable Byron discovery in the poet's Albanian costume, now at Bowood in Wiltshire. I was seeking her advice over an exhibition of Art Deco I was organising for an American museum. I told her in passing that I was a kinsman of Scrope Davies. I forgot entirely that I had mentioned this – but she did not.

Early in 1976, John Murray, head of the publishing firm, telephoned me. We already knew each other well, as I was writing a book for him and had been at Magdalen College, Oxford, with his son John. I had attended many delightful parties in those fine rooms which Scrope Davies, as well as Byron, must have known so well. 'Jock' Murray said to me: 'Doris Langley Moore says you're a kinsman of Scrope Davies. Will you write down for me everything you know about him, especially about his family and descendants? I'm afraid I can't tell you at this stage what it's all about – but you will know eventually.' I did what he asked, and thought no more about it.

Foreword

On 3 November 1976, I received a letter from Mr Christopher Norman-Butler, director of Barclays Bank at 1 Pall Mall East. Mr Norman-Butler, who himself happens to be a descendant of Thackeray, wrote:

Dear Mr Hillier,

I am sure you will be interested to learn that earlier this year we made an important discovery of literary documents in one of the strongrooms of our 1 Pall Mall East branch. This was a locked trunk deposited by your ancestor, Scrope Berdmore Davies, in 1820, which was found to contain a mass of correspondence from Lord Byron, Thomas Moore, John Cam Hobhouse, Charles Skinner Matthews, Augusta Leigh, etc., together with some important manuscripts of Byron and Shelley poems . . . The papers are being lodged by the Bank on loan with the British Library to protect the possible rights of ownership . . . I am afraid that it will prove extremely complicated and difficult – and perhaps impossible – for such rights to be established, owing to the fact that your ancestor died intestate and without issue in 1852, but any rights of ownership are in no way prejudiced by the papers being on loan with the British Library . . .

Mr Norman-Butler added that he had also written to Martin Davies, and that he and I would be welcome to come to the bank and examine the papers. He also said that he was in touch with Sir Denis Hamilton at *The Times* with whom he was 'coordinating arrangements for breaking the news to the public'. I at once wrote to Sir Denis and suggested that, as I was a kinsman of Scrope Davies, with some prior knowledge of his life, and as, further, I had begun my professional life as a Home News Reporter on *The Times*, I might be allowed to write the account of the discovery for them. Sir Denis Hamilton and the Editor, Mr William Rees-Mogg, agreed to this.

So I now went to the bank in Pall Mall East for my first look at the papers. It was a thrilling occasion. If one had been writing a novel, the circumstances of the discovery could hardly have been more theatrically romantic: a piratical chest of crumbling leather, brass-studded and with a brass plate on top engraved 'Mr Scrope Davies'. Mr Norman-Butler gave me a room on my own in which to study the

3

papers for several days. They included an original manuscript of *Childe Harold's Pilgrimage*, canto III, early versions of Shelley's 'Hymn to Intellectual Beauty' and 'Mont Blanc', with two unpublished poems of Shelley, many unknown letters from Byron, and others from Moore, Hobhouse, Lady Frances Webster and Augusta Leigh. There were also drawings of Napoleon sent home by Samuel Decimus Davies, and sketches and a plan of Longwood, St Helena, showing Napoleon's quarters.

Apart from these valuable papers (*how* valuable, was to be a subject of gloating speculation by the press), there were several of Scrope's betting books and bills on spikes: in the excitement of his first viewing of the papers, Jock Murray pricked his hand on one of them and quipped, 'Wake me up in a hundred years time'. There were invitations from Lord and Lady Holland and the Duke of Wellington; a receipt for gooseberry wine; lists of Latin and English aphorisms, perhaps prepared by Scrope for 'spontaneous' delivery at dinner parties; a bill from his boot-maker, George Hoby, for a pair of tennis shoes and a pair of red slippers; a summons on a debt of £7000; a bill from his shirtmaker, C.H. Hemans, for twelve long cloth shirts (12 gns.) and six Indian muslin handkerchiefs (£3.15s.); and a statement of account from Elphick & Son, late breeches-maker to the Emperor of Russia. Engraved visiting cards bore the names of Mr Murray, Albemarle Street, of Lord Frederick Montague, Berkeley Square, Mr Hanbury Tracy of Dover Street and Rear-Admiral Leveson Gower of 37 Queen Anne Street. The trunk was, in Martin Davies' phrase (much quoted in the press), 'a mini-Pompeii'. He and I tried on Scrope's white kid gloves, which had also been thrown into the chest, and found them a perfect fit.

From Christopher Norman-Butler, I heard more about the discovery of the papers. In 1820 Scrope Davies, like Beau Brummell four years before, had had to leave England in a hurry to escape his gambling creditors and other demands. He stuffed his papers chaotically into the studded leather chest and deposited it with his bankers, Ransom, Morland & Co., one of twenty private banks which came together at the end of the 19th century to form Barclays Bank. In 1976 Barclays were making alterations to 1 Pall Mall East, their principal West End office. In reorganising the premises they took a look at a private deposit vault containing a mass of old deed boxes and papers, which had been deposited more than a century before.

Foreword

Mr Norman-Butler believed that the vault might contain items of historical interest. He asked the bank's archivist to come and open cases, breaking them open where necessary. They worked on the principle that only boxes which had been on deposit and unopened for more than a hundred years, and in which no company or corporate body had rights, might be opened. One chest bore the brass name-plate of Scrope Davies. Mr Norman-Butler said: 'We were not entirely unaware of what the trunk might contain because Byron banked at 1 Pall Mall East, and we knew that Davies was a friend of his.' (Byron frequently wrote to the Hon. Douglas Kinnaird, senior partner of Ransom, Morland & Co., and 1 Pall Mall East is now called Kinnaird House.) 'We thought we might be on to something good', Mr Norman-Butler said, 'but we had no idea of what was going to be in the box until we opened it. We were absolutely staggered. To obtain confirmation of what we thought we had discovered, we consulted the Secretary of the Royal Commission on Historical Manu-scripts, Mr Davis, saying that we wished to lend the papers to the British Library.'

Mr Davis suggested that the bank get in touch with Jock Murray as Murrays had been Byron's publishers. The first work of verification was done by the bank's former archivist, Mr A.N. Harrison, Jock Murray and Dr Daniel Waley of the British Library. One difficulty was the legal ownership. The bank made a search at Somerset House which showed that Davies had not left a will and that a grant of administration had been made to his eldest sister, Isabella. On Jock Murray's advice the bank wrote to Martin Davies and myself.

The value of the papers was hard to assess. Considering that the manuscript of Byron's *Beppo* had fetched £55,000 at Sotheby's earlier in 1976, I suggested in *The Times* that the value of the papers could be assessed at between £250,000 and £500,000. By the evening of the day my article appeared, the figure of £1m. was already being bandied about the press, and by the next day was taken as a certainty by newspapers and by the television broadcasters, who persistently called Scrope 'Scroap'. (In fact his Christian name – one of the ancient family names of England, which appears in Shakespeare plays – rhymes with 'soup', not with 'soap'.)

Martin Davies and I decided at an early stage that we would make no attempt to claim the papers. We thought it right that they should be permanently accessible to the public in the British Library. That did not prevent a number of surprising claimants from springing up. The present Lord Byron, cabling from Australia, said he thought the papers were his by right. Scrope Davies' old Cambridge college library at King's felt they had a moral claim to the papers because King's had given Scrope a roof over his head during his disreputable tenure of his Fellowship there, and a number of amiable lunatics presented their claims. Jock Murray, who like Martin Davies and myself had no intention of putting in a claim, said that if the Byron papers belonged to anybody, it was to John Murray as the 'sole legal representative of the Late Lord Byron' and because John Murray II had bought Byron's copyrights.

However, the papers were brought to the British Library by horse-drawn coach, where a beaming Lord Eccles (Chairman of the British Library Board) received the battered trunk on the colonnade from the Deputy Chairman of Barclays Bank, while press flash-bulbs popped. There the papers have remained, and there I hope they will remain.

The press had a field day — several field days — over the papers. I took a professional interest in seeing how quickly my rather deadpan original story was mangled and mutilated and megaphoned. Apart from the enormous sums of money postulated, the *Daily Mail* conferred most improbable Holy Orders on Scrope, calling him the Rev. Scrope Davies throughout. Scrope, one feels, would have been the most speedily unfrocked parson in the history of the Church.

The cartoonists also enjoyed themselves hugely. In *The Times* 'Marc' (Mark Boxer) showed a harassed bank manager with his hand over the telephone receiver, telling his assistant: 'It's his shirtmakers, demanding compound interest.' Osbert Lancaster, in the *Daily Express,* showed Maudie Littlehampton examining a compromising Byron letter from the trunk and saying to her husband, 'But Willy, darling, you've never told me that your great-great-grandmother had even *met* Lord Byron.' 'Jon' portrayed Mr Healey (then Chancellor of the Exchequer) being told by a Bank of England official, 'Sorry, sir, the only manuscripts in our vault are IOUs and some poems by Mary Wilson.' 'Chic' in the *Evening News* had a bank manager composing an 'Ode to a Persistent Overdraft'. 'Mac' in the *Daily Mail* drew two bank robbers refusing money pushed through the grille by a cowering bank clerk, and demanding 'old love poems' instead.

The drawing that amused me most was not meant to be funny.

Foreword

Harper's magazine in America commissioned a Chinese girl to illustrate a brilliant article on the Davies papers by Richard Holmes, the biographer of Shelley. She drew the trunk and the tattered papers and the notebook containing *Childe Harold*, canto III, faithfully enough. But, misinterpreting the paragraph in which I recorded that the trunk contained a *bill* for red slippers, she added a pair of very 1970s leather slippers to the contents spilling out of the chest.

The Guardian, meanwhile, made mock of the newly discovered Shelley sonnet 'To Laughter' — admittedly a youthful and immature work — with a parody headed 'Bysshe shot':

> Bysshe, we are past condolence who believed
> Thee wedded to the higher forms of art,
> Brother to Keats, dear to the bleeding heart
> Of Byron, and are roughly undeceived.
> Shorn of the skill to scan, thy fickle muse
> Gave thee an extra line to compensate.
> Can it be thine? Or did some reprobate
> Impostor seek thine honour to abuse?
> Sonnet to Laughter? Wherein lies the joke?
> Who slaps his thighs and helpless falls about?
> Or was it bitterness thy verse ground out,
> Nor mirth but melancholia that spoke?
> Yet dead thou art and, poesy or prank,
> The secret died with thee in Barclays Bank.

At least one newspaper provided some unintended humour when it printed the first line of 'To Laughter' as 'Thy friends were never mine, tho' heartily fined' instead of '. . . thou heartless fiend'.

All this was good fun, and a boon to jaded journalists in the pre-Christmas silly season. But behind the ribaldry and extravagant guesses lurked some real questions. Of what value to scholars were the newly discovered papers? What did they reveal of Davies, Byron and Shelley?

Though he was perhaps the most intimate of all Byron's friends, Davies has remained until now a shadowy figure. Others of Byron's circle had direct descendants to keep their names green. John Cam Hobhouse (later Lord Broughton) somewhat disapproved of Byron's and Davies' rakehell ways and, as the newly discovered Byron letters show, was held in less affection than Davies by Byron. Yet a book (no

Foreword

doubt justified by his more distinguished career) has been devoted to
him – *My Friend H* by Michael Joyce (1948). The only longish
accounts of Scrope's life until the present book were a few paragraphs
by the unreliable 19th-century memoirist Captain R. H. Gronow and
chapters in *Beaten Paths and Those Who Trod Them* by Thomas Colley
Grattan, published by Chapman & Hall in 1865, and in *Eight Friends
of the Great* by William Prideaux Courtney, published by Constable &
Co. in 1910.

In January 1816 Byron thus dedicated his poem 'Parisina': 'To
Scrope Berdmore Davies Esq. the following poem is inscribed by one
who has long admired his talents and valued his friendship.' Benjamin
Disraeli who hero-worshipped Byron (even taking over his rooms in
Albany and his servant) and may either have known Davies or heard
reminiscences of him, borrowed his Christian names for a character in
Vivian Grey, Sir Berdmore Scrope. After that, Scrope's name sank into
near-oblivion.

Even so, leading writers on Byron have recognized his importance
in the Byron set. Peter Quennell in *Byron: the Years of Fame* (1935)
wrote of 'Davies, whose "dashing vivacity", whose hard-headed
devil-may-care cynicism made an agreeable contrast to the strain of
diffidence, of morbid, almost feminine sensibility that ran through
and pervaded Byron's nature. He admired and envied such masculine
recklessness.' I like this image of my kinsman – a sort of Regency
Bulldog Drummond – but it was based, perhaps, on rather flimsy
evidence. Even now, we do not know enough about Scrope to talk
about him in such assertively confident terms.

Mrs Langley Moore also had something to say of Davies. In *The Late
Lord Byron*, she suggested that Scrope may have been the friend of
Byron who approached Augusta Leigh in May 1824, the month after
Byron's death, with the proposal of writing his life. More tantalis-
ingly, she wrote of Davies, in the same book: 'He is known to have set
down, in his latter years, very voluminous recollections of his friends
which have never come to light. It may be that in some French
library, some village or provincial town, a delightful verbal portrait of
Byron by one who saw him both in grief and gaiety remains to be
discovered.'

The Davies papers were not allowed to languish in the British
Library. A selection of them was quickly put on show to the public;
and a British Library scholar, Mr Tim Burnett, undertook the task of

8

researching into them. The result has been this, the first book (and perhaps the last) to be published on Davies.

It is a masterly treatment of the subject. Mr Burnett's task was not easy. Even with the contents of the chest, our knowledge of Scrope is still rather limited. While meticulous in his investigation of facts, Mr Burnett belongs to that breed of scholar which is not afraid to speculate intelligently. He even considers (and rejects) the possibility that Scrope might have been homosexual. He has had to immerse himself in the arcana of Regency England, rather as a 'method' actor allows himself to be commandeered by the part he is playing. A man who works under the same roof as chaste classical marbles and monkish illuminations, he has had to become an expert on unsavoury financial dealings, on the game of hazard (ancestor of the modern 'craps'), on the Turf in the early 19th century, Regency clubland, gunsmiths and slang and the codes used by noblemen in their diaries to indicate sexual escapades.

His book succeeds triumphantly on three counts. First, it shows Scrope as the friend – the blood-brother, almost – of Byron. With Scrope, Byron could laugh at the old-womanish scoldings which the intermittently pious Hobhouse administered. As with all great friends, their foibles were part of their attraction for each other. And in his palmiest days Scrope was (as Byron admitted) more than a match for the poet in the verbal duel of wits: Byron even pirated one of his *bon mots* in a poem.

Second, Tim Burnett brings out fully Scrope's characteristic role as a go-between – a role for which his detachment, his 'dandy impassivity', well qualified him. He took on the thankless task of interceding between Byron and his wife. He was a literary go-between, too, a courier of cantos. He was a carrier, but not a victim, of that epidemic disease of the early 19th century, the Romantic Agony. He was immune from its fevers himself, as Byron wryly observed after their great friend Matthews was drowned in 1811. 'Scrope Davies has been here,' he wrote to Hobhouse on 30 August, 'and seemed as much affected by late events, as could be expected from one who has lived so much in the world.' In politics too – and this is another respect in which Mr Burnett's book is full of new insights – Scrope maintained his usual urbane detachment, obliging his friends by canvassing here, or chairing a meeting there, without sharing their passionate conviction. He stayed on the outer fringes of the inner councils. His brief

Foreword

appearance in the arena of politics has brought him to the notice of historians who do not usually take into account the dandy friends of dissolute poets. It earned him three glancing mentions in *The Philosophic Radicals: Nine Studies in Theory and Practice, 1817–1841* by William Thomas (Clarendon Press, 1979). Mr Thomas's treatment of the subject is forensic and profound; but Mr Burnett amplifies Thomas's account with beguiling personal detail. One of the most evocative passages in the book describes the 'rustic summer' Scrope and his cronies spent with Sir Francis Burdett at Ramsbury, where Scrope trolled out songs with the Misses Burdett and for once was out-witted, by Thomas Moore. Like Byron, Burdett found Hobhouse somewhat prosy, if not actually a dull dog, and was openly relieved when Scrope arrived to enliven the party.

Finally, Tim Burnett gives us the Age of Scrope. Not every Regency male was a buck, rake or dandy: but these men, with a pleasure-loving prince at their head, set the tone, in much the same way as interior decorators, couturiers and photographers (with their own sympathetic Prince of Wales) would a century later. The definitive *zeitgeist* was their creation. A nursery like the Eton described so vividly by Mr Burnett was unlikely to loose tame, demure young men on the world. The Cambridge where Scrope and Byron first met did nothing to check the ardent strain. The young men had their hour; by the mid-19th century, those who had not perished already were landed gasping on the strand of Victorian morality — terrible old figures, bogeymen to the young, antique rouged roués like Lord Steyne in *Vanity Fair*, which appeared four years before Scrope Davies died. Even in his last years, Scrope, wizened, name-dropping and still trotting out his pet and pat quotations, remained faithful to his age, still playing the part which history expected of him.

BEVIS HILLIER

1

Beginnings

Scrope Berdmore Davies was born towards the end of 1782 at Horsley in Gloucestershire, of which parish his father Richard Davies was the Vicar. On New Year's Day 1783 he was baptised, his sonorous forenames being derived from his late maternal grandfather, the Reverend Dr Scrope Berdmore, Vicar of St Mary's Nottingham, himself the son of the Reverend Samuel Berdmore and his wife Martha Scrope. Scrope Davies' father had been born in 1747 at Caio, Carmarthenshire, the son of a tenant farmer.[1] He had entered the Church, and after serving as curate at Caio and at Tewkesbury, had been presented by the Bishop of Gloucester to the Vicarage of Horsley in 1774. In 1792 he was elected to the Vicarage of Tetbury, and held both livings until his death in 1825. His seems to have been the tranquil existence one would expect for a country parson who lived in the age of Jane Austen.

Scrope was the second son in a family of six sons and four daughters. Such evidence as we have indicates that he remained on good terms with his family, though he can have had little enough in common with most of them. With two of his brothers, however, he maintained closer contact. The next to himself in seniority, Thomas, was at Eton with him, and thence proceeded to Merton College, Oxford. Despite — though it is probably naive to use the qualification — being a Fellow of that Society and in Holy Orders too, Thomas seems to have been something of a rogue, and may even at one time have adorned a debtors' prison. Certain it is that his name is joined with Scrope's in countless documents which concern the raising of loans.

Scrope's youngest brother, Samuel Decimus, passed a life which, while short, was as full of incident as his own. During his service as a

---

1 Venn's *Alumni Cantabrigienses* is incorrect in giving Scrope's father's name as David. Foster's *Alumni Oxonienses* is incorrect in all details there given as to the parentage, age and academic record of the Rev. Richard Davies. These errors are perpetuated in W.P. Courtney's otherwise excellent chapter on Scrope Davies in *Eight Friends of the Great* (1910).

midshipman in the Royal Navy he took part in the burning of the city of Washington in 1814, and was on the *Northumberland* when she conveyed Napoleon to exile in St Helena the next year. He wrote a spirited account of each of these events which were preserved in Scrope's trunk, and are printed in the anthology. Scrope took an interest in his brother's career, and made him an annual allowance of £40. Samuel Decimus' other letters, in which he fervently desires to rise in the service, thanks Scrope for his help, and explains how hard it is to make ends meet, are pathetic reading when we remember that Scrope the gambler was winning or losing in an evening more than his brother could hope to earn in a lifetime. Samuel Decimus died in Jamaica on 8 December 1824, two weeks after accepting promotion to Master's Mate, and without ever reaching the longed-for rank of Lieutenant.

The family of Scrope's mother was quite distinguished in the academic and ecclesiastical sphere. It had supplied two other vicars of St Mary's Nottingham in addition to his grandfather, and a Master of the Charterhouse. There was also a first cousin of his mother's who directed in his will that his epitaph should read 'acquired an ample and liberal fortune by Tooth Drawing'. The family had found this indelicate. The memorial tablet itself bears the words 'By the Profession of Dentist'. When Scrope had become an ornament of society, the intimate of Lord Byron and Beau Brummell, he was to find this picturesque connection the source of something less than pride. Writing to their mutual friend John Cam Hobhouse in January 1809 Byron confided:

I have lately discovered Scrope's genealogy to be ennobled by a collateral tie with the Beardmore, Chirurgeon and Dentist to Royalty, and that the town of Southwell contains cousins of Scrope, who disowned them, (I grieve to speak it) on visiting that city in my society. — How I found out I will disclose, the first time 'we three meet again' but why did he conceal his lineage, 'ah my dear H! it was *cruel,* it was *insulting,* it was unnecessary!

Of Scrope's early childhood nothing is recorded. The first event of which we have knowledge was that which was, for good or for evil, to shape the rest of his life. His mother's brother, Scrope Berdmore the younger, had been a King's Scholar at Eton from 1755 to 1763, proceeding thence to Merton College, Oxford, of which he was

Beginnings

Warden from 1790–1810. Inspired by the example, Scrope's father secured him a nomination for a King's Scholarship, and he was duly elected. Not that election was difficult. The only qualification was the ability to reply, in Latin, to the questions, also couched in Latin, 'What is your name and surname?' 'How old are you?' 'What was the day and month of your birth?' 'From what village or town do you come?' and 'In what country?' Some easy Greek and Latin then had to be construed.

Since Eton must have shared to a large extent in the formation of Scrope Davies, it may well be revealing to examine the strange institution that it was in his time, and to trace what we can of his career. Eton turned the simple clergyman's son into a wit, a dandy and a scholar with the entrée to the grandest drawing-rooms of London. At the same time it made him a gambler, a drunkard and a spendthrift who ended his days in ruin. Of even greater interest, however, than the reflections naturally excited by this moral balance sheet is the fact that it moulded a man who won the affection and admiration of Lord Byron, and who shared with the poet not a few of the vicissitudes of his life.

The situation of a King's Scholar at the end of the 18th century, a time when Eton, in common with most other English educational establishments, had sunk to its nadir, was paradoxical. On the one hand, by securing a Scholarship a boy was almost certainly set up for life. King's College, Cambridge, the sister foundation of the royal architect, the saintly Henry VI, had a foundation of seventy Fellows and Scholars taken together, the numbers of each class not being fixed. All the Scholars had by statute to be drawn from the ranks of the Scholars of Eton. Moreover, Scholars of King's were by ancient custom exempt from University examinations and after three years residence almost invariably became Fellows for life. A boy elected to a Scholarship at Eton had therefore a good chance of passing a secure and comfortable existence as a Fellow of King's or, should he wish to marry, as the incumbent of one or more college livings.

On the other hand, the conditions in College, that part of Eton reserved for the Scholars, were so appalling that even the most hard-hearted parents hesitated to subject their children to them. The result was foreseeable. In 1799, when Scrope was at the top of the fifth-form and his brother Thomas, also a Scholar, was about half-way up, there were only forty-eight Scholars out of the possible

13

seventy, and in the next year the number reached its lowest ever, forty-three. The only incentive to become a Colleger, as the Scholars were generally called, was that King's College Fellowship at the end. In order to achieve this while minimising the sufferings of their unhappy boys many parents would allow them to remain Oppidans (boys who were not Scholars) until the age of sixteen (the statutes permitting boys who were 'specially well read' to become Scholars up to the age of seventeen), and transferred them into College at the last possible moment. Scrope was not so fortunate. On the evidence of the list of Baptismal Certificates preserved at the school, he seems to have entered College in September 1794, at the age of eleven.

Well might a boy abandon hope who entered there. The surroundings, the routine and the diet that confronted Scrope on his arrival at Eton must have struck terror into the boy from a quiet country vicarage. Here indeed was the other face of the 18th century, the face unglimpsed in Jane Austen's novels, brutal, filthy and corrupt. Henry VI's intention that the Collegers should be housed round a spacious quadrangle was never fulfilled, and the boys were crammed into the original late 15th-century school building, embattled and picturesque from outside, but very different within. The upper storey contained the infamous Long Chamber, a plain room 172 feet long, 27 feet wide and 15½ feet high. This was the sole dormitory for the Collegers until early in the 18th century, when Thomas Carter, the Usher, or Lower Master, moved into a private residence, and gave up his quarters at the east end of Long Chamber. This increase in accommodation was lamentably offset by the consequent ending of any form of supervision. The Provost and Fellows had wisely ordained in 1661 that the Master and Usher should 'lodge in their chambers at the ends of the Long Chamber, to prevent disorders', but henceforward, the Head Master having long since departed to more luxurious quarters, between the hours of 8 o'clock at night, when they were locked in, and 7 o'clock the next morning when they were released by the Head Master's servant the boys were left totally to their own devices. No master even slept in the same building, and how, in the course of rather more than a century, there was not a disaster resulting from fire it is impossible to imagine. The total lack of privacy combined with this want of control not only meant that study was virtually impossible, but also resulted in cruel bullying and sexual malpractices.

Beginnings

The College provided no breakfast and no tea, while dinner invariably consisted of roast mutton and mashed potatoes, the latter being withdrawn in the season when they were too small to mash. The quantities were so inadequate that the wretched Collegers were, and still are, known to the Oppidans as 'Tugs', an abbreviation of 'Tug-Mutton'. He who tugged least ate least, and the smallest boys subsisted on bread dipped into cold gravy. Beer was also provided, but an old Colleger wrote 'I do not think — writing as I do calmly some eighty years after — that any beverage was ever so vile, villainous, and detestable . . .' Supper was dinner's mutton served cold, but few availed themselves of it, preferring to make their own arrangements elsewhere. As a result a quantity of scraps was left lying in Long Chamber which was devoured during the night by the rats which infested it in large numbers. The same old Colleger wrote 'They came out in troops, well fed and wary, and were heard scurrying about the fireplaces, and up and down all night long.' The hunting of these rats (at one time they were carefully skinned when caught, and the skins nailed up above the fireplaces), together with drinking (supplies were thrust through the bars of one of the windows by a man from the local inn), fighting and gambling formed the principal amusements of the Collegers during the hours of their nightly imprisonment.

It must not be supposed, however, that everything about Scrope's new situation was black. His surroundings were venerable and beautiful, and he had the prospect of a comfortable academic career before him. The teaching, while confined almost exclusively to the Classics, was probably as good as could be obtained, and his companions and classmates included members of the oldest, noblest and most powerful families in the land. What was more, the proximity of Windsor Castle and the great fondness of George III for Eton meant that Scrope's sovereign was a familiar and frequent sight. The world of rank and fashion, of politics and power was revealed at first hand to the boy from rustic Tetbury. Moreover, with the passage of time, servitude was exchanged for privilege, and the wretched fag became the master of three or four such. With so many attentive valets and footmen dirt and squalor could be left behind for elegance and something approaching luxury.

Among the more surprising items found in Scrope Davies' trunk were an almost complete set of half-yearly bills sent to his father from Eton on account of Scrope and his younger brother Thomas, covering the years 1796–1802. Eton boys' bills are not unknown, indeed the earliest extant was sent to Sir Gilbert Dethick, Garter King of Arms during the reign of Mary Tudor. The Davies brothers' bills, however, are detailed, and by a stroke of luck one of Scrope's is supported by individual bills from the many tradesmen in the High Street. They enable us to gain a glimpse of the boys' everyday life, and its cost to their father. Scrope's earliest preserved bill reads as follows:

Mrs Harrington's Bill to Xmas 1796

195   Mr Davies

half a year in College 26 Decr 1796	5- 5-
addition for candles in college	5- 3
omitted it in the last half year	5- 3
Dr Heath	2- 2-
Mr Keate	4- 4-
small school expenses	5-11
Care of bed and desk 2/- bedmaker 2/-	4-
man attending long chamber 1/- waterman 2-6	3- 6
shoes cleaning	10- 6
shoes mending	2- 9
boughs and brooms in July	1-
Money home in Aug.st	1- 5-
man to carry trunk	1-
parcel 1/2 letters 1/7	2- 9
money the 14th Oct^r	2- 6
subscription to Walkers lectures	1- 1-
man attending long chamber	1-
extra washing	18- 6
allowance 14 weeks	14-
servants	10- 6
	18- 5- 5

Pitt	1- 3- 4	
Charters	8- 9	
Egelstone	2-	
Miller	18- 3	
Atkins	14- 4	
Brads	4- 8	
	3-11- 4	3-11- 4
		21-16- 9

Beginnings

Mrs Sarah Harrington had been a 'dame' since 1787, and was to act in that capacity for both Scrope and his brother.[2] It is interesting to see that even Collegers' bills did not emanate from the school itself. Despite the Founder's injunction to the contrary, it appears that Mr Davies was required to pay five guineas a half year to the College, two guineas to the Head Master, Dr Heath, and four guineas to Scrope's tutor, Mr Keate.

George Heath, known to the boys as 'Ascot Heath' after the racecourse with which they were no doubt familiar, was appointed Head Master in 1792. He was a strict disciplinarian, and on one occasion is said to have flogged seventy boys at one session, if that is the word, administering ten strokes to each. As a result 'he was laid up with aches and pains for more than a week'. In 1798 he gave fifty-two boys 'a round dozen each'. Despite these severities he quite failed to suppress the driving of tandems around Eton and Windsor, and on two occasions during Scrope's time at Eton virtually the whole school failed to appear for Absence. On the first occasion they preferred to attend the first ever cricket match between two public schools, Eton against Westminster, and on the second they made an excursion by boat up the river to Maidenhead.

John Keate was to become the most famous Head Master of Eton in all its long history. He achieved this not as a great reformer or benefactor, but by adopting an extremely harsh and menacing tone towards the boys, and by a fondness for the birch which has passed into legend. The occasion is still recalled at Eton when Keate confused the list of those to be confirmed with that of those to be punished, and flogged the confirmands with a will reinforced by their apparently blasphemous protestations. A. W. Kinglake left a marvellous sketch of Keate:

> He was a little more (if more at all) than five feet in height, and was not very great in girth, but in this space was concentrated the pluck of ten battalions. He had a really noble voice, which he could modulate with great skill, but he also had the power of quacking like an angry duck, and he almost always adopted this mode of communication in order to inspire respect; he was a capital scholar, but his ingenuous learning had *not* 'softened his manners'; and *had*

2 Oppidans lodged with landladies known as dames. Even Collegers needed a dame. She provided washing facilities, breakfast, and a room in which they could be nursed when sick.

'permitted them to be fierce' — tremendously fierce; he had the most complete command over his temper — I mean over his *good* temper — which he scarcely ever allowed to appear: you could not put him out of humour — that is, out of the *ill*-humour which he thought to be fitting for a headmaster.

Yet Keate was at heart a kind man, and when teaching a small number of boys, such as the sixth form, he was accounted a brilliant exponent of the classics. Scrope was, therefore, unusually lucky to be placed under such a tutor, though he may not always have appreciated it at the time.

One of the items in Scrope's bill reveals an attempt to broaden the curriculum. One guinea was charged as a subscription to 'Walkers lectures'. Adam Walker, who lived from around 1731 to 1821, was originally a schoolmaster at Macclesfield, and later a travelling lecturer in Natural Philosophy, what would nowadays be called Science. In 1778 he was persuaded by Joseph Priestley to give lectures in London, and after this did so every winter. Edward Barnard, Provost of Eton from 1765 to 1781, invited him to lecture there, and this example was followed by Westminster, Winchester and other schools.

Most of the other items on the bill are self-explanatory, but some require elucidation. Candles for the occupants of Long Chamber were supplied by the Dame, and had to be fetched from her house. Even candlesticks were not provided, and these were fashioned out of the cover of a book bent double, with a hole cut through the centre. The watermen supervised the boys' bathing in the river. According to a writer who was for a time in College with Scrope, though a few years younger, they were 'excellent swimmers, men appointed by the head master, such as Shampo Carter and others [who were] always on the spot to prevent any accident, and [were] regularly paid by the boys for that purpose'. 'Shampo' also hired out boats. Skewered on one of four spikes found in Scrope's trunk was a bill from him to 'Mr Davies Major' for 'the use of Boats & c.' from 11 March to 13 July 1802, in the sum of £1-8-9. On that occasion payment was not so regular. The receipt is dated February 20th 1804. The writer mentioned above also explains the mysterious item 'boughs and brooms in July'. Electiontide, at the end of July, was the season when the Provost of King's, accompanied by two of the Fellows, would travel from Cambridge to

Beginnings

Eton in a yellow coach drawn by four horses in order to assist his brother of Eton in the election of Scholars to the two foundations. There was always a great influx of visitors at that time, and it was realised, to quote another Colleger who was there from 1811 to 1822, that Long Chamber's 'daily garb and general appearance was neither inviting of itself, nor to the credit of the Authorities'. Two courses were adopted fraudulently to disguise this fact. Firstly, for a week previous to Election Saturday, the day the party from King's arrived, the occupants of Long Chamber indulged in the custom of 'rug-riding':

> Some lower boys' rugs are tied up at one end, in which a bolster is placed, and to the other end of it a rope is affixed; an upper boy then takes his seat, and a certain number of other boys are fagged to run up and down Long Chamber, with as great speed as possible; this continuing for a week, it is scarcely possible to conceive the beautiful gloss which the old oak boards receive: the space between the bedsteads is also scrubbed with hard brushes, to correspond with the other . . .

> [Secondly,] on the Thursday previous [to Election Saturday], waggon loads of beech boughs, from the College woods, are brought, with which the whole of the chamber is decorated, from one end to the other. On the Saturday morning, green rugs, with the College arms, are placed on every bedstead. Company is then admitted to view it, and really it is a very pleasing sight – a complete vista of foliage: and considering the moving scene between, the Captain's bed at the top of the chamber, surmounted by a handsome Flag, the boys in their gowns, and the fragrance of the boughs, render it almost a magical delusion – in short, it is a magical delusion, in comparison with the appearance which the dormitory exhibits, without the assistance of these extraordinary supplies.

It is sad to reflect that not only were the parents and friends of the boys subjected to this fraud, but were also, as Scrope's bill shows, expected to pay for it. One shilling was not a great sum, but the charge reveals yet again the cynicism of the governing body.

The names at the foot of the bill are those of tradesmen in the town. Pitt was a draper, while Charters seems to have been a haberdasher, but also sold soap and toothbrushes. Egelstone was a hatter, Miller a

19

tailor, and Atkins a shoemaker. Brads seems, appropriately enough, to have been a carpenter or handyman. His bills relate to the repair of various items of furniture. It is amusing to see that there is no bill from Pote, the bookseller.

For that half-year to December 1796 the Rev. Mr Davies had escaped with a bill of only £21-16-9, College and tradesmen together, perhaps £1500 by today's prices, though the equivalents are hard to calculate. As Scrope got into his stride, however, and rose to be a swell in the sixth form his father's liabilities more than trebled. On 21 August 1800 Mrs Harrington wrote

> Sir I enclose your Gentlemens acc^{ts} which I apologise for not sending by them, but I was from home on account of my health — I hope they arrived safe and are enjoying their holidays. My regards to them wth best comp^{ts} to Mrs Davies — I am Sir Your truly Obligd and Obd^r S Harrington. The trades peoples bills I keep to send with the Gentlemen at Xmas.

Mrs Harrington's indisposition seems to have worked to our advantage. It is the 'trades peoples bills' which she proposed to send at Christmas which alone have survived.

The tradesmen's bills give an interesting picture of the boy's standard of personal hygiene, and his attention to dress. Scrope's bill with M.A. Charters in 1799 reveals him buying a piece of soap on 21 July, 15 September, 10 October and 16 November, all at 1/-. A toothbrush was purchased on 1 December for 6d. In the course of the next seven months he bought of William Smith a hair-brush and soap for 1/7 on 17 Jan, a toothbrush on 9 February, soap on the 25th, the same on 22 March, 'Spences tooth powder', a toothbrush and more soap on 11 May, a nail-brush and comb on 4 June, and another piece of soap on the 22nd. It appears that the new standards of personal cleanliness often credited to Brummell were surprisingly quick to catch on among schoolboys, not usually believed to be a fastidious tribe. It may be, however, that Scrope was already an exception in this respect. Of William Smith he also bought woollen, kid and other gloves in 1800, often when he went there for a haircut. This service was performed on 29 January, 27 February, 23 March, 24 April (on which occasion Scrope also had a shave for 4d.), 5 May, and 4 June (the King's birthday).

Many of Scrope's purchases in 1800 reflect his new status as a

Beginnings

sixth-former. He entered sixth form at the beginning of the Lent Half as the Etonian term is called and on 22 January he went to Pennington's and bought a tea-pot for 1/6, a cream-pot for 1/-, a coffee-pot for 2/-, six coffee-cups for half-a-crown, together with six cups and saucers, six plates, six knives and six spoons for a total of 13/-. The whole bill came to £1-3-0. Clearly he intended to do some entertaining in the study for which he paid the Headmaster £1 per half-year, the room being surplus to that worthy's requirements. On the same day Scrope bought a 'Pair of Pearl Sleeve Buttons' for 9d at Smith's, where, three days earlier he had invested in a 'Pair of Best Silk Elastic Braces with Morocco Straps' at 7/-. Altogether that January he ran up bills amounting to £4-9-10½d. In the first half of the year 1800 he spent £35-1-6d to the benefit of Eton High Street, approximately £2,600 at today's prices, surely a formidable sum for a schoolboy.

The principal area of expenditure, as might be expected, was clothes. Scrope seems often to have bought the materials himself and had them made up by the tailor, though on some occasions the latter's bill includes the price of cloth. Between 26 November 1799 and 27 February 1800 he bought fifteen items from John March, the draper, including six yards of 'Huccaback' at 11/-, a yard of 'blue and buff Toilinett' [3] for the same price, two yards of 'Cotton buck^m Silk and twist' at 4/4d, 'Buttons Canvas tape thread' 10d., '5 yds. silk binding & Silk' £1-1/-, '1 yd printed India Dimity' 7/-, and '1 ⅜ yds Flannell' 3/2½d. Huckaback was a stout linen with a rough surface, used for towels, and even tablecloths. Toilinet was a fine woollen cloth, used for waistcoats. Dimity was a stout cotton fabric, woven with raised stripes or figures, and again was probably intended for a waistcoat.

James Miller, the tailor, submitted a bill of thirteen guineas for the period between 30 November 1799 and 15 July 1800, consisting of forty-nine items. Among them were the following, a touching mixture of schoolboy repairs and dandy finery:

4 Dec	Seating & Mend breeches & Covered buttons	0- 1-8
12 Dec	Making a Coat Lappold button sleve	
	Crimp Coller	0- 8-6
	Spunging a Coat	0- 1-6
16 Dec	Coat 6 brest Gilt buttons & all trimmings	
	Velvat Colar	0-13-6

3 Beau Brummell's morning dress included a blue coat and a buff waistcoat.

17 Jan	Mend breeches & Coverd & Mettel buttons	0- 1-0
31 Jan	Making breeches & Coverd buttons	0- 5-0
3 Feb	Mend a Coat	0- 0-9
4 Feb	Making Under Wastcoat faced	0- 2-6
25 Feb	Grafting & Mend a Coat	0- 2-0
	Mend a Gownd & Cloth	0- 1-2
28 March	Mend a Coat & New Coller	0- 2-0
	5 Nales of Velvet	0- 5-0

A 'nail' was a measure of length for cloth, equalling $2\frac{1}{4}$ inches, or the sixteenth part of a yard. 'Mend breeches' recurs on 8 March, 20 March (kneeing & Mend breeches), 21 May, 31 May, 28 June, 5 July and 11 July. Leaving aside repairs, new clothes that Scrope had had made during the period were five waistcoats, four coats, six pairs of breeches, and two gowns.

Two other items give glimpses of Scrope's life. On 11 June is the entry 'Making panterlunes In to breeches & Coverd buttons 0-4-6'. Collegers were forbidden to wear trousers, and this was strictly enforced, even though Oppidans might wear what they pleased. Apart from this ordinance, and the wearing of gowns by Collegers, there was no suggestion of uniform at that date. Scrope's bills reflect the ordinary civil dress of the period. On 9 May appears the item 'Making a Cricket Jacket dubbel brested 0-5-6'. Scrope was accounted a notable cricketer by his contemporaries, and had already played for Eton against Westminster at Lords in 1799 (the famous series of annual matches against Harrow, for whom Byron played, did not begin until 1805). On that occasion he had been one of the opening batsmen, but had been bowled out for a duck by Agar. The match was abandoned when Westminster were 13 for 5 wickets. Eton had managed 47 all out, having gone in first. The betting, for the bookies were not expelled from Lords until 1817, had been 5-to-4 on Eton. The next year, resplendent in his new 'Cricket Jacket', Scrope fared somewhat better. Once again he was an opening bat, and had scored 11 when he was run out. Eton beat Westminster by an innings and 128 runs. Scrope's final appearance for Eton against Westminster at Lord's was on 31 July 1801. Yet again he opened, scoring 21 in the first innings before he was run out (he was either unlucky in his partners, or somewhat rash), and 1 in the second, being bowled by Ecles. Ecles was no doubt glad to get his revenge, for he had been caught by Scrope in Westminster's first innings. Nevertheless Eton, once again the favourites at 5-to-3 on, won by 129 runs.

The latest bill from Eton is that submitted by the 'Christopher' for the period from 7 November 1801 to some time in the middle of June 1802. The 'Christopher' was an inn that stood right in the middle of Eton, almost opposite the College Chapel. Although strictly speaking out of bounds, it was in fact extensively patronised by the boys, who could always pretend that they had called there to collect a parcel. The pot-boy from the 'Christopher' it was who used to thrust liquid supplies through the bars of Lower Chamber to the Collegers within during their nightly incarceration. The deficiencies of the College diet have been described. Scrope's bill shows how they were made up. The total amount of the bill is £38-10-11d, but of this £30-2-3d is carried forward from a previous bill. On six occasions Scrope had breakfast, generally at a cost of between twelve and sixteen shillings, at which price he must surely also have been treating some friends. On ten occasions he had wine, usually accompanied by 'Cake & Oringes', 'Cake & Buiscuits' or fruit. On 28 February the wine was 'muld'. His expenditure on wine was usually in the region of two shillings on each occasion, but on 31 May he spent sixteen shillings, one hopes entertaining his friends, while on the Fourth of June, the King's Birthday, twelve and ninepence was very properly laid out on wine and fruit. 16 February must have been a chilly day, for Scrope consumed milk punch, wine and fruit, and breakfast for a total of fifteen and sixpence. Some days he would just drop in for a 'Sanwich' at sixpence, or a plate of cold beef or cold pork at a shilling, but on others more substantial fare was called for, such as 'Fish Dress^d & Sauce' at one and six, a shilling's worth of 'Loves Butterd', or even 'Grisking & Pottatoes', also at a shilling (Griskin is the lean part of the loin of a bacon pig).

The first step in the translation of Scrope Davies from Eton to Cambridge was taken at Electiontide in 1801 when, at the age of eighteen, he had risen high enough in the ranks of the Collegers to be included in the indentures prepared by the electors. In accordance with the statutes they chose 'a number of Scholars larger than that of the actual vacancies at King's College', no doubt 'disregarding the instances, prayers or requests of kings, queens, princes, prelates, noblemen or others, and looking rather to the proficiency of the boys in grammar and to their moral character.' However this may have been in former times, and it is doubtful if the Electors were ever very

Beginnings

good at resisting the instances of either kings or prelates, by Scrope's day the Collegers were elected strictly in the order they occupied in the School List at Eton, regardless of ability.

The next step was to await a sufficient number of resignations at King's for Scrope's place on the indentures to be reached. This was an alarming business. At the time of the next Election, the end of July 1802, he would already be nineteen. If he had not gone up to King's by then he would be superannuated, and lose his chance for ever.

A further source of anxiety was the fact that 1802 was to be one of the triennial 'Montem' years. The origins of the procession 'Ad Montem' ('To the Hill') are lost in the mists of antiquity. It was already ancient when first mentioned in 1561, and was abolished in 1847, greatly against the wishes of Queen Victoria, who, like her royal grandfather, was much attached to the ceremony. On the Tuesday in Whitsun week all the boys in the school would dress up in a variety of costumes, military and civil, and march in a column, accompanied by regimental bands, to an insignificant hillock near Slough called Salt Hill. The organisation of the column was military, the Captain of the School being the Captain of Montem, while the remainder of the sixth form shared among themselves the subordinate ranks, such as Mareschal, Ensign, Colonel, Lieutenant, Steward, Sergeant or Salt Bearer. These great officers were attended by the younger boys in the guise of servants, while the rank and file were designated 'pole-men' from the wands which they carried. Once arrived at Salt Hill, the Ensign flourished his flag from the top, and the ceremonies were over. Until 1778 the dirtiest boy in College, dressed as the Clerk, was then kicked down the hill by another Colleger dressed as the Parson, but Queen Charlotte, who with George III regularly attended Montem, was so shocked by this performance that it was discontinued. The company then dispersed to the various taverns which neighboured the hill for an excellent dinner, and afterwards, according to Hone's *Year Book*:

> The boys along the garden strayed,
> With short curved dirk high brandished
> Smote off the towering onion's head,
> And made e'en doughty cabbage feel
> The vengeance of their polished steel.

On one occasion they even succeeded in felling a large apple tree.

24

The important business of the day, however, was being enacted elsewhere. The Salt Bearers, one a senior Colleger, the other the Captain of the Oppidans, were attended by twelve boys of the middle rank, called servitors. These were armed with staves having mushroom-like tops, and very early in the day they dispersed to the principal bridges over the Thames and the main roads in southern Buckinghamshire. They were accompanied by toughs hired for the occasion, and thus emboldened would stop all travellers and demand 'salt', that is to say, money. In return the passer-by received a ticket, and if he demanded to know by what right this exaction was being made, the boys could point to the mottoes painted on their staves among which were 'Mos pro lege' (Custom instead of Law) or 'Nullum jus sine sale' (No Justice without Salt). The travellers seem generally to have paid up with a good grace, and in the meantime the lordly Salt Bearers, who did not leave the confines of Eton, would have collected fifty guineas from King George, and a similar sum from his Queen. The result of the day's work was that the Captain of Montem, having paid his expenses, and they were many, went on to Cambridge furnished with anything between £600 and £1200.

This day of unexampled glory with its pecuniary bonus was within Scrope's grasp, but it was dangerously close to the dread date of Election Day, somewhat less than two months later. Of the Scholars elected with him, Knapp went up to King's in December 1801, Ripley was admitted there on 30 March 1802, and Martin Thackeray on 2 April. This left only John Tompkyns, who in later life was to go to Spain with the First Dragoons, be called to the Bar, and become Dean of Theology at Kings.[4] If there should be a death or a resignation at King's, and the summons should arrive at Eton at any time before midnight of the twentieth day before Montem, Tompkyns would have to leave before the great day, and his Captaincy would revert to Scrope. So strongly was the drama of this situation felt that it was the custom in College to sit up until midnight of the last day listening for the fatal hoof-beats and the cry of 'Resignation' from the messenger. If none had come by the time the clock on Lupton's tower had finished striking midnight, a shout of 'Montem sure!' went up in Long Chamber, the ends of the previously raised oak bedsteads were dropped

4 H.C. Blake, author of *Reminiscences of an Etonian* also records that he was 'a famous hand at making "Bumble" a beverage composed of swipes and brown sugar' and the only method known which could render College beer potable.

on the floor, and the shutters were slammed with a will, the whole contributing to make a din that could be heard in Windsor. So it was in the case of Scrope. There was no resignation, and his only consolation was a sum of money, probably £50, which the successful Captain generally agreed to give his rival in the event of being himself assured of Montem.

The incidence of Montem must have contributed substantially to the Rev. Mr Davies' expenses. Scrope took part in three, and his brother Thomas in two. On his first appearance, 17 May 1796, Scrope was but a humble poleman, and as such his costume was not a matter of personal choice. Polemen wore blue coats with four gilt buttons, white waistcoats, white knee-breeches, silk stockings, and buckled shoes. By 14 May 1799 Thomas, taking part in his first Montem, was a poleman, but Scrope had risen to the rank of servitor. As such he was allowed to indulge his own taste as concerned his costume. It is therefore a great pity that the tradesmen's bills in the trunk do not cover the period when Scrope and his fellow servitors were ordering their 'dresses of selected colours – pink, blue violet, and red with combinations, plumed hats, buff boots, and silken bags to hold the salt'. The school bills, however, reveal that Thomas paid 1/- for his Montem pole (his would have been of plain deal), 8/- for dinner, and 2/6 for Montem money, his contribution to the Captain's expenses. Scrope on the other hand paid 4/- for his Montem pole to be varnished. Thomas had to buy a new pole since those carried by the polemen were usually hacked to pieces before the procession left Eton. Scrope would have inherited his servitor's staff, with its painted motto, but no doubt wished it to be restored to its original beauty.

On 8 June 1802 Scrope, even if disappointed of the Captaincy, was nevertheless glorious as College Salt Bearer. Since the officers who bore military titles wore military uniform, the Salt Bearer's costume gave the greatest scope for imagination and splendour. In this latter year he appointed Thomas one of the servitors, so both brothers would have looked very grand. Once again there are unfortunately no bills revealing the details and cost of their dress, but the latter must have been considerable. Perhaps their father felt that his purse had suffered enough, but at any rate this was to be Thomas's last half as well as Scrope's. On 5 July 1802 Thomas matriculated at Oxford, having been nominated to a Postmastership at Merton, of which College his uncle, as we have seen, was Warden.

Beginnings

Montem out of the way, Scrope's next concern was to get safely to Cambridge before the arrival of Election Day. The earliest letter to Scrope found in the trunk is from Edward Jones, Junior, addressed to him at Eton, and dated 29 June 1802. In it Jones says 'Had I not been favoured with your letter which I received yesterday noon, I had otherwise purposed the sending of my Resignation to Kings time enough to enable the Captain of Eton to save the Commencement. I now purpose writing to the Provost of Kings to this effect, by the Post subsequent to the date of this, which I hope will allow sufficient space of time for the saving of the Term —'. The explanation of these mysterious remarks is that the statutes of the University required an undergraduate to reside for twelve terms before becoming a Bachelor of Arts. This meant beginning residence in the Easter term which was inconvenient to the University since the academic year began with the Michaelmas term. It became accepted, therefore, that any student who was admitted to a College during the Easter term was deemed to have kept it. Scrope was admitted to King's on 8 July. The term ended on the 9th. During that first week of July Scrope had to undergo one final piece of Etonian mummery, that of being 'ripped' by the Provost. His gown was sewn up in front, and he presented himself to the Provost, who, taking a knife, ripped the gown in two. Scrope was no longer an Etonian.

Eton made Scrope Davies. It introduced him to the great world, and allowed him to be on terms of easy familiarity with the ruling class — indeed, placed him in a position of superiority and command over many of its future leaders. Since he had the intelligence to profit from it, he was given a good grounding in, and genuine love of, classical literature.

On the debit side, games of chance in Long Chamber, where sums of £18 could be won or lost in a night, gave him his love of, and skill at, gaming. The readiness of the tradesmen to allow him credit doubtless encouraged him in those habits of extravagance which were to prove his downfall. The availability of an army of fags, and the comprehensive choice of shops and services in the High Street, enabled him to cultivate that fastidious attention to personal appearance, and that meticulous interest in dress, which, together with an attitude of effortless superiority, which it is also easy to attribute to Eton, were to make him the very model of a Dandy. Such ceremonies as Montem, and the passion of the denizens of Long Chamber for

27

amateur theatricals also no doubt fired his interest in clothes, and gave him that style which was to excite the admiration of Byron. Scrope himself retained a fondness for the place. He is to be found in the list of Stewards at the Eton Anniversary Dinner held at the 'Crown and Anchor' in the Strand on Saturday 18 May 1811, and in the last year of his life during one of his rare visits to England he was seen at Eton.

2

The Friend of Byron

Scrope Davies was an attractive and entertaining character in a colourful age when dandies, gamblers and wits were by no means hard to find. A few anecdotes, a few quotations, a few accounts of extravagant behaviour would have sufficed to keep him in the footnotes of history. One vital particular, however, distinguished him from the other disciples of Beau Brummell. He was one of Byron's two closest friends – the other being John Cam Hobhouse. In attempting to understand a character as complex as Byron, it is of value to know the friend he admired and liked so much, and to study the reasons he gave for his affection.

When Byron returned to Trinity College, Cambridge on 27 June 1807, after an absence of almost a year, he was much cast down to find that most of his former friends had departed. He accordingly announced his intention of leaving the University for ever. Almost without exception the friends of his first year had been Harrovians, and, apart from Edward Noel-Long, had been chiefly companions in dissipation, to whom he was attached by little except sentimental memories of Harrow. A week later, however, he had resolved to reside at Trinity for another year. He had made a new set of friends, men of a very different stamp from the cronies he had lost. With the exception of John Cam Hobhouse, who had been at Westminster, they were all Etonians. They were intellectuals, and among them were fledgling poets, like Byron himself, wits, scholars, politicians and free-thinkers.

With Hobhouse Byron had been acquainted before, but Hobhouse had disapproved of him because, Byron wrote, 'I wore a *white hat*, and a *grey* coat, and rode a grey horse (as he says himself) . . .' Now that Byron was a poet with his works in print (*Hours of Idleness* was on the point of publication) Hobhouse saw him in a different light. Another new friend at Trinity was Charles Skinner Matthews, who had occupied Byron's rooms during his absence, and been much amused by his tutor's warning that he should pay 'attention not to damage any of the movables, for Lord Byron, Sir, is a young man of *tumultuous passions*'. He and Hobhouse were devoted to each other. With these two Byron 'became really friends in a morning'. Hobhouse aspired to be a poet, and had political ambition too. His views were those of the Whig reformers. Matthews was witty, brilliant, up to all kinds of mischief. He was, as Byron put it, 'a most decided atheist, indeed noxiously so, for he proclaimed his principles in all societies'. His political views were equally advanced, earning for him the nickname 'Citoyen', the French Revolution's equivalent of 'Comrade'.

A third member of Trinity with whom Byron must have become acquainted at that time, though he was not to become a close friend until later, was Douglas Kinnaird. A younger son of the seventh Lord Kinnaird, his mother had been a Miss Ransom, of the banking firm Ransom and Morland. The firm's premises occupied the same site as that branch of Barclays in which Scrope's trunk was found, and it was as a partner in the bank that Kinnaird came to play an important part in Byron's financial affairs. In 1815 they were both concerned in the management of the Drury Lane Theatre, and a fondness for the drama, for actresses, and for old brandy, formed a further link. He was one of Byron's advisors during the separation crisis, tending to take a hard line, as he was later to do in Westminster politics, each time with unfortunate results. His character is difficult to define. Augusta Leigh, who became so devoted to Scrope, called Kinnaird 'that shallow *brained* & *hearted* man, who will do all the mischief he can'. This, however, was in 1819, when she was distressed at the possibility that Byron would return to England. That same year, when Kinnaird won a by-election at Bishop's Castle, Hobhouse in his diary summed up his friend. Again we must remember that they had been rivals for the Reform nomination in Westminster, and Hobhouse had recently failed in an attempt to enter Parliament. Hobhouse wrote:

(Kinnaird's) return I take to be a very auspicious event — and he may make it a very important one — but what he wants is *genius* he has none whatever — no livelyness — stock of general information — no classical learning nor even historical to any extent whatever — yet he gets up a subject well — and explains with perspicuity what he understands correctly — his voice and manner are good — his elocution ready and generally correct — his fault is tediousness — and confusion and when he has got beyond his tether there is nothing happy in his mode of retreat.

The Friend of Byron

Hobhouse and Matthews already knew Scrope Davies when they first became friends with Byron, and no doubt it was through them that Scrope joined the circle of the poet's friends. Matthews, though an Oppidan, had been a contemporary of Scrope's at Eton, and Hobhouse must have met him by 1805, for in 1820 he noted in his diary that he had known Scrope for at least fifteen years. That they soon became good friends is revealed by one of the many pocket-books found in Scrope's trunk. It contains an account of expenses incurred on a tour of the Highlands made by himself and Hobhouse during the months of August and September, and despite its damaged and fragmentary nature can be dated to 1806. Hobhouse also seems early to have become involved in the tangle of Scrope's finances, for his name appears under the date 4 August 1807 in a list of 'Annuities Granted by Scrope Berdmore Davies Esq.' which was among Scrope's financial papers.[1]

Byron and Scrope rapidly became the most intimate of friends. Their friendship was to remain almost unclouded, with only two brief periods of coolness. One occurred when Byron failed to keep an appointment and Scrope was offended, and the other when in 1808 Scrope unwisely took it upon himself to invite a mutual friend to Newstead. Byron was not amused, and wrote somewhat sharply.

What was it in Scrope that earned him Byron's trust and friendship? In the first place he was an intelligent and entertaining companion. His contemporaries esteemed him a 'ripe scholar', though we must perforce take their word for it, since the few papers devoted to learned matters found in his trunk are insufficient to enable us to form our own judgement. He certainly corresponded on the subject of correct latinity in monumental inscriptions and other learned matters with Samuel Parr, known as the 'Whig Dr Johnson', and not a man to suffer fools gladly. Hobhouse on the other hand, summing Scrope up in his diary after the latter had come to say farewell on the occasion of his final ruin, wrote 'He did not know much – but what he did know he knew well and from perpetually turning over Shakespeare, and Bacon's essays, particularly, had a fund of agreable quotation and ingenious remarks ever at hand'. Hobhouse had, however, just lost £250 as a result of Scrope's defalcations, and there had always been an element of rivalry which underlay their long-standing friendship.

1 Hobhouse's name is linked, apparently as introducer, with that of the lender in the entries for two annuities. The granting of an annuity was the commonest way of repaying a money-lender.

Byron certainly respected Scrope's intelligence, even in matters concerning his own works. On several occasions he accepted his advice as to what could or could not be printed, or agreed to alterations which Scrope proposed. He wrote, for example, on 5 March 1818, when Canto IV of *Childe Harold* was being seen through the press, '. . . I bow to Scrope's alteration of the preface, and I request that it be adopted forthwith'. An intelligent friend is for a poet a sounding board, and thus partakes, in however small a way, in the process of composition.

As to Scrope's wit, in a letter to Robert Dallas after the death of Matthews in 1811, Byron wrote:

> He [Matthews], Hobhouse, D[avies] and myself, formed a coterie of our own at Cambridge and elsewhere . . . D[avies], who is not a scribbler, has always beaten us all in the war of words, and by his colloquial powers at once delighted and kept us in order. H[obhouse] and myself always had the worst of it with the other two; and even M[atthews] yielded to the dashing vivacity of S[crope] D[avies].

Byron's letters from exile called again and again for news of Scrope and his jokes, and in his 'Detached Thoughts' compiled in October and November of 1821 he recalled several of Scrope's sallies. Although Byron thought them worthy of record, they scarcely bring a smile to the lips of the modern reader. Like those of so many wits, famous in their day, Scrope's jokes, out of context and lacking his own delivery, seem thin as wine too long in the bottle. One, however, has earned immortality, for Byron stole it, readily confessing to the deed:

> When Brummell was obliged . . . to retire to France, he knew no French; and having obtained a Grammar for the purposes of Study, our friend Scrope Davies was asked what progress Brummell had made in French, to which he responded, 'that B. had been stopped like Buonaparte in Russia by the *Elements*'. I have put this pun into 'Beppo', which is 'a fair exchange and no robbery'; for Scrope made his fortune at several dinners (as he owned himself), by repeating occasionally as his own some of the buffooneries with which I had encountered him in the Morning.

Byron liked to be thought of as a nobleman who chanced to be a poet, rather than the reverse. He would gammon earnest admirers

32

with horrid fabrications. Scrope and his other 'men of the world' friends he could not gammon, and with Scrope one has the impression that he was completely relaxed. By 1814 Byron habitually wrote to 'Dear Scrope', while Kinnaird only became 'Dear Douglas' after his visit to Byron in Venice in 1817, and Hobhouse remained 'Dear Hobhouse' in perpetuity. Scrope possessed sound commonsense, not alas in his own financial affairs, but in a way most helpful to Byron. As the son of Francis Hodgson, a friend of both Scrope and Byron, recounted:

> Byron, when absorbed in thought and indulging in reckless speculation, used often, as he expressed it, to suffer from 'a confusion of ideas', and would sometimes exclaim in his most melodramatic manner, 'I shall go mad.' Scrope Davies, a true friend, and a charming vivacious companion, who had a quaint dry manner of speaking and an irresistible stammer, used quietly to remark in answer, 'Much more like silliness than madness.'

Writing to Hobhouse on 20 September 1811, and referring to the death of Matthews the preceding month, Byron observed:

> Our friend Scrope is a pleasant person, a 'facetious companion', and 'well respected by all who know him', he laughs with the living, though he dont weep with the dead, yet I believe he would do that also, could it do them good service, but good or bad we must endeavour to follow his example and return to the dull routine of business or pleasure . . .

In Scrope Byron found a confidant. A letter to him, which was in the trunk, contains what appears to be the first mention by Byron of suicide, that theme so fascinating to them both, as to a great number of their contemporaries. Happily they both resisted its temptations even in their darkest days. In a letter to Byron Scrope recalled that his friend had once invited him to leap from the church tower at Harrow — a chance to win immortality which we must be thankful that he declined.

From time to time in his letters Byron attempted to sum up the character of his closest friends. In the letter to Dallas cited above he wrote: 'Matthews was indeed an extraordinary man . . . there was the stamp of immortality in all he said or did . . . My poor Hobhouse doted on Matthews. For me, I did not love quite so much as I honoured him; I was indeed so sensible of his infinite superiority, that though I did not envy I stood in awe of it' Byron's opinion of Hobhouse was more equivocal. In a letter to Scrope, written from Patras on 31 July 1810 he said '. . . I have got rid of Hobhouse. I determined after one years purgatory to part with that amiable soul, for though I like him, and always shall, though I give him almost as much credit for his good qualities as he does himself, there is a something in his manner & ͨ in short he will never be anything but the "Sow's Ear".' In justice to Hobhouse it must be remembered that a year's travelling with one companion would put considerable strain on any friendship. In less exasperated mood Byron could say '. . . I was engaged in taking leave of Mr Hobhouse . . . — he is the oldest — indeed the only friend I have — and my regrets are equally *social* and *selfish* — for if I had attended to his advice — I should have been anything but what I am — and in parting with him I lose "a guide philosopher and friend" I neither *can* nor *wish* to replace.'

This passage reveals an aspect of Hobhouse not found in Scrope. Hobhouse was ever ready with advice and strictures upon Byron's conduct, though happily for posterity he did not succeed in making Byron anything but what he was. He did not however preach from a position of unimpeachable moral rectitude. Even apart from the question of sexual conduct, which perennially fascinating subject we will examine shortly, he did exhibit certain other lapses. From his diary we learn that in 1811, during his brief career in the Army, when he was on piquet on the cliffs at Dover, in the frontmost line of defence against Napoleon, he was 'roaring drunk' all night. Hobhouse was no prig and no sobersides — his letters are racy and witty and he was ready to drink deep in company, if not as deep as Scrope or Byron — but he was more prone than Scrope to two dangerous weaknesses. He was ambitious, and he was inclined to be earnest — a characteristic which can so easily lead to insensitivity, self-deception and lack of balance.

Byron himself tried to define the quality in Scrope which made him, despite, or perhaps in alliance with, all his shortcomings, a most delightful companion. Writing to Hobhouse on 20 September 1811, and speaking of John Claridge, a friend from Harrow days, Byron said:

now here is a good man, a handsome man, an honourable man, a most inoffensive man, a well informed man, and a *dull* man, and this last damned epithet undoes all the rest; there is S B D[avies] with perhaps no better intellects, and certes not half his sterling qualities, is the life and soul of me and everybody else . . . – Alas 'Motley's the only wear'.

Byron was well aware that the hyper – if not the hypocritical might consider that Scrope had not applied his talents in the most worthy manner. On one occasion, he referred to him as 'our Yorick', and on another, when allotting eighteenth-century personalities to his friends he concluded that Scrope would have to be Gay. Nevertheless, he never lost his respect for Scrope. It is noticeable that in his letters Byron very seldom makes fun of him, while poor Hobhouse is his constant butt. His affection led him to stress Scrope's importance, and to gloss over his imperfections. Writing to Hobhouse in 1819 he declared:

> I am glad that *'us youth'* have made our due noise in the world – you and the Dougal[2] have turned out very promising politicians in the honesty line – as well as orators; William Bankes hath made a stupendous traveller – Michael Bruce too is a fine fellow – and then there is the 'Poeshie du Roi vot' maitre;' in short we are a fine batch including Scrope – the most celebrated of the six in his line . . .[3]

Consideration of Byron's most particular friends inevitably brings us to a certain aspect of their lives. His exotic and frenetic sex-life has been from his day to our own a continuing source of rumour, innuendo, scandal and entertainment. He was certainly bisexual, and there is cause to believe that he may have committed incest with his half-sister. Such alarming aberrations must cause us at least to ponder the sexual proclivities of his closest friends.

Hobhouse had a somewhat unsatisfactory time of it. He was extremely ill at ease with women of his own class. There are frequent entries in his diaries where he bewails his *mauvaise honte* – for example, when he had not the courage to be introduced to the dazzling Bessy Rawdon, she whom Scrope and Byron escorted to the theatre at Cheltenham, and who so fascinated the Emperor Alexander at a ball that he leant on the back of her chair all night, and even picked up her fan. Like many in his condition Hobhouse sought consolation in the

2 Douglas Kinnaird
3 His line was of course gambling.

arms of the ladies of the town. For many years he entered each occasion in his diary, using the Greek word for whore, χαμαιτυπη, subsequently shortened to χαμ, and then to the unrevealing symbol 'X'. He also generally recorded the price. The earliest entry relates to a girl in Chepstow, perhaps an unlikely candidate for the modern Babylon, but no figure is given. The most expensive lady he permitted himself in London asked £1-5-; the cheapest one shilling. His penchant for young persons of the lower orders has been noticed by other writers, who have quoted from his diary for 12 June 1812, the day he left Newstead after staying there with Byron. The passage has, however, been given inaccurately as: 'This whole week passed in a delirium of sensuality —house maid at N.' The entry is in fact less specific as to the nature of the sensuality, a term which could be used to cover drunkenness as well as lechery, but possibly more so as to one element of its cost. In the diary it stands thus upon the page:

set off from Newstead at 8. slept at Woburn —house-maid at N — 0-11-0
This whole week passed in a delirium of sensuality —

On the face of it there need be no connection between the sensuality and the housemaid. Hobhouse may merely have tipped her 11/- at the end of his visit for looking after him in other and quite decorous ways. If there was indeed more to it than that, then we may feel that Byron ought to have provided his friends with obliging housemaids on the house.

At a period when homosexual relations were a crime not only punishable by death, but for which men were in fact hanged, few were bold enough to make reference to such practices even in the most guarded manner. It is striking, therefore, how often Byron wrote on the subject to Matthews, and Matthews to him and Hobhouse. We are forced to conclude that in Matthews Byron saw someone especially sympathetic to that side of his nature. It is true that Byron referred to such matters quite often in letters to Hobhouse and other friends, but not in a way which suggested that they might share such delights — one assumes that Byron's assertion to Henry Drury in a letter of 25 June 1809 that 'Hobhouse further hopes to indemnify himself in Turkey for a life of exemplary chastity at home by letting out his "fair bodye" to the whole Divan' is intended to be humourous. On 22 June 1809 while waiting to sail from Falmouth, Byron and Hobhouse wrote a joint letter to Matthews. Byron employed a not particularly opaque form of covert language, in which the Latin quotation from the *Satyricon* of Petronius, which was to remain a favourite with him, and the references to Hyacinthus, a boy loved by the god Apollo, would not have been lost upon the recipient:

> I take up the pen which our friend has for a moment laid down merely to express a vain wish that you were with us in this delectable region, as I do not think Georgia itself can emulate in capabilities or incitements to the 'Plen. and optabil. – Coit.' the port of Falmouth and parts adjacent. – We are surrounded by Hyacinths and other flowers of the most fragrant nature, and I have some intention of culling a handsome Bouquet to compare with the exotics we expect to meet in Asia.

In his part of the letter Hobhouse also referred to homosexual matters, but he employed a term which was somewhat less transparent than those used by Byron. The word was – how shocking to the followers of Wesley had they known – 'Methodism'. While no doubt not un-appreciative of the humourous effect of this usage, the friends had etymology on their side, for the Greek word 'methode' has the meaning 'practice'. Hobhouse wrote: 'I should not however forget to inform a Methodist, that by a curious accident we overtook Caliph Vathek [William Beckford, author of *Vathek*, and a notorious homosexual] at Hartford Bridge; we could not obtain a sight of this great apostle, he having closed the shutters on the outside.'

With Scrope Davies matters are more clear cut. True, as a leading dandy he may be open to the charge of narcissism. He cultivated, however, the reputation of an ardent womaniser. On 3 February 1817 Byron wrote in a letter to Douglas Kinnaird:

> Tell me of Scrope – is he as full of 'fierce embraces' as when I last saw him? – he had made then innumerable conquests – according to his own account – I wish he would marry and beget some Scrooples – it is a pity the dynasty should not be prolonged – I do not know anyone who will leave such 'a gap in Nature'.

Scrope's activities were more than a matter of reputation. On 11 April 1818 when Hobhouse went round to his rooms in St James's to consult him upon a political question, it was to find Scrope in bed with a girl. Hobhouse knew that Byron would enjoy this item of

The Friend of Byron

tittle-tattle, and when he wrote to him on 5 June he reported 'The Scrope is occasionally amorous, and has intrigues, Sir —intrigues with milliners who scratch his face and make him look unseemly'.

A curious point is that Scrope made something of a speciality of taking up with Byron's discarded loves. On one occasion, indeed, as Hobhouse related to Byron in a letter of 4 November 1818, he ran them in double harness — 'S B D is got into the hands of Lady C[aroline] L[amb], and is in deep with Lady F[rances] W[ebster]. As they are in some measure *de tiennes*, I suppose he makes love to one and hate to the other with your poetry'. We know from the letters of Augusta Leigh that the two predatory females in question were very friendly at that period. Whether they agreed between them to share the hapless Scrope we do not know. It is however certain that the report was not mere gossip. In Scrope's trunk there were found no fewer than twenty-one letters to him from Lady Frances, couched in that tone of high-flown despair which Byron before him had known so well. [4] Scrope was also on extremely good terms with Byron's Countess of Oxford, Jane Elizabeth Harley, and was supposed by his friends to have been among the numerous lovers of that notoriously unfaithful lady. So varied was the paternity of her many children that they were called by the wags the 'Harleian Miscellany', the title of a work published by her complaisant husband. Part of Scrope's attraction for these women may, of course, have been the fact that he was known to be an intimate of Byron, and could be a bridge to the man whom they had once, or indeed still, loved. Lady Frances's first letter to Scrope contains the lines 'If Lady F. mistakes not Mr Davies is but lately returned from Venice [she did mistake], If so — how fares that favoured Child of Taste and Genius from whom an anxious and admiring World now vainly asks fresh drops of Etherial Essence —'.

Womanising can be, of course, as it was perhaps in the case of Byron himself, a sign of the bisexual, who finds it difficult to form a lasting relationship with one member of the opposite sex. Scrope appears to have been privy to Byron's 'violent, though *pure*, love and passion' for the Trinity College chorister, John Edleston. The only MS. of poems by Byron found in Scrope's trunk other than the two famous notebooks containing Canto III of *Childe Harold* and *The Prisoner of Chillon* was a copy not in Byron's hand of 'To E—' and 'The

4 For an account of Lady Frances and her relationship with Scrope Davies see the Anthology, where also a fine specimen of her epistolary style is printed.

38

The Friend of Byron

Cornelian', two of the poems inspired by that love. It has long been thought probable that 'To E—' was addressed to Edleston, despite the fact that it is dated 'November, 1802' in Byron's first printed work, *Fugitive Pieces*. This MS., where the two poems share one sheet of paper, provides confirmation that it was.[5] The fact remains, however, that there is no evidence whatever that Scrope at any time shared Byron's homosexual inclinations, or even formed a passionate relationship with another man. In his letters to Scrope from Falmouth in 1809, and from Greece in the next year, Byron does not refer to the anticipated or actual delights of pederasty, as he did in his letters to so many of the others. The fact that Scrope never married is explained in part by the statutes of King's, for marriage would have entailed forfeiture of his Fellowship, and after his ruin the dividends were his sole source of income. Bearing in mind the all-absorbing delights of gambling, it seems clear that Scrope could never contemplate any tie which might stand as an obstacle between him and his obsession. The delights of love had to be fitted in to what little time remained after the exigencies of St James's and the Racing Calendar. When ruin might have freed him for marriage, the prospect of losing his Fellow's dividends imprisoned him in celibacy. A passage in a letter from Hobhouse to Byron written on 28 September 1818 seems to bear this out. Writing of Scrope he said 'How his concerns go on, no soul alive knows; his being in love looks suspicious, for he was never known to be so when in money'. This could be taken to mean that only impending financial disaster could drive him to contemplate matrimony, as a means of mending his fortune. Alas, when the crash came, it was too sudden and too complete for that course to be open to him.

Douglas Kinnaird adopted a different approach to amatory affairs. With commendable fidelity he lived in more or less domestic bliss with the same mistress for the better part of a decade. This interesting fact is confirmed by a pun which Byron could not forebear to perpetrate in a letter to John Murray on 23 September 1820. Speaking of his 'Hints from Horace', written in 1811 and in 1820 still unpublished, he said 'It has been kept too *nine years* — nobody keeps their piece nine years now a days — except Douglas K — he kept his nine years and then restored her to the public'.

5 The MS. also contains a third poem, 'On the Death of a Young Lady, Cousin to the Author, and very Dear to him.' It was written by Byron in memory of another idealized passion, Margaret Parker, with whom he had been in love at the age of twelve.

The Friend of Byron

Since it was in 1818 that she and Kinnaird finally parted it must be to her that Byron was referring when he told Hobhouse in a letter written on 9 November 1811 'Baillie and Kinnaird I saw yesterday, K with his Piece, she is pretty & but pretty, perhaps only prettyish.' There was however more to her than prettiness, for on 15 April of the next year Hobhouse noted in his diary that he had seen 'Kinnaird's girl—a nice one'. Her name was Maria Keppel, and she was a singer by profession. So long was she a part of Kinnaird's establishment that she rose to the dignity of being referred to by his friends as 'Mrs K' (it was of course convenient that both their surnames began with that letter), and indeed she bore her keeper a child. When Hobhouse after his absence abroad called on Kinnaird on 5 February 1818 he found 'Mrs K. and the bastard there'. By that time her days as Kinnaird's mistress were numbered. Hobhouse was pleased when she departed, writing in his diary for 27 March the brutal entry 'D.K. has finally discharged his whore'. Byron felt more regret. On 23 April he wrote to Kinnaird who had informed him of this new development:

> 'Poor Maria' um!—I do not understand the particulars—nor wish to hear them—all I know is that she made your house very pleasant to your friends, and as far as I know made no mischief—(which is saying infinitely for a woman) and therefore whatever has or may happen—she has my good will, go where she will;—I understand that you have provided for her in the handsomest manner—which is your nature—and don't *surprize* me—as far as Prudence goes—you are right to dissolve such a connection—and as to provocation—doubtless you had sufficient—but I can't help being sorry for the woman—although she *did* tell you that I made love to her—which by the God of Scrope Davies! was not true—for I never dreamed of making love to any thing of yours except sixty pints of Brandy sixty years old—all or the greater part of which I consumed in your suppers.—God help me—I was very sorry when they were no more.

To Hobhouse he wrote the next day: '—I can't help being sorry for D[ougla]s Kinnaird's piece—she gave me sixty bottles of brandy—the very best I ever drank—poor dear woman—she will be a great loss—I shall never see the like again'. Maria being out of the way, Byron told Kinnaird when he wrote to him on 27 May 'I hope you will *marry*.' His hope was not fulfilled. When Kinnaird died in 1830 he was still a bachelor.

The Friend of Byron

It has long been considered that Hobhouse was Byron's dearest friend. Hobhouse himself was certainly of that opinion. Never the object of any passionate affection on the part of Byron, he was nevertheless the dependable 'man-of-the-world' to whom Byron turned for support in practical matters, a loyal companion in time of crisis. The papers found in Scrope's trunk, however, together with the scattered traces of his life in collections of correspondence and volumes of memoirs, show that he had a claim at least equal. The image of Scrope the jester, Scrope the gambler, has hidden the man whom Byron trusted and respected. Because Scrope was prepared to give his friendship without trying to change Byron, and to be loyal without being solemn, he seems more of a lightweight than Hobhouse. He was not blind, however, to Byron's faults. According to Captain Gronow, whenever he asked Scrope for his opinion of Byron the reply was the same — 'vain, overbearing, conceited, suspicious and jealous'. This clear-sightedness was nevertheless united with genuine devotion. As he put it in one of his letters to Byron: 'There is no man with whom when present I am more delighted, or of whom when absent I more often think, than Byron.'

Hobhouse and Scrope themselves perceived that they were rivals for Byron's affection, and Byron would have been less than human if he had failed to enjoy the jealousy which he inspired. In the letter cited earlier written to Scrope from Patras, Byron related with glee that Hobhouse had borrowed Scrope's brilliance in order to shine in company:

> I think of you frequently, and whenever Hobhouse unlawfully passed off any of your *good things* as his own, I immediately asserted your claim in all cabins of Ships of war, at tables of Admirals and Generals, Consuls and Ambassadors, so that he has not pilfered a single pun with impunity. I tell you with great sincerity that I know no person, whom I shall meet with more cordiality [than yourself].

Hobhouse was the less independent, the more sensitive, quick to feel slights. In his diary for 9 February 1816 he wrote: 'Byron's "Seige of Corinth" and "Parisina" I bought today. It is to be published on Tuesday. He showed me that the first was dedicated to John Hobhouse, Esq. The poem is inscribed by his Friend. He thought this sublime. I should have liked it better if he had not dedicated

41

"Parisina" to S.B. Davies. I told him this'. The dedication to Scrope reads 'To Scrope Berdmore Davies Esq. The following poem is inscribed, by one who has long admired his talents, and valued his friendship' — rather more fulsome than that to Hobhouse. Scrope, however, was not above making digs at his rival. In November 1808, declining an invitation to visit Newstead, he wrote to Byron: 'Newstead is too far from London and too near to Hobhouse for me — he like some paintings appears to greater advantage at some distance — Curtis asked me his address — I told him H. was gone out as male scullion (how do you spell the word) to the British army in Spain —' then repenting — 'I really very much wish to see Hobhouse and remember me to him most affectionately'.

To dandies such as Scrope and Byron, Hobhouse's linen seems to have been of a questionable cleanliness, for Scrope makes a further gibe of the same kind in a letter to Byron written in April 1809. 'Remember me to Matthews and Hobhouse — I would recommend you to take advantage of the present heavy rains, and travel to town after placing the latter outside, it being the only chance of cleansing my worthy friend.' Scrope was so entranced with his own joke that he wrote it down in one of the notebooks found in his trunk. Matthews was no kinder. On being shown the famous monument at Newstead inscribed 'Here lies Boatswain a Dog', he asked Byron why he did not adorn the other face with the legend 'Here lies Hobhouse a Pig.' It was a coterie in which a man had to know how to look after himself. It is perfectly clear, nevertheless, that Scrope and Hobhouse were extremely fond of each other, even if underlying tensions sometimes broke through in quarrels. The latter's diaries witness how constantly they were together, and how intertwined were their fortunes, during the decade and a half of their friendship.

Hobhouse's unconventionality and radicalism were transmuted by time into respectability and a peerage. He therefore appears to possess more *gravitas* than Scrope, whose career ended in ruin and exile. Moreover, the fact that Hobhouse wrote his memoirs while Scrope Davies it appears, despite frequent expressions of intent, never did has caused an imbalance between their two reputations. We should not however allow this to make us undervalue Scrope's part in Byron's life. Much of the evidence for the importance of that part remained until recently buried in his trunk.

3

Among the Dandies

When the Lent term of 1808 at Cambridge began, Byron was unable to return by reason of his debts. Scrope chose not to do so and the two friends plunged into a life of dissipation in London. In Byron's case it was chiefly whoring and gambling, in Scrope's gambling and drinking. In his 'Detached Thoughts' Byron recalled one of Scrope's more noteworthy achievements:

> One night, Scrope Davies at a gaming house (before I was of age), being tipsy as he usually was at the Midnight hour, and having lost monies, was in vain intreated by his friends, one degree less intoxicated than himself, to come or go home. In despair, he was left to himself, and to the demons of the dice-box. Next day, being visited, about two of the Clock, by some friends just risen with a severe headache and empty pockets (who had left him losing at four or five in the morning), he was found in a sound sleep, without a night-cap, and not particularly encumbered with bed-cloathes: a Chamber-pot stood by his bed-side, *brim-full* of — *Bank Notes*! all won, God knows how, and crammed, Scrope knew not where; but *there* they were, all good legitimate notes, and to the amount of some thousand pounds.

A picture of the earlier part of one of these convivial evenings is provided by a bill found in Scrope's trunk. It dates from a year later, but no doubt differs not at all in essentials. Scrope and Byron it appears had agreed to split the price of a dinner consumed by themselves and three friends at the Coffee House run by one Robert Joy. The bill reads as follows:

N 14	5 Gents —
Bread & c	0- 1-8
Soup & Bullies	0- 5-0
Turbot Dressing	0-14-0
Lobster Sauce & c	0- 3-6

Lemmon /	0- 0-4
Turkey Dressing	
Oyster Sauce &c	
Sausages	0-10-0
Roast Beef	0- 7-0
Potatos	
Brocoli	0- 2-0
Sallad	0- 1-0
Escollops Oysters ///	0- 3-9
Tart /	0- 2-6
Jellys ////	0- 2-6
Cheese & butter	
Cellery	0- 1-6
Beer //	0- 1-4
Bottled Porter //	0- 2-0
East India Mad^r /	0-10-0
Claret ///	1-10-0
Port /	0- 5-0
Orranges	0- 2-0
Apples	0- 1-0
Olives	0- 1-6
Nuts	
Biscits	

$$£5- 8-1^1$$

$$£ \quad s \quad d$$

Lord Byron   3- 5-0
    Feby 27th 1809
Settled John Egling for Robert Joy
Dinner Bill   5- 8-1
Supper &c   1- 3-5
             6-11-6
             3- 5-0 Settled
          £3- 6-6 for Mr Davies
    March 2^d 1809
    Settled with Mr Davies Remaining Share of
    this Bill 3- 6-6
   Waiter fee &c 11-6
       £3-18-0
           John Egling for Robert Joy

---

1 Some £240 in today's money.

Among the Dandies

In terms of drink it seems to have been a relatively abstemious occasion, at least by their standards, with only three bottles of claret, two each of beer and porter, and one each of madeira and port being drunk by five men. No doubt, however, they intended to go on to some gaming hell or other place of low resort where more would be consumed. It is interesting to note that claret cost twice the price of port, perhaps a reflection of the Napoleonic Wars, though in that case it is hard to explain why madeira should have cost so much.

By the end of February 1808 the two friends were played out. Byron wrote to Hobhouse on the 27th 'I am buried in an abyss of Sensuality, I have renounced *hazard* however, but I am given to Harlots, and live in a state of Concubinage, I am at this moment under a course of restoration by Pearson's[2] prescription, for a debility occasioned by too frequent Connection . . . Scrope Davies is meandering about London feeding upon Leg of Beef Soup, and frequenting the British Forum,[3] he has given up hazard, as also a considerable sum at the same time'.

Hazard was the form of gaming which Scrope chiefly practised. It was, with the exception of backgammon, the only game with dice generally played, and its nature was such as to favour an intelligent player. It was the ancestor of the modern game of 'craps', the name of which indeed is derived from one of the losing throws at hazard, known as 'crabs'. The rules were as follows. One player, the 'caster', threw two dice together until he scored five, six, seven, eight or nine. His score on that occasion was called the 'main'. He then threw again. If his second score equalled the main (in the case of a main of six or eight twelve was also good, as was eleven in the case of a main of seven) he was said to have 'nicked it', and he won all the stakes. If he threw 'crabs', that is to say, two or three, or if he threw eleven or twelve (except of course in the cases mentioned above when eleven or twelve were winning throws) then he 'threw out', and lost. If, however, he

2 Probably George Pearson, physician.

3 The British Forum was a London debating society run by John Gale Jones. Some idea of its, and perhaps of Scrope's, politics may be gained by the fact that in 1810 Jones was imprisoned for advertising for discussion the question 'Which was the greater outrage on public feeling, Mr. Yorke's enforcement of the Standing Order to exclude strangers from the House of Commons, or Mr. Windham's recent attack upon the liberty of the press?' Sir Francis Burdett was sent to the Tower for supporting Jones.

neither nicked it, nor threw out (if for example the main were seven, and he threw four, five, six, eight, nine or ten) then he had to continue throwing until he either equalled the main, in which case he lost, or his second score, known as the 'chance', in which case he won. So far so simple. The interest of the game, and the advantage it afforded Scrope, lay in the notorious fact that it is easier to throw some numbers than others. There are, for example, six chances in thirty-six of throwing a seven, and but three chances in thirty-six of throwing a four. A player with a main of seven and a chance of four has odds of two to one against him. As the learned Jones, reviser and corrector of the 1814 edition of *Hoyle's Games*, judiciously remarks 'It is necessary to be perfectly master of these odds, in order to play the prudent game, and to make use of them by way of insuring bets in what is called hedging . . .' By intelligent hedging it was often possible to ensure a win. The odds against each possible result remained fixed, so that for instance a bystander watching the player mentioned above could place a bet of five pounds at evens that the player would throw his main, and a bet of three pounds to win six that he would throw his chance. Scrope, whose contemporaries esteemed him a 'first-rate calculator', would have had no difficulty in mastering the odds, whereas no doubt many of his opponents lacked both his mental powers and his application.

Half way through March 1808 Scrope returned to Cambridge. Byron wrote on the 14th to Hobhouse, who had virtuously remained there 'Scrope Davies has mounted a pyeballed palfrey, and quitted London'. Byron did not forget his reprobate friend, for on the 26th he asked Hobhouse to 'Greet in my name the Bilious Birdmore'. Hobhouse had meanwhile been given an account of Byron's proceedings by Scrope, and saw fit to read him a lecture 'I learn with delight from Scrope Davies that you have totally given up dice — to be sure you must give it up. For you to be seen every night in the vilest company in town! Could anything be more shocking? . . . I know of nothing that should bribe me to be present once more at such horrible scenes . . .'

Hobhouse may also have made it tolerably clear to Byron's concubines that he disapproved of them too. In a letter to the Reverend John Becher written on 26 February 1808 Byron had rather inappropriately informed the reverend gentleman that his 'blue-eyed Caroline' had 'been lately so charming' that they were 'commanded to repose,

Among the Dandies

being nearly worn out'. Caroline remains unidentified, but in a letter to Byron written in November 1808 Scrope reported 'Caroline was at the play on Monday parading the Lobby – she came up to me, and without any ceremony commenced the most violent attack on Hobhouse I ever witnessed – an interview between the two, would be no bad interlude between the play and farce –'. That Caroline was 'parading the Lobby' can give us no very lofty notion of her virtue.

The high-minded Hobhouse failed to realise that Byron was deeply wounded by the hostile reviews of his *Hours of Idleness* – especially that in the *Edinburgh Review*. In his Journal for 22 November 1813 Byron wrote '. . . I remember the effect of the first *Edinburgh Review* on me. I heard of it six weeks before, – read it the day of its denunciation, – dined and drank three bottles of claret, (with S.B. Davies, I think,) neither ate nor slept the less, but, nevertheless, was not easy till I had vented my wrath and my rhyme, in the same pages, against every thing and every body'. This was how Byron would have liked it to have been. In truth, he was shattered, and his round of debauchery with Scrope was in part a necessary anaesthetic.

In July 1808 Byron was plunged into further melancholy by Hewson Clarke's attacks upon him in *The Satirist*. Scrope and Hobhouse accompanied him to Brighton, perhaps with a view to restoring his spirits. They all lodged together at 1, Marine Parade. It was a most remarkable excursion, with elements of what would nowadays be called 'high camp'. Byron was accompanied by one of his concubines disguised as his cousin, though some say as his brother. Scrope gave an account of two incidents concerning her to Miss Frances Williams Wynn, of whom he saw a good deal during the later years of his life. According to her:

> The name of the young lady who played Kaled to the noble poet's Lara was Gordon.[4] Dressed in boy's clothes, she accompanied him to Brighton, where he introduced her as his cousin to several of his friends. She was riding on the Downs with Davies, when Lady P[erceval] joined them, and, entering into conversation with the supposed lad, asked where he had got such a pretty pony. 'It was *gave* me by my cousin George'. 'That young gentleman is no cousin of Lord Byron's', whispered Lady P. to Davies, and rode off.

4 It appears that Miss Williams Wynn was understandably confused about the girl's name. Such evidence as we have suggests that her name was Cameron, and that Byron passed her off as his brother Gordon (see Marchand, *Byron*, vol. i, pp. 150–1)

47

A round game was got up for this damsel's amusement at his Lordship's lodgings, and she was detected in cheating. He spoke angrily to her, and she rose to leave the room, vowing she would kill herself. 'Stop a minute, madam,' and he rang the bell. 'Fletcher' – to the servant – 'place a bottle of laudanum and my Turkish dagger on Miss Gordon's dressing-table, and fasten a rope to the top of the bedpost. Now, madam, you have your choice of deaths'. She resumed her seat sobbing: 'You want me to kill myself, and I won't'.

This was not the only occasion on which Byron had to exercise his skill in defusing a would-be suicide. He recalled in his 'Detached Thoughts':

At Brighthelmstone (I love orthography at length), in the year 1808, Hobhouse, Scrope Davies, Major Cooper, and myself, having dined together with Lord Delvin, Count (I forget the french Emigrant nomenclature) and others, did about the middle of the night (we *four*) proceed to a house of Gambling, being then *amongst us* possest of about *twenty guineas* of ready cash, with which we had to maintain as many of your whorson horses and servants, besides house-hold and whore-hold expenditure. We had, I say, twenty guineas or so, and we lost them, returning home in bad humour. Cooper went home. Scrope and Hobhouse and I (it being high Summer), did firstly strip and plunge into the Sea, whence, after half an hour's swimming of those of us (Scrope and I) who could swim, we emerged in our dressing-gowns to discuss a bottle or two of Champaigne and Hock (according to choice) at our quarters. In course of this discussion, words arose; Scrope seized H. by the throat; H. seized a knife in self-defence, and stabbed Scrope in the shoulder to avoid being throttled. Scrope fell bathed in blood and wine – for the *bottle* fell with him, being infinitely intoxicated with Gaming, Sea-bathing at two in the morning, and Supplementary Champaigne. The skirmish had past before I had time or thought to interfere. Of course I lectured against gambling –
'Pugnare Thracum est',
and then examined Scrope's wound, which proved to be a gash long and broad, but not deep nor dangerous. Scrope was furious: first he wanted to fight, then to go away in a post-chaise, and then to *shoot* himself, which latter intention I offered to forward, provided that

he did not use *my pistols*, which, in case of suicide, would become a deo-dand to the King. At length, with many oaths and some difficulty, he was gotten to bed. In the morning, Cool reflection and a Surgeon came, and, by dint of loss of blood, and sticking plaister, the quarrel (which Scrope had begun), was healed as well as the wound, and we were all friends as for years before and after.

When it came to 'whore-hold' Scrope may have experienced some trouble with the newly re-introduced stays. Inviting him and Hobhouse to Geneva in 1816, Byron wrote 'don't forget to urge Scrope into our crew – we will buy females and found a colony – provided Scrope does not find those ossified barriers to "the forefended place" – which cost him such a seige at Brighthelmstone.'

Next to his friendship with Byron the most celebrated aspect of Scrope Davies's existence is the position he occupied as a leading dandy. It was a side of him which interested Byron, who was proud to have been accepted by the dandies as an equal. In his 'Detached Thoughts' he wrote 'The truth is, that, though I gave up the business early, I had a tinge of Dandyism in my minority, and probably retained enough of it, to conciliate the great ones at four and twenty'.

Scrope was the dandy best known to Byron, and it seems probable that it was he who had the major part in introducing Byron to that life. He was some five years older than the poet, a significant gap at the age of twenty, and already a man of the world. It is not surprising if Byron was impressed by his wit, his self-assurance and his imperturbability. Despite what he said, Byron remained something of a dandy throughout his life – though in Italy his dandyism became more flashy and continental in character – and in his exile, if we are to believe Trelawny:

> His conversation was anything but literary except when Shelley was near him. The character he most commonly appeared in was of the free and easy sort such as had been in vogue when he was in London . . ., and his talk was seasoned with anecdotes of the great actors on and off stage, boxers, gamblers, duellists, drunkards, etc., etc., appropriately garnished with the slang and scandal of that day . . .

Such a way of life may appear at best frivolous, at worst reprehensible, but it was to be justified in a manner hard to foresee. In the words of Byron himself, writing to Douglas Kinnaird from Venice on 26 October 1819:

As to 'Don Juan' – confess – confess – you dog – and be candid – that it is the sublime of *that there* sort of writing – it may be bawdy – but is it not good English? – it may be profligate – but is it not *life*, is it not *the thing*? – Could any man have written it – who has not lived in the world? – and tooled in a post-chaise? in a hackney coach? in a Gondola? against a wall? in a court carriage? in a vis a vis? on a table? – and under it?

Byron's dandy existence did not only equip him to portray the world of fashion in his greatest poem. It is to his excursions into low life, surely undertaken in the company of Scrope, that we are indebted for such memorable passages as his description of the footpad in the nineteenth stanza of Canto XI, written in the flash cant of the underworld:

> He from the world had cut off a great man,
>   Who in his time had made heroic bustle.
> Who in a row like Tom could lead the van,
>   Booze in the ken or at the spellken hustle?
> Who queer a flat? Who (spite of Bow Street's ban)
>   On the high toby spice so flash the muzzle?
> Who on a lark with black-eyed Sal (his blowing)
> So prime, so swell, so nutty, and so knowing?

Barbey D'Aurevilly in his *Of Dandyism and of George Brummell*, averring that 'Don Juan' was 'throughout essentially dandyesque in tone', claimed that Brummell might have been one of the muses of the poem, albeit invisible to the poet. Given the mixture of high life and of low life which distinguishes Byron's greatest work, it seems that rather than the excessively 'fine' Beau Brummell, he who shuddered to reveal that he had once eaten a pea, the invisible muse of *Don Juan* was Scrope Davies.

What was a dandy? The idea, and its embodiment, continued to fascinate and at times appal the remainder of the 19th century and our own. To quote D'Aurevilly again 'Dandyism is almost as difficult a thing to describe as to define'. He dismissed with scorn Carlyle's famous definition 'A dandy is a Clothes-wearing Man, a Man whose trade, office and existence consists in the wearing of Clothes' with the retort 'Dandyism is social, human and intellectual. It is not a suit of clothes walking about by itself!'. Indeed Carlyle's definition does not go very far. It does not answer the question what sort of people became dandies, nor what was their motivation, nor what climate of ideas gave rise to such a motivation. For D'Aurevilly dandyism 'springs from the unending struggle between propriety and boredom'. It does not, as does eccentricity, openly revolt against the established order, but rather plays with the conventionalities. On a less exalted level Mrs Catherine Gore, in her novel *Cecil; or, the adventures of a coxcomb*, published in 1841, threw some light on who became a dandy. One of her characters is described as 'a nobody, who had made himself somebody, and gave the law to everybody. This was accomplished per force of some talent and much impudence.' In our own time Ellen Moers, in her admirable work *The Dandy*, attempted a definition by negatives. The dandy, she pointed out, had no coat of arms, no ancestral portraits, no obligations, no attachments, no wife, no child, no occupation and no obvious means of support.

Attempts to define the dandy prove to be largely attempts to describe the movement's founder, George Brummell. In the same way we can use what we know of Scrope Davies to add further to the picture, and at the same time to determine the extent to which Scrope was and was not typical of the dandies. By his contemporaries he was regarded as typical. Captain Gronow, himself a former dandy, wrote of Scrope 'His manners and appearance were of the true Brummell type: there was nothing showy in his exterior. He was quiet and reserved in ordinary company, but he was the life and soul of those who relished learning and wit.' The description makes clear the distinction between a dandy and a fop. Brummell's rules of dress insisted on dark colours and understatement, with any element of arrogance confined to the perfection of cut, an arrogance discernible only to the cognoscenti. To attract attention by one's dress was the supreme mortification, and yet paradoxically to dress in such a manner was in itself a defiant statement, expressing scorn for the values of ordinary men. In conduct, too, coolness was all, coolness in the sense of effrontery, but also in the sense of imperturbability and reserve. The dandy, unlike the fop, was not a chattering fool. Scrope had more in common with Brummell than his manners and appearance. Ellen Moers' definition fitted him as well as Brummell. He too was unmarried, of comparatively humble origin, with no occupation but the social round, and of limited financial resources. There were respects, of course, in which Scrope differed from Brummell. He was not cold-blooded. Scrope had mistresses, while Brummell, it appears, did not. He was not 'fine' as was Brummell. It is hard to imagine Brummell sharing Scrope and Byron's enthusiasm for pugilism and athletic pursuits, though it is true that Brummell did own a pair of sporting guns. Moreover Scrope was more a man of action than was Brummell, as we shall see when we consider his political career.

Dandy characteristics were the antithesis of the aristocratic. It was in an age of revolution that the dandy movement was born, an age when the institutions of monarchy and aristocracy were hated and despised as seldom before. Camus saw the dandy as a revolutionary, and it is interesting to find that Scrope was involved in radical politics. The dandies set up a rival aristocracy, one so arbitrarily exclusive that real aristocrats might seek to enter it in vain. The dandy aristocracy, however, had no power base. Its members were largely middle-class, and without great fortune. Their tyranny could only be maintained by a sham, by sheer nerve, by unconquerable self-assurance. The stories of Brummell's insolence are many and well known. That Scrope was master of the same techniques we learn from the diary of his friend Hobhouse. On 31 March 1814 he wrote 'dined with S.B. Davies and two of his brothers and Solomon Norton at the Piazza Coffee House. The Empire assumed by my friend Scrope over Solomon is most singular partly kept up by the grossest flattery and partly an air of superiority.' Wit was the essential weapon, and in Scrope's notebooks are to be found pages of aphorisms, observations and what were called at the time 'good things', some original, but most lifted from the storehouses of literature both classical and modern. The professional diner-out worked hard at his profession, albeit in secret.

Scrope was accepted as an intimate by the leading dandies of his day. He was in a position to reveal to Hobhouse secrets concerning Brummell's financial state, and he was among those to whom Brummell appealed for help during his last desperate days in England. Scrope used his knowledge of Brummell's affairs to avoid throwing good money after bad in what he knew to be a hopeless cause. The exchange of notes has passed into legend:

> My dear Scrope, send me two hundred pounds. The banks are shut and all my money is in the three per cents. It shall be repaid to-morrow morning. — Yours
>
> George Brummell.

Among the Dandies

My dear George, 'tis very unfortunate, but all my money is in the
three per cents. — Yours

S. Davies.

Barbey D'Aurevilly comments admiringly 'Brummell was too much
of a Dandy to be wounded by such a letter . . . Scrope's answer,
though cruelly caustic, was not vulgar. Their honour, as Dandies,
remained untouched.' In fact the answer was uncharacteristic of
Scrope. Hobhouse wrote at the time of his friend's crash that he had
'been guilty of one or two indiscreet, that is, very generous, actions
towards those with whom he played successfully'. In the case of
Brummell there was more to the matter than a desire on Scrope's part
to protect himself from loss. In the course of his final collapse
Brummell, together with Lords Alvanley and Worcester, had entered
into a scheme to borrow £30,000 on their joint securities despite the
fact that he knew he was unable to repay even the interest. Richard
Meyler, a man of fashion whose wealth was founded on sugar, heard of
this fraud, as he saw it, perpetrated against his friend Worcester, and
denounced Brummell at White's club. At the same time he resolved
in future to cut Lord Alvanley, who riposted by calling Meyler a
damned methodistical grocer among other choice epithets. The
correspondence found in Scrope's trunk reveals him to have been a
friend of Meyler, or 'Dick the Dandy-killer' as he came to be known,
and this no doubt coloured his attitude to Brummell.

The most celebrated of Scrope's generous actions was recounted by
Gronow. According to him Scrope:

seldom played against individuals; he preferred going to the regular establishments. But on one occasion he had, by a remarkable
run of good luck, completely ruined a young man who had just
reached his majority and come into the possession of a considerable
fortune. The poor youth sank down upon a sofa in abject misery,
when he reflected that he was a beggar; for he was on the point of
marriage. Scrope Davies, touched by his despair, entered into
conversation with him and ended by giving him back the whole of
his losses, upon a solemn promise that he never would play again.
The only thing that Scrope retained of his winnings was one of the
little carriages of that day, called a dormeuse, from its being fitted
up with a bed, for he said, 'When I travel in it I shall sleep the
better for having acted rightly'. The youth kept his promise; but

53

when his benefactor wanted money, he forgot that he owed all he possessed to Scrope's generosity, and refused to assist him.

The story is quite obviously too good to be true. And yet, on more than one occasion Hobhouse makes mention of Scrope's *dormeuse*, while among his financial papers the latter kept a coach-builder's detailed bill from which, although the type of vehicle is not named, it is possible to understand that an elaborate travelling carriage has been refurbished and re-upholstered, and Scrope's crest new-painted upon the doors. It is tempting to see this as the moment when Scrope took possession of his newly won *dormeuse*.

It was at Eton that Scrope Davies became a dandy. We have seen from his bills that he had already adopted the Brummell style of dress, and the beau's fastidious cleanliness, while still a schoolboy. He had also been given a vision of the world of rank and fashion. It was, however, a temporary situation, made possible only by the nature of school life. Eton over, there would be nothing for it but the parochial, fusty life of a Cambridge don or the humdrum if admirable existence of a country parson, unless the ascendancy, which his wit, his style and his effrontery had already given him over his superiors by birth, could be maintained in a greater arena with the same weapons. To a character innately weak, the choice was not difficult to make.

How did Scrope spend his time? The question may be considered in two parts, the division of his year, and the activities which he pursued. In the early nineteenth century, as indeed later, the season and the annual migrations of the fashionable were governed by the sittings of Parliament. It was important to be in London while the nation's destiny was being decided, but the task was rendered less onerous by the fact that Parliament only sat from January until July, and not at all for the rest of the year. In addition to these important dates in the social cycle, Scrope was of course bound by his duties as a Fellow of King's College. These do not appear to have been burdensome. Perusal of the addresses on letters written and received by him, and of his friends' journals, reveals that he managed to reconcile the demands of the great world with those of Cambridge by confining his attendance at the University very largely to the Autumn months, when in any case the Craven and the two October meetings at Newmarket would render the neighbourhood of Cambridge more attractive. Nevertheless he was wont to complain bitterly when compelled to reside there. In November 1808 he wrote to decline an

invitation from Byron to stay at Newstead in the following terms:
'Nothing but an absolute certainty of incurring a penalty of 20£ could
induce me ever to remain one hour in the quiet ugliness of Cambridge', and again, nine years later in 1817, he repeated the unflattering expression in a letter lamenting that lack of funds prevented him
from travelling out to Venice in order to see Byron. To modern ears
such a description of Cambridge must sound strangely, but we should
remember that to eyes accustomed to the elegance of neo-classical
London the picturesque medieval and Tudor architecture of Cambridge must have seemed sadly barbaric. Moreover, Cambridge
shared in that decline of academic institutions which we have already
noticed in the case of Eton. To be a don was not, and indeed has never
been, a fashionable occupation, and the Fellows of Scrope's day were
very many of them drunken, idle – indeed, they were called upon to
do very little – uncouth, parochial and pedantic, and as far as society
was concerned, in the words of a despairing patron who realised that
his candidate for a bishopric would never do, 'unproduceable'.

Scrope confined his attendance to the Michaelmas Term, with
short excursions to Cambridge at other times. He must however have
attended to University matters more than he pretended, for Byron on
one occasion congratulated him on an award in his favour, and in
1814 Hobhouse remarked that his reputation there stood higher than
that of any man of his years. He had indeed pleasant rooms at King's,
the first floor set nearest the Chapel in the Gibbs building, and it is
apparent from his friends' letters that he kept a good cellar for them
and for himself as Byron writing from exile in 1817 reminded
him. In view of this it is disappointing that the Cellar Book which
survived in his trunk records nothing as to vine-yards or to years. The
entries mention only the broad divisions Port, Burgundy, Claret and
Madeira – the last it appears was kept under the window. There was,
however, a bill in his trunk from Messrs. Wombwell Gautier from
which it appears that on 8 April 1812 Scrope paid £20-13-0 for three
dozen bottles of Clos Vougeot.

During the time that he was not engaged in his academical pursuits, Scrope divided his year much as would any other dandy. During
the season he was in London, but with the arrival of August he betook
himself off to various watering places or to stay with friends. In the
summer of 1808, for instance, he was with Byron at Brighton, in
1811 he went to Harrogate, while the Autumn of 1812 found him

and Byron at Cheltenham. The summer of 1816 was occupied by his tour to Switzerland with Hobhouse, 1817 found him marooned by lack of funds in England, while the summers of 1818 and 1819 were spent in part at Sir Francis Burdett's place at Ramsbury in Wiltshire or with the Harley family on the Isle of Wight. The various resorts had of course theatres, clubs for gambling, racecourses and other such diversions.

Scrope's migrations were closely tied to the Racing Calendar. Newmarket was for him, as it was for English racing as a whole, headquarters. Not only did he keep a bank account there, no doubt a wise precaution on the occasions when his winnings were substantial, but he also was a member of the Coffee Room attached to the Jockey Club and at one time seems even to have had some form of permanent apartment there. So much we may deduce from a letter found in his trunk dated Newmarket 19 May 1817, written by one John Newman: 'S^r I am inform'd Mr Crockford have Bought the Part of the house that your Tapstery is in and If you have Not Sold it to Mr Dayless I should Be Glad to Know wither you Would Like for me to get it Carefully taken Down and Packed up and Sent to Cambridge for its Likely if there is Nothing Seen After it it will be Spoiled in taking down'. Crockford, of the famous 'Hell' in St James's Street, had purchased what was later known as Rothsay House in order to open a hazard saloon at Newmarket. He had found the proceeds of gaming to be more profitable than the ownership of racehorses.

From Scrope's trunk there emerged a number of small pocket-books used by him to 'book' the various and many bets that he made. A few of the bets relate to such events as the likelihood of the French being in possession of Cadiz on or before 11 July 1810, but the vast majority concern the results of horse-races, and of matches, for contests between two animals were still run, though their popularity declined steadily throughout Scrope's racing career. Almost all of Scrope's bets were with other gentlemen, many of them well-known owners and members of the Jockey Club, but the ill-omened name of Crockford is also to be found. Scrope not only backed horses against the field, but also one animal against another within a race, or even various combinations, as in the 1810 Claret Stakes at Newmarket (so called because a hogshead of wine was added to the stake money) when he bet Mr Townley '6/5 Mares v. Horses'. He would make as many as twenty-five or more separate wagers on the same race, laying as well as taking odds. He also took care to lay off if he felt exposed. For example, in the case of the 1810 Derby he recorded twenty-two separate wagers, and on the facing page wrote down the financial implications of any given result. The best for him would have been a win by Lord Egremont's bay colt out of Carthage, when he would have cleared £600, and the next best a win by O.P. (no doubt named after the Old Price riots in 1809 caused by an increase in the price of seats at Drury Lane), when he would have collected £560. The worst result would be a win by the favourite Whalebone, against whom he had rashly laid odds of five to one and three to one, in which event he would lose £191. Whalebone started two to one favourite and duly won. He was followed home, ironically enough, by Lord Kinnaird's chestnut colt The Dandy.

Scrope's careful computations suggest that he may have acted at times as a semi-professional bookmaker. Gambling, after all, provided by far the greater part of his income, and he could afford to neglect no possible source of cash. There were by his time professional 'legs' or 'Ring men', most of them former grooms or 'horsey' persons of equally humble extraction, but a great deal of betting still went on between gentlemen, despite the fact that the professionals had a somewhat higher reputation for integrity than the amateurs. No doubt the borderline between the two groups was indistinct. Betting had become to some extent institutionalized, with a regular Ring at Newmarket, while in London the premises of Tattersalls, the famous auctioneers of horses, provided a forum for betting men of all classes. There was a room for bookmakers from 1815, and fixed settling days, not always punctiliously observed by losers, some of whom had the gall to turn up and collect such winnings as they had only to decamp before encountering their creditors.

In the last summer of his life in England, that of 1819, Scrope was involved in a betting coup apparently cooked up by his friend Richard Rodes Milnes. Milnes was a gambler and spendthrift whose activities encompassed the ruin not only of himself but of his brother, the father of the future Lord Houghton, friend and mentor of the poet Swinburne. Perhaps Scrope's involvement in Milnes' scheme is a reflection of his own increasing desperation. A series of letters from Milnes in the country to Scrope in London record the progress of the affair. On 17 July Milnes wrote 'Take for me the very best odds you can get to one hundred about Mr Peirse['s] horse (out of Lisette) for the S^t.

Ledger'. The St Leger was due to be run on Monday 20 September. Mr. Henry Peirse's bay colt Wrangler, by Walton out of Lisette, was well fancied. Milnes himself had a horse entered, The Laird, but he continued to be more impressed by Wrangler's chances, for on 20 July he wrote to Scrope:

> I wish the best odds you can get from good men to 300 about Mr Peirse's horse [out of] Lisette (Harry Peirse) for the St. Ledger – I should not care if 200 of it was about Mr. Peirse winning the Produce at York & the St. Ledger, if they will bet you more odds – If he cannot win the Produce he cannot win the St Ledger – *Never* mention it is for me, or I shall be in a terrible scrape – Do it on Thursday if you can, as he will soon be first favourite.

Four days later Milnes wrote again with news of his own runner. Scrope had evidently found Wrangler increasing in popularity.

> You [are] a stupid fellow for getting the money on on such bad terms. I think the Laird's case is now so desperate that I bet whatever you can for me against him – I do not think you will find people to back him outright, but you may between horses. I should like to back [Wrangler, out of] Lisette, Palmerin, Wolsey, [Jenny Wren, out of] Tom Tit['s dam], Sir Walter *on any terms* against the Laird.'

On 17 August Milnes wrote again. In the meantime part of his strategy had paid off, for Wrangler had finished first in the Produce Stakes at York, starting second favourite at odds varying between two to one and five to two against. Milnes' latest communication read:

> Bland told me at York races that you had been betting for me how he found it out I cannot understand as I have never mentioned it to any living soul –
> You will probably have observed that the Laird is creeping up into favour again very fast & they greedily took 11/1 about him – I am writing this from his stable door & I am afraid he has no chance. I am very anxious to keep him up a favorite & at the same time I wish very much to get off all the money I can, now he is in favour –
> . . . I hope you will be able next Monday at Tattersalls to do something for me –

By 21 August the situation had changed completely. On that day Milnes wrote:

> I am afraid you will think me very troublesome but I wish to change my mind entirely about betting about the Laird – The horse is going on so well . . . that I feel confident the Laird will soon be a great favorite again. I do not wish to bet anything against him till nearer the time. Pray let me hear from you; I am very anxious to hear the news about Sultan.

Sultan, owned by Crockford of gaming hell fame, was strongly fancied for the race. On 3 September Milnes reported further progress. 'The Laird got up a very great favourite at Pomfret & they took 8/1 about him – I really think he will continue to rise & be one of the very first favourites –' The odds against The Laird were shortening fast. Among Scrope's papers was a copy of *Hunt's List*, the race-card for the September meeting at Pontefract. At the foot is recorded the betting at Tattersall's on 1 September. Sultan was favourite at thirteen to four against, followed by Wrangler at seven to two and Sir Walter at eleven to one. The Laird was offered at sixteen to one against. On the back of the list some unknown informant (the signature is heavily erased) has conveyed to Scrope the latest state of the market, presumably at Pontefract:

7 to 2 a[gainst] Lisette
4 to 1 a[gainst] Sultan
8 to 1 a[gainst] the Laird taken to a good pile of Money
    Mills bet [?Brunston] a Thousand Gs the Laird beat Sir Walter

Yours Truly.
[   ]

As it proved, Scrope and Milnes could scarcely have chosen a worse race than the 1819 St Leger on which to speculate. In the words of the *British Statesman* the day 'presented a scene of confusion unprecedented in the records of the Turf'. An inauspicious beginning was made when Sultan, the favourite, broke down during his morning gallop. The more enterprising of those punters who had witnessed the tragic event galloped off to Doncaster and other near-by towns in order to hedge their bets or otherwise profit from this piece of exclusive information. Wrangler succeeded Sultan as favourite at seven to four against, with Sir Walter and Agricola as joint second favourites at six and seven to one. When the race started Sir Walter, Agricola and three others failed to get off. The Laird started, but was unplaced. The race was won by a rank outsider, Antonio, followed by Wrangler and Archibald. The result caused a sensation, and to quote the *Racing Calendar*, 'In consequence of a representation to the Stewards, that several horses prepared for starting, had not gone off with the rest, the above was, in the first instance, declared a false start, and a fresh race was run . . .' Wrangler and Archibald prepared to make the trip again, as did Jenny Wren, Tablet and the Irish horse Shamrock. They were opposed by five fresh horses, including the joint second favourites. Antonio and the Laird, among others, did not attempt another trial. The Starter, however, one Mr Lockwood, when invited to start the race for the second time threw down his flag in disgust, and declined to officiate. The race was accordingly started by an obliging bystander. The gallant Wrangler and Archibald finished second and third again, beating Agricola, but they could not prevail against Sir Walter.

The Stewards had now got themselves into a complete muddle, and were confronted by a serious riot. With a view to quelling the disturbance they posted the following notice: 'It has been determined by the Stewards and the gentlemen of the Doncaster Racing Club that a reference shall be made to the Jockey Club to decide whether the race shall be given to Antonio; and if not, whether the second heat shall be deemed a race, the horses not having been started by any person deputed for the purpose.' The anxious owners and even more anxious punters were constrained to wait until 5 October before they learnt their fate. On that day the Jockey Club gave it as their opinion that 'the race should have been adjudged to *Antonio*, and consequently that the Stewards should not have allowed a second race'. A horse considered by no-one had won, and Scrope and his confederate, unless they followed the example of the many losers who used the confusion as an excuse to cry off their bets, were left ruefully to contemplate the ruin of their hopes.

Not all of Scrope's time in the country was taken up with racing and with gaming. When he first took up shooting is not known, but on the occasion of the Highland tour which he made in company with Hobhouse in 1806 he acquired a new gun. A small pocket-book in which Scrope kept an account of their expenses also contains a few notes, and on 25 August, while they were at Dalwhinnie on their way from Perth to Inverness, he wrote 'Fired my new gun – shot very bad – killed a brace and a half of grouse and a snipe –' Two days later at Pitmain he noted 'Shot 2 brace of grouse'. The shot which he stigmatised as being so poor he had bought for 10/- five days earlier at Perth. When and where he acquired the new gun the notebook, which is in a very fragmentary condition, unfortunately does not reveal. Other necessaries for the journey had been purchased in Edinburgh. On 14 August they bought various items which suggest a somewhat dandified approach to the tour, for they included knives and forks, books and pencils, lavender water, cloaks, essences and an umbrella, the last item costing £1-15-0.

On the 18th, however, a more serious spirit prevailed and Scrope bought a shooting jacket for £1-9-0, a 'gun oil can' for 7/-, an oilskin for 4/- and Mr Murray's Tour for 10/6d. They evidently hoped to indulge in sport as well as admiration of the picturesque for they were accompanied on their travels by dogs, whose food is a recurring item of expense at the various inns where they put up. The dogs would probably have been setters, a breed which had replaced pointers in popularity as sportsmen took to shooting birds flying. Scrope's reference to the badness of his shot reminds us of the technological obstacles faced by sportsmen before the invention of the breech-loading gun. Until the end of the eighteenth century the weight of the gun, the time which elapsed between pulling the trigger and the actual ignition of the powder, and the nature of the shot which was not spherical but simply cut out of sheets of lead, had made it virtually impossible to shoot game other than on the ground or in the branches of trees. By the time of Scrope and Hobhouse's tour technical advances had made it normal to shoot birds on the wing, and in 1807, only a year later, the Rev William Daniel announced in his *Rural Sports* that it was 'not exactly at present the *custom for Gentlemen* to shoot on the ground'. Scrope's gun would, nevertheless, still have been a muzzle-loading flintlock – the detonator was not invented until the next year and even then was slow to catch on owing to its unreliability – and there would still have been a delay of one tenth of a second between trigger and combustion. Driven birds were therefore unknown. All game was walked up and taken as soon as possible going away. Scrope's very small bags were therefore by no means unusual. Even the best shots of that time were content with four or five brace of mixed game after a whole day of strenuous walking.

Scrope retained his enthusiasm for shooting, for in 1814 he ordered a new gun from Joseph Manton, the earliest of the great London gunsmiths. This was an investment equivalent to buying a new pair of Purdeys nowadays. Manton not only built beautiful, perfectly balanced guns, but was also extremely inventive. His entry in the *Post Office London Directory* for 1819 proudly announces that he is the 'Patentee for Detonating Guns, Gravitating Stops, and for Chronometers going in Vacuo, Gun-maker to their RH the Prince Regent, the Dukes of York, Cambridge, Gloucester etc'. There are other, possibly better, claimants to the honour of inventing detonators, but Manton also introduced an 'elevating rib' to prevent shooting low, and the use of platinum for touch-holes. His 'Gravitating Stop' was a safety device to prevent accidental discharge. Manton's bill to Scrope survives, but is unfortunately torn and much is missing. Enough, however, remains for us to see that Scrope's gun incorporated all of Manton's refinements. It reads as follows:

May 20. A Double Gun w
             Elevation, Hammers,
             and Gravitating Stop
             holes & finished in the
             manner in a Ma [?hogany]
             furnished –
             Brown Leather &

The receipt, which is fastened to the bill with a wafer seal, and signed by Manton himself reveals that on 3 March 1815 Scrope paid £67-2-0 for what must have been an extremely handsome gun. The very next year Walter Scott had a character in the *Antiquary* say 'It's a capital piece; it's a Joe Manton, that cost forty guineas'.

Manton occupied an additional position of importance. In an age when even Prime Ministers engaged in duels it was advisable to be proficient with a pistol. Manton not only made them, but also kept a gallery behind his premises where gentlemen could practise shooting, or challenge each other to a pacific contest firing at targets. In his Journal for 17 November 1813 Byron, fearing that a letter of his to Lady Frances Wedderburn Webster had fallen into the hands of her husband, wrote 'If so – and this silence looks suspicious – I must clap on 'my musty morion' and 'hold out my iron'. I am out of practice –

but I won't begin again at Manton's now. Besides, I would not return his shot. I was once a famous wafer-splitter; but then the bullies of society made it necessary.' So proverbial was the excellence of Manton's weapons that Byron used his name both as a noun and as a verb. In one letter he asked Kinnaird why Hobhouse, who had been challenged to a duel by the aged Reformer Major Cartwright, had not 'wafered him with Mantons', and in another he assured Hobhouse himself that although 'that lust for duelling of which you used to accuse me in the Stevens's Coffeehouse days has long subsided into a moderate desire of killing one's more personal enemies' he would have 'Mantoned old Cartwright most readily'.

By all accounts — or at least by Byron's, who as we have seen should have been a good judge — Scrope too was formidable with his pistols. In his 'Detached Thoughts' Byron, remembering the companions of his youth, wrote:

> A private play being got up at Cambridge, a Mr *Tulk*, greatly to the inconvenience of Actors and audience, declined his part on a sudden, so that it was necessary to make an apology to the Company. In doing this Hobhouse (indignant like all the rest at this inopportune caprice of the Seceder) stated to the audience 'that in consequence of *a* Mr. Tulk having unexpectedly thrown up his part, they must request their indulgence, etc., etc.' Next day, the furious Tulk demanded of Hobhouse, 'did you, Sir, or did you not use *that* expression?' 'Sir,' (said Hobhouse) 'I *did* or *did not* use that expression.' 'Perhaps' (said Scrope Davies, who was present), 'you object to the *indefinite article*, and prefer being entitled *the Mr. Tulk?*' The Tulk eyed Scrope indignantly; but aware, probably, that the said Scrope, besides being a profane Jester, had the misfortune to be a very good shot, and had already fought two or three duels, he retired without further objections to either article, except a conditional menace — *if* he should ascertain that an intention, etc., etc.

Despite his proficiency, Scrope was not a bully, and was prepared to accept an apology on the two occasions of which we have any knowledge. On the first of these Byron acted as Scrope's second — a service which Scrope in his turn performed for him on at least two occasions, and would have been requested to perform again had Byron ever carried out his long cherished plan of returning to England, or at least to Calais, in order to settle accounts with Henry Brougham. About 6 August 1813 Scrope wrote:

> My dear Byron A circumstance took place last night which I am desirous of laying before you, that I may know your opinion how I should act – and in the event of your sentiments coinciding with my own, I hope you will not be unwilling to attend me in that character in which I should prefer you to any man breathing – Words have passed between Lord Foley and myself which I cannot pass over – Pray let me see you at *one* –.

Byron accepted the part of 'present peacemaker or future second', and was successful in the former role, as he recounted to Thomas Moore:

> By the by, I was called *in* the other day to mediate between two gentlemen bent upon carnage, and . . . I got one to make an apology, and the other to take it, and left them to live happy ever after. One was a peer, the other a friend untitled, and both fond of high play – and one [Scrope], I can swear for, though very mild, 'not fearful', and so dead a shot, that, though the other is the thinnest of men, he would have split him like a cane. They both conducted themselves very well, and I put them out of pain as soon as I could.

In London Scrope's activities were many and varied. The principal one, however, was gaming, for it was not only his passion but his major source of income. The age was notoriously one of high play, and Scrope would not have lacked for opportunities at Eton, at Cambridge and of course in London to become acquainted with the pastime which was to become an addiction. Of Cambridge Byron wrote 'this place is wretched enough, a villainous Chaos of Dice and Drunkenness, nothing but Hazard and Burgundy, Hunting, Mathematics and Newmarket, Riot and Racing . . .' Byron made at least one attempt to define the attraction of gambling:

> I have a notion that Gamblers are as happy as most people, being always *excited*. Women, wine, fame, the table, even Ambition, *sate* now and then; but every turn of the card, and cast of the dice, keeps the Gamester alive: besides one can Game ten times longer than one can do anything else . . . I have thrown as many as fourteen mains running, and carried off all the cash upon the table occasionally; but I had no coolness or judgement or calculation. It was the *delight* of the thing that pleased me.

Among the Dandies

Thomas De Quincey, on the other hand, said of Dickens that he 'misunderstands the true impulse in obstinate incorrigible gamesters: it is not faith, unconquerable faith, in their luck; it is the very opposite principle — a despair of their own luck; rage and hatred in consequence as at the blind enemy working in the dark'. Scrope and Brummell and all other middle-class dandies were doomed from the first moment they took up gaming. They were hopelessly out-gunned not only by the proprietors of the gaming clubs but above all by their fellow gamesters, magnates and landowners whose resources were so vast that they were bound to win in the end. Nevertheless Scrope Davies does not seem to have been the classic type of gambler described by De Quincey. He managed to amass a small fortune by gambling, and to remain solvent for nearly fifteen years.

To gamble Scrope had to have a venue. In Regency London there was no shortage of establishments only too willing to extend their facilities to the unwary. In addition to these 'hells' of extremely doubtful honesty there were many well-established and reputable clubs where play took place. The club was the natural habitat of the dandy, and it is no surprise to find that Scrope belonged to several. He was a member of Watiers, the dandy club *par excellence*, from 1814 at the latest, for on 17 July of that year he received a card with the welcome news that for that month he was £6,550 in credit. Watiers was founded at 81 Piccadilly by the Prince Regent's chef, and was renowned for the quality of its dinners. It was famous for high play, but in this respect was perhaps too successful for in 1819 it closed, most of its leading members being ruined.

Scrope never achieved membership of the most prestigious club of all, White's, despite the fact that his friends Brummell and Lord Alvanley were leading members, but in 1816 he was elected a member of Brooks's, the headquarters of the Whigs. It may be that, as so often, politics had an influence on his social existence. At Brooks's too he was able to engage in play, though to judge by his monthly accounts he did not risk such large sums there as he did elsewhere, and indeed by his time high stakes were discouraged in the two leading clubs. Vast gains and losses were however a feature of the Union Club, founded in 1799, and with premises in St James's Square. Although respectable, the Union was until 1821 little more than a gaming-house. A list of the founding members contain such names as Sheridan, Charles James Fox, Burdett, and the Dukes of

Bedford and Norfolk, suggesting that Scrope would have found several individuals there whose politics were compatible with his own. Byron became a member in 1812. Another club to which they both belonged was the Cocoa Tree, originally a chocolate house in the reign of Queen Anne. It lacked the *cachet* of White's and Brooks's, but it seems to have been a favourite haunt of Scrope's and Byron's during the years that they spent together in London. There too gambling for high stakes was the order of the day.

In addition to his less reputable, if conventional, London pastimes Scrope engaged in other activities which reflected a change in the attitude of the English gentleman. That passion for athletics and for games which was to become a distinguishing feature of the race had been unknown to the eighteenth and earlier centuries, for whom sport had meant either killing a variety of birds and animals, or betting on the outcome of horse-races, or of gladiatorial combats between dogs, bears, bulls, game-cocks, boxers, or any other species that could be induced by greed or natural ferocity to batter each other to insensibility or death. These activities continued during the period of the Regency, though a reaction was setting in against cock-fighting and the baiting of bulls and bears, but beside them there grew up an interest among gentlemen in engaging in strenuous exercise themselves. The interest grew into a passion, and 'Gentleman' John Jackson, who had only fought in three prizefights himself before setting up as instructor to the amateur, was said to number a third of the peerage among his pupils. There are numerous references in Byron's correspondence to his sparring either in his own rooms, or at Jackson's 'academy'. Scrope also was a keen student of this form of exercise, and would spar with Byron in the latter's rooms. On occasion he could turn his studies to practical use. According to James Holmes the painter,[5] who late in 1815 took miniatures of Scrope and Byron for them to exchange, Scrope

> who was a small thin man, but extremely handy with his fists, told Holmes of an adventure he had had at one of the coal wharves on the Thames, whither he had gone on some business or other. Some of the coal-heavers and others about the wharf, seeing the dapper little gentleman got up in the most dandified manner, began to make fun of him. Davies replied, and from the bandying of words there

5 Alfred T. Storey, *James Holmes and John Varley*, 1894, pp.55–56.

soon came threats, and before the smart gentleman well knew where he was, he found himself confronted by a big broad-shouldered fellow, squaring up to him in lusty anticipation of soon putting him *hors de combat*. 'I knew,' said Davies, 'that a blow from his big fist would do for me, and took my precautions accordingly. He made a lunge at me, which I warded, and then let him have one with all my might in the wind. He instantly fell all in a heap. His friends crowded round him, thinking he was dead, and I, while their attention was thus occupied, took to my heels and ran for my life.'

Parallel with this interest in participation was an endeavour by the 'fancy' to regulate the sport and make its conduct more respectable, a foreshadowing of the Queensberry Rules. To this end a 'Pugilistic Club' was formed, with a view to its occupying the same place in boxing as the Jockey Club already did in racing. In Scrope's trunk was an invitation to one of its functions. It takes the form of a printed card postmarked 11 June 1816:

The honour of your Company is requested to meet the Noblemen and Gentlemen of the P.C. to Dinner, at the St James's Coffee-House, on Saturday the 22nd of June, at Half past Six o'clock.

Tickets to be had at the Bar of the St James's Coffee-House, or of Mr Jackson, at his Room in Old Bond-Street; and it is particularly requested they may be applied for before the 20th.

Another pastime of ancient origins which enjoyed a renewed vogue in Scrope's time was tennis. This was not lawn tennis, which was not devised until the end of the century, but the original game played with a hard ball in a large court with four walls, round three of which ran a penthouse in imitation of the cloisters in which the game was no doubt originally played. By 1816 Scrope's renown as an amateur was sufficient to draw a large crowd when he took on the marker (that is to say, the professional) at Geneva. In his trunk were two relics of his interest in the game, a little notebook in which his account with a professional was kept, and a draft of proposals for the foundation of a club. The notebook which covers January to July of 1818 (effectively the London season) is divided into two parts. The first two pages are occupied by a record of Scrope's losses and gains at betting on the outcome of sundry matches — for even this healthful exercise could not be divorced from wagering – while six later pages have been used for an account of his expenses. The record reveals that Scrope's reputation as a useful player was not exaggerated. In the course of January and February he won £27-16-6, £26-5-0 of it from Colonel Ponsonby (throughout the account his most frequent opponent), in April and on one day of May £35-14-0, and during the rest of May, June and up to 10 July a further £59-6-6. In all, the unfortunate Ponsonby was obliged to part up with 59 guineas. Scrope also won six guineas from the Duke of Argyll, and on 20 June he took fifteen guineas off Mr Osbaldeston, a feat of which he must have been proud, for George Osbaldeston was accounted 'The Atlas of the Sporting World', supreme in his time among athletes, and a man who had beaten champions at royal tennis. Scrope's winnings totalled £122-17-0. Over a slightly longer period, that is up to 27 July, his losses were £72-9-0. He was a tolerably regular player, his attendance at the court varying between four days in January and in March, eleven days in April and ten days in May and in July. When he was there, however, the exercise he took was often strenuous. On 3 June for example he not only played five sets with the professional, R. Matt, but also took on Mr Howard and Colonel Ponsonby. Small wonder if that day Scrope had to lay out two shillings on brandy and water, and five shillings on two new handles. That was the only occasion on which he took brandy. His normal refreshment was soda water or lemonade. Other expenses were the professional's fee when Scrope played against him, which varied between about five and seven shillings a set, the hire of the court at a guinea, new rackets at two guineas each, balls at a shilling each, and the restringing of rackets at twelve shillings a time. Scrope also bought various items of clothing. A new pair of socks cost him 3/-, while a shirt cost only one. At 16/- tennis shoes were a greater expense.

It was in early 1819, only a year before his ruin, that Scrope and some friends drew up draft proposals for the foundation of a club of tennis players. The document records that the founding members were Messrs. Cuthbert, Davies, Lukin, Osbaldeston, Badot and Grant. There follows a list of those who are to be invited to join. Clearly the founders hoped that their club would comprise the very height of the *ton*, for the list begins: Duke of Argyll, Lord Jersey, Lord Granville, Hon. Colonel F. Ponsonby, Lord Apsley, Lord Clanwilliam, Hon. W. Howard and continues with another twenty-eight names of similar lustre, not excluding Lord Alvanley himself. The club was in fact established with Mr Lukin as its secretary. It flourished until 1866 in James Street, now Orange Street, where the walls of the court can still be seen not a hundred yards from Number 1, Pall Mall East.

Scrope Davies' frequent sojourns in London necessitated somewhere to live. In the early years he seems to have favoured Limmer's hotel in Conduit Street. Limmer's was the headquarters of the more fashionable members of the pugilistic 'fancy', and no doubt Scrope found many congenial spirits there. An hotel was probably too expensive for long stays – on 8 June 1811 he settled a bill with Stephen Limmer for £118-16-0 – and as he began to spend more and more time in London it was sensible to make other arrangements. Already in November 1808 he was writing to tell Byron that he had taken lodgings in Jermyn Street opposite Batt's Hotel, and the next year, at the time when Byron was leaving for the Levant, Scrope was living above a shoemaker in the same street, perhaps at the same address. A receipt dated 10 August 1810 still describes him as Mr Davies of Jermyn Street, but by March 1814 he was lodging at 3, Little Ryder Street, just off St. James's Street, and he was still to be found there in November. When it ceased to be his London address is not known, but on 28 February 1816 Hobhouse wrote in his diary 'Went to London. Put up at 11 Gt. Ryder Street the lodging of S.B. Davies Esqre'. That was to remain Scrope's address when in London up to the time of his ruin. Perhaps it was in connection with a recent move to what he hoped would be a permanent London abode that on 13 January 1816 he purchased of Edmund Lloyd, Patent Stove Grate Manufacturer and Furnishing Ironmonger of 178, Strand, one set of steel fire irons, one gothic fender, a pair of steel standards, and an improved coffee pot, all for £11-4-6 which included fitting the standards to the fender, bronzing the fender, and supplying an open packing case. Evidence of intention to keep the rooms for some time is surely supplied by a bill from Messrs. James and Cousins, Carpenters, dated 22 March 1819 'To fixing Shower bath and Putting Line D° 4 hours 9 yards of sashline 1^h . . . 6² of 1 deal 2 1½ Pulleys', for a total of 5/6d. The sashline and pulleys suggest that the shower was of the simple type favoured by boy-scouts, comprising an overhead bucket and a length of rope.

Some idea of the cost of Scrope's lodging and what he received for it can be gained from a bill found in his trunk. It is due to Victoire Barringer, doubtless the wife of the respectable proprietor of Messrs. Barringer & Co., coal-merchants, who are listed in the *Post Office London Directory* as occupying either No. 10 or No. 11, Great Ryder Street until 1840. The bill reads as follows:

To acct deld to 7 May 1818	166- 8- 0
8 Weeks Lodging from 7 May to 1st July 1818 at 4 guineas per Week	33-12- 0
10 Weeks do at 3 Guineas do	31-10- 0
4 do Washing	1- 0- 0
Letters and early Post	2- 0- 1
Wine	4-14- 6
Paid a Basket Fish and Box	9-10
Fish &c for a Dinner	5- 7
Mr. S. Davies	2- 2- 0
Broken Glass	2- 0
Epsom Races	10- 0
	£243- 4- 0

According to *The Picture of London for 1815*, a guide book for visitors to the Metropolis, Scrope was paying a very fair rent for his lodgings. Nevertheless he was, characteristically, over a year in arrears. He subsequently paid 18 guineas on account, and later £140, leaving £84-6-0 owing. Whether or not that debt was ever discharged is unknown, but when Scrope fled to the Continent Hobhouse believed him to owe £80 to his lodgings. Mrs Barringer seems to have provided a normal range of services, including an item which was perhaps a hamper to be taken to the Derby and Oaks meeting at Epsom from 27 to 29 May. Evidently Scrope gave dinners in his rooms, but for the most part he ate out, either in one of the coffee-houses which abounded all over London, or else in one of his clubs.

Scrope's magnificent existence had, unfortunately, to be paid for. His family were no more than comfortably off, and he had many brothers and sisters. There is no evidence that he ever received any family money. On the contrary, it was he who supported his youngest brother. Scrope's habits were extravagant, and he spent his life in a society characterised by reckless expenditure. The only income on which he could count was his share, as a Fellow, of the annual revenues of King's College. For the year 1816/1817 it totalled £140, or £111-13-0 nett, after taxes and deductions. For the year 1811 his outgoings (made up both of current expenditure and of repayment of loans) as revealed by his papers – and no doubt they by no means reveal all – were £1939-15-8. To bridge the very considerable gap Scrope had recourse to two common but fatal expedients, gambling and 'the Jews'.

The details of a dandy's finances were almost by definition obscure. It was a tenet of their creed that such matters were beneath notice or discussion. So it was with Scrope. Even a friend as close as Hobhouse, writing to Byron and speculating on the state of Scrope's affairs, was compelled to admit 'but who by searching can find out Scrope?' No doubt a man trying to pass as rich among rich men had every reason for keeping quiet about the extent of his wealth, while a professional gambler would wish to maximise his credit. With the discovery of his trunk we are in a position to go through his papers, a privilege he would have denied most emphatically to his friends.

Hobhouse believed that Scrope Davies' entire fortune was derived from gambling, and this belief is confirmed by his papers. On the occasion when he bade farewell to Hobhouse before going into exile Scrope himself gave a sketch of his pecuniary rise and fall. In 1815 he had been worth £22,000, and a good income besides, but when he went to Switzerland in 1816 he was worth only £5,000. These statements are supported by Scrope's papers. His run of luck had begun in 1814. On 11 June he told Hobhouse that the previous night he had won £6065 playing macao at Watiers, and his account with that club dated 17 July does indeed show a credit of £6550. For Scrope 1815 was the *annus mirabilis*. It was in that year that he spent £86-12-6 on the restoration of a luxurious carriage, and that he paid for his Manton gun. He spent £70 at his tailor's, the appropriately named William Taylor, of 30 Bury Street. His luck held, and on 6 November he paid one thousand guineas into his account at Newmarket. His statement covering the decline of his fortune is also reflected in his papers. On 16 May 1816 his account with Eaton Hammonds was £4624-1-6 in credit. Even that may have owed something to a fortunate stroke. Hobhouse recorded in his diary that on 11 April 1816 Scrope had gone to the Union Club after dinner and won £3700. On 8 June he told Byron in a letter that Scrope had

'reduced his body pecuniary of late at the Union' and that he had
brought himself round to the point whence he started that season.
The year 1817 started well – on 7 March Byron wrote 'Scrope
flourishing by the account' and on 14 April 'Scrope has won back
£3,000 – which is something and augurs well for the rest' – but by the
autumn Scrope could describe himself as steeped in poverty 'to the
very lips'. His account from Watiers, dated 17 September, tells at
least part of the sad tale. He started the month with a credit balance of
£13-12-6, and at first he prospered, winning 110 guineas on the 8th,
and 700 on the 9th. He then hit a disastrous streak, losing 1050
guineas on the 11th, 995 on the 13th and 105 on the 15th. Happily
he won back 270 the next day, but this still left him with a debit
balance of £1110-13-0. By 5 February 1818 Hobhouse could note
that 'S.B.D. has partially recovered himself'. During that year, to
judge by his papers, Scrope was able to keep up with his payments to
moneylenders, and appeared reasonably prosperous. The next year,
1819, his last in England, was not so happy. Perhaps the approaching
doom of two great dandy institutions is foreshadowed in three little
cards. They are Watiers accounts for 8 April, 18 June and 12 July
1819. All are for the same amount, £38-19-8, made up of £25-0-8 to
cash and the previous year's subscription, £2-18-6 to House Account,
and £11-0-6 to subscription for 1819. If Scrope was neither paying
his bills nor attending the club then the writing was on the wall for
both of them.

Scrope Davies was early into debt. On 10 April 1805, not three
years after he first went up to Cambridge, he paid £18-13-0 at the
suit of a creditor, a sum which included costs and even bail. Among
his papers was a list of 'Annuities Granted by Scrope Berdmore Davies
Esq'. The earliest is dated 23 February 1807, and the latest 28
December 1809. There are thirty in all amounting to a sum borrowed
of £14,520, and involving annual repayments of £2422-2-8 excluding interest. Scrope had already acquired an impressive burden of
debt. The granting of an annuity to the lender was at that time the
normal method of securing repayment of a loan. The annuities seem
usually to have run for six or seven years. In addition there were
periodical, usually half-yearly, sums of interest to be paid. A feature
of the business which on occasion caused Scrope and others extreme
agitation was that money-lenders customarily obtained by means of a
legal fiction a court order against a borrower before he had seen a

penny of his loan. This meant that literally the minute any payment was overdue the lender had only to notify the court, and the Marshal would drag the debtor away to the Marshalsea. Scrope's papers reveal that he never escaped from the hands of the money-lenders. The process of robbing Peter to pay Paul continued, with new debts being incurred in order to pay off old. It was a life of anxiety combined with cheerful irresponsibility, the flavour of which is well conveyed by a letter written 27 April 1814 to Scrope at Newmarket by his friend and fellow dandy Lord Alvanley:

Dear Davies

My non appearance at Newmarket and the continent being open must have considerably alarmed you for your five hundred — the fact is that I began to fear that I had lost
'Persuasion's breath to lull the raging Jew
His blackening mists dissolve to golden Dew
Teach him to dun no more, and lend anew.'
I have however happily overcome my difficulties and hope still favente Moses to Pay you next week. I trust you have had better fortune than when in London and am

Yours most Truly
Alvanley

An expedient which Scrope adopted parallel to his dependence on money-lenders was to maintain a number of different bank accounts. His principal account was with John Mortlock Esq and Sons of Cambridge. At Newmarket he maintained an account with Messrs Eaton and Hammond. In London he had accounts with the banks on whom Mortlock, and Eaton and Hammond, drew, that is to say Sir James Esdaile and Co. in Lombard Street and Biddulph, Cocks Ridge and Co. in Charing Cross. He also had accounts with George, Caesar, Charles and Edmund Hopkinson of St Alban's Street and of course with Ransom, Morland & Co. of 56 Pall Mall, the bank in which Douglas Kinnaird was a partner and with whom Scrope left his trunk when at last he was forced to flee. Large sums of money were moved by Scrope from one to another of these banks, and although the transfers from Newmarket were no doubt the results of fortunate speculations, one cannot help suspecting that some of them were attempts to use the same sum of money to placate several different banks — a technique which has survived to this day. It appears that Scrope's bankers had similar suspicions. On more than one occasion Mortlocks wrote to ask Scrope to address business letters to the bank rather than to individual partners, since the latter procedure caused delay. In a letter dated 19 July 1819, a time when Scrope was already in deep financial trouble, the bank wrote:

> Dear Sir We have received your letter apprizing us of having drawn a Draft for £800, and we will attend to your instructions respecting it.
>
> With regard to the £1000; instead of remitting it to us by post, as you propose, would it not be better to pay it at once to our Credit with Sir Jas Esdaile & Co, whose advice we should receive on Wednesday Morning?

Already in 1813 Scrope's way of life inspired anxiety in his bankers. On 25 June J.C. Mortlock wrote: 'I . . . have requested Messrs Esdailes to honor your drafts to the amount of £1140-11-6. I trust you will pardon my adding that these *Cash advances* are contrary to our rules of business, particularly with you Gentlemen of the Turf, as such you will excuse my adding that I rely upon punctuality.'

It was perhaps inevitable that the financial affairs of two such irresponsible young men as Scrope and Byron should become entangled. In the process Scrope came to be credited by later generations with assisting Byron in a way which, ironically enough, the contents of his trunk show never to have happened. Nevertheless, he did perform a service for his friend which if not so dramatic as the legend would have had it at least called for considerable courage and forebearance.

The story began in 1808. On 12 May of that year Byron wrote to a certain Mrs Massingberd 'I shall call with Mr Davies and the rest at five today to finish the business. I hope you and Miss M will be at home and disengaged.' Mrs Thomas Massingberd, an impoverished widow, ran, with the assistance of her daughter, a superior lodging house in Piccadilly. Mrs Byron had taken her son there in 1800 during his school holidays, and he used their house as a base in London on subsequent occasions. In 1805 he explored the possibility of going to 'the Jews'. He soon discovered that a minor needed a guarantor, and his sister Augusta refusing to act, Mrs and Miss Massingberd agreed to fill the role. Their action was not only irresponsible but worse, for Mrs Massingberd received a handsome 'rake-off' from the money-lenders for each negotiation. Thus began Byron's involvement in a web of debt from which he was not to escape for many years. In the list of annuities mentioned earlier as having been granted by Scrope, Mrs Massingberd's name is linked, perhaps as joint security, with those of the lenders of loans totalling £2,700, eight made on 8 March 1808 and four totalling £1,800 made on 13 May 1808, the day after the date of Byron's letter. It would seem that Byron introduced Scrope to Mrs Massingberd, and that both friends then used her as a go-between, and her house as a rendezvous with usurers.

It should be remembered too that Byron did not attain his majority until 22 January 1809, so Scrope's presence could have been necessary as a guarantor. Later evidence shows that at least once, possibly on that very occasion, Scrope undertook the part. A loan made to a minor was legally irrecoverable, so that money-lenders tried to avoid direct transactions with such borrowers. In one case they actually insisted that Byron should not be in the room. It is therefore possible that the £4,500 borrowed by Scrope with the assistance of Mrs Massingberd was in fact destined for his friend.

Scrope's involvement in Byron's financial affairs, together with a flurry of letters between them on such matters just before Byron's departure, have led biographers of the poet to conclude that it was a loan from Scrope which enabled him to set out in 1809 on that journey to the Levant which was to give the world *Childe Harold*. Scrope's ability to make the loan has even been attributed to a win at the tables. No writer has been clear, however, as to what the amount of the loan was, or even whether it was a straight loan, or a guarantee. The papers found in Scrope's trunk help to throw more light upon the matter. Sad though it must be to bid farewell to a picturesque legend, there does not seem to be any evidence that about the middle or end of June 1809 Scrope either made or guaranteed a loan to Byron. Indeed, the correspondence which took place at that time and later between the two, and with others, all points to the transaction in question being that which took place in the Spring of 1808.

Since the autumn of 1807 Byron had been constantly thinking of foreign travel. His bad relations with his mother meant that he had no home, or considered that he had none, and a variety of ideas for protracted voyages make their appearance in his letters. Finally plans crystallised around Greece and Turkey, and from the beginning of

April 1809 Byron was telling his friends that he had reserved a place in May on the Malta packet. In the event it did not prove easy to raise the money for a prolonged sojourn abroad, the less so since Hobhouse, who was to accompany Byron, could not afford his share. As late as 26 April Byron was writing to his solicitor John Hanson 'I wish to know before I make my final effort elsewhere, if you can or cannot assist me in raising a sum of money on fair and equitable terms and immediately'. In a postscript to the same letter he asked 'Is my will finished? I should like to sign it, while I have anything to leave' – it was finally signed on 14 June. By 23 May his situation was no better: 'I have not five pounds in my possession. – I do hope the money will be procured for I certainly must leave England on the fifth of June, and by every power that directs the lot of man, I will quit England if I have only cash to pay my passage', – and by 19 June, the day he left London for the port of Falmouth, desperation had driven him once more to the 'tribes of Israel'. He wrote to Hanson:

> Sir, – In consequence of the delay, I have been under the necessity of giving Thomas [a money-lender] an annuity for his bond, and taking up further monies on annuity at seven years purchase to the tune of four hundred per annum altogether including T's bond. – For the payment of this half yearly you will deduct from the money of Sawbridge when complete, and be good enough to place three thousand in Hammersley's hands . . .

Colonel Sawbridge was a friend of Hanson's partner Birch, and it was his agreement to lend Byron £6,000 which allowed him at last to make his departure. Hammersley was the international banker on whom Byron drew in Malta and Constantinople. There was some delay in the receipt of Sawbridge's loan, as Byron's letter shows, but it was received and from it were made available the funds which he used in the Levant. It is at this point that Scrope makes his appearance, with a letter written to Byron on or about 20 June:[6]

> In consequence of your permission, I opened your will, and, to my great disappointment, found no mention made either of me or the annuities, unless you include them in the word 'debts' – But how am I to substantiate my claim in the event of your death? I have no

6 As is usual with Scrope the letter is undated, but presumably he wrote it after Byron had left London. It was enclosed by Byron in a letter to Hanson dated 21 June and it is now British Library Egerton MS. 2611, ff.291, 291b

grounds at all on which I may proceed —

A person has this morning offered ten years purchase on your Rochdale property, by way of annuity — this would save you 700 £ per annum — and, however inconvenient, I will pay for the papers — Pray write to me by return of post, and inclose (after consulting some person in the law about the necessary form) an instrument authorising Mr. Hanson to accept this offer, and enjoin him to do it — for God's sake do not inflict murder on one who has been guilty of kindness only towards you — Under my present anxiety existence is intolerable — I cannot sleep — and much fear madness —

Mr Hanson says there is nothing to pay the interest of the annuities — why not tell me this? Write to me immediately or you shall hear of such things as the day would quake to look on.

Scrope was clearly afraid that some annuitants, or lenders, would come upon him for their capital and interest if Hanson were unable to find the money. Furthermore, the uncertainty of travel in the Levant could mean that Scrope faced sole responsibility for those debts should Byron die. He therefore encouraged Byron to raise a loan on the security of his estate at Rochdale. Part of the estate had been illegally alienated by Byron's predecessor, and Hanson was proceeding in his usual dilatory fashion with the business of recovering it with a view to sale. Byron hoped that the proceeds of this sale, and of another estate at Wymondham in Norfolk, would redeem his debts.

It is this letter of Scrope's, written just before Byron's departure, which has given the impression that it was he who stepped into the breach at that critical juncture. Other letters written at the time and later, however, some of them discovered in Scrope's trunk, show that he was referring to an earlier transaction for which he, as guarantor, would be left responsible while Byron was abroad. The poet's imminent departure had brought home to Scrope a sense of his extreme vulnerability. In his despair he decided to try a two-pronged attack, and to mobilise humour as well as reason. He wrote a facetious account of the consequences to Byron of forcing Scrope to do away with himself, and enclosed it either in the letter just cited, or possibly in another written shortly thereafter.[7]

7 The account itself has no greeting or ending, so does not appear to have been an independent letter. It is not dated, but the reference to Falmouth and the similarity of certain phrases to those found in the letter, show that it must have been written at much the same time. At the head of the first page is a drawing of a figure hanging from a gallows.

Among the Dandies

Yesterday was executed pursuant to his sentence at Newgate Lord Byron for the horrid and unnatural murder of S.B. Davies late of Jermyn street St James's of which murder the following is a full, true and particular account.

The deceased S.B.D. for some time lived on the most intimate and buffooning footing with L⁽ᵈ⁾B. who was accustomed to laugh at whatever he said and did. This intimacy for which the world did in vain attempt to account continued for the space of two whole years during which time the deceased was always merry and his lordship always well pleased with his company. However, about the beginning of May last the deceas'd was observed to get tipsey oftener than common and to talk in a strange incoherent manner about the receipt of frequent letters, the Cocoa tree club and many other unaccountable matters . . . But as the month of May advanced these peculiarities in his conduct increased . . . He became every day more lean and less laughable, and about the beginning of June began to show other symptoms of disease as he not unfrequently talked about life annuities, ten years' purchase etc. and of dying the next day in the same breath. His friends sometimes thought he had formed an imprudent love-connexion somewhere in Piccadilly, as he was heard to mention the name of one Mrs Massingberd living in that street . . . At this Juncture L⁽ᵈ⁾B. left London apparently very disconsolate at the situation of his friend, and giving no cause for suspicion of the horrid catastrophe that he was about to cause. His lordship had been only one day at Falmouth, when he received a letter from the deceased of which a duplicate had been deliberately forwarded to the same place in case of accidents. This letter informed L⁽ᵈ⁾B. that the deceased was at the time of writing or at least would soon be insane, and that unless his Lordship enter'd into some arrangement with the Lady in Piccadilly before mentioned, the deceas'd would do a desperate deed at which the world would quake. L.B. pretended not to understand this, and giving not a satisfactory answer, heard by the next week's post that the said S.B. Davies had swallowed a pint of Laudanum in his daily dose of double distilled Brandy and died in great torments still talking of life annuities. A coroner's inquest immediately set upon the body and after considering much, and in vain looking for the letters of which he so frequently talked, brought in a verdict of willful murder against a person or persons unknown. Thus this horrid transaction was likely never to have been traced to the true author, if the letter written by the deceas'd to L^dB. had not fortunately been discovered in Falmouth Street. On this discovery his Lordship was immediately taken into custody and convey'd to London, where after a confinement of some months in the Tower he took his trial in Westminster Hall in which place his immediate predecessor was also tried for his life. On the trial it appear'd that the deceas'd had given his lordship fair warning that he would upon the refusal to do as he wish'd, make away with himself: and as L^dB. had nothing to say in his defence, but that he thought the deceas'd to have been only in joke – he was unanimously convicted, and soon afterwards condemned. Wednesday being the day fix'd for his execution, his lordship took two pills on Tuesday Evening for fear of getting fat, forgetting that he was to be hang'd the next morning. The same kind of indifference appear'd in his whole conduct, and he died as he had liv'd, very impenitent . . . ('Vivant Rex et Regina')[8]

On 26 June[9] Byron sent Scrope a letter (it was found in the latter's trunk) with a view to allaying his fears:

Since your epistle I have received a codicil from Hanson, which I trust will prevent the sad catastrophe of the triple suicide, yours, Mrs. & Miss Massingberd's – We are shortly to sail, and I hope by this time Hanson has prepared the cash requisite to suspend your 'ensuing insanity' (at least for the present) and I further trust that a few months will make you free, the old woman like Æson[10] with renovated youth, and me independent. – Pray let me hear

8 On the verso of the second page are four pen and ink caricatures. Two are entitled 'Two Authors of the Satirical Miscellany', the third 'Ld B. as an Amatory Writer', and the fourth 'The Satirist.' Of the first two, one has Hobhouse's characteristic nose, and next to the other have been written the initials C S M, so perhaps it represents Matthews. Hobhouse was busy at the time with *Imitations and Translations*, 1809, which he called his 'Miscellany', though Matthews all too prophetically insisted on referring to it as the 'Miss – sell – any.' It would be pleasant to think that the fourth caricature was of Scrope himself, but there is no evidence to support this. A possible candidate is Hewson Clarke who continually attacked Byron in a journal called *The Satirist*.

9 The letter is dated 22 June, but the wrapper has been dated by Byron 24, while the postmark is 26 June.

10 In Greek myth the father of Jason, restored to youth by his daughter-in-law Medea.

from you, your letters are always amusing particularly the tragical ones, I hope I shall not behold any catastrophical paragraphs in the 'Malta Mercury' — Seriously, dear Scrope, you are one of the few things in England I leave with regret & shall return to with pleasure, I hope God or the Devil (it matters not which if the end is the same) will prosper you at Newmarket, at the Union, at Racket's, at the Cocoa Tree, I am sure in my absence you will laugh when you think of me, I wish I may be able to do the same and to furnish you with many Oriental anecdotes wherewithal to astonish your gregarious audience at the various clubs of which you form so distinguished an ornament . . .

At the same time Hobhouse wrote to Scrope as well. His letter, dated 24 June and also found in the trunk, is the first to make it reasonably clear that Scrope's worries related to an earlier transaction, and not to a recent loan:

Dear Davies,

Since the receipt of your letters & since B. gave you an answer, Mr Hanson has sent down a codicil to be annex'd to your friend's will, by which a particular acknowledgement is made of the debt due to you, and an injunction is addressed to the executors to see that the sum be properly discharged. I trust that this will entirely allay all apprehensions of any accidents that can accrue by this oriental tour, as far as respects the payment of the principal. B. has seal'd sign'd & deliver'd the writing after all the proper forms and has transmitted the paper to Mr Hanson. Your friend likewise assures me that the interest will be regularly paid, & of this indeed as it always has been so, & as several sums have been by him set aside to answer this demand I cannot see any reasonable doubt, altho the agent either from peevishness or disappointment at this tour does not appear to have given you quite such satisfactory answers to your queries as you might have wished & expected. I hope, however, that your mind is entirely at ease on both these points, or at least will be, the moment you know of this codicil . . . Our amusements yesterday were a little diversified by seeing a lady whipp'd at the cart's tail thro'out a pleasing perigrination of the dirty districts of this Town. If the delight occasion'd to us by this spectacle had not been a little damped by a recollection of the catastrophe probably acting at that time at N° 81 Jermyn Street,

we should have been tolerably merry, which we do not again expect
to be exactly until we have heard from you that you are actually
alive & in spirits . . .

In the meantime Byron had referred Scrope's suggestion about
Rochdale to Hanson, and given him instructions as to the disposal of
the £6,000 which he was to borrow from Sawbridge. At the same
time he asked him why he had not honoured a certain draft. Hanson
replied on 24 June, pointing out that Byron had not left him enough
money to meet the draft, and that furthermore there was £537-10-0d
to be paid to the annuitants. If Hanson were to pay Byron's other
drafts, the annuitants would have to wait, which they would be most
unwilling to do. 'Consequently', said Hanson, 'I must go back on Mr
Davies and Mrs Massingberd which I wish to prevent'. This was just
the kind of outcome that Scrope feared. As far as Rochdale was
concerned:

> I think it would be quite an unnecessary Work and certainly a very
> expensive one to give any Charge on the Rochdale Estate . . . Why
> not give Mr Davies a Bond of Indemnity which will appease his
> fears — I have just now seen him and as he informs me you are
> willing to give him such a Bond I have prepared and now enclose it
> for your Lordship to execute in the Presence of a Witness.

The reference to the impatience of the annuitants must refer to a loan
contracted some time in the past — they would scarcely have become
anxious for their interest after only a week.[11] Even with Hanson's
support, however, Scrope was not to get his longed-for indemnity.
On 30 June Byron wrote to Hanson:

> The Codicil [to Byron's will] supersedes the necessity of a bond to
> Mr Davies who professes himself merely to be anxious for security
> in case of my demise, besides it is for 10000 £ and Mr. D only stands

11 Impaled on one of the spikes in Scrope's trunk was the following document (now Scrope
Davies Papers, Vol. 4, f.214), confirmatory of this hypothesis:
Received the 26 Novr 1808 of Scrope Berdmore Davies Esquire the sum of sixty seven pounds
ten shillings for One Quarters Annuity due from Massingberd and others for Lord Byron on
£300 per Annum after deducting property Tax the 13th Instant —

Quarters Anny	£75- 0-0	
Property Tax	7-10-0	
	£67-10-0	[Signed] J H Moore

pledged for £6000, it is true I offered to sign any satisfactory instrument for Mr. Davies, but I think the codicil sufficient, without a Bond of indemnity which shifts the responsibility completely, now as there must be a reliance either on my part upon Mr. D. or on Mr. D's upon me, I see no reason why it should not stand in its present state, as the annuities are fully intended to be redeemed the moment the estates are sold.

Byron's departure abroad in 1809 with his affairs in such a condition was an act of considerable irresponsibility. He did, however, genuinely believe that within a few months sufficient of his property would be sold to free himself and Scrope from worry. Hanson's unforgivable procrastination ensured that this was not so.

The longer Byron stayed abroad the more anguished Scrope became. On 17 July 1810 he wrote to Byron:

> I was happy to hear from you, but should be more happy to see you – I not only am not relieved from responsibility, but am obliged to pay the Arrears – Your Agent must have concealed all these things from you, or I am sure, you would long since have returned to England. – I can say no more at present but that I am subject to an arrest day after day and nothing but your return can relieve me – God bless you –.

Scrope's plight was not entirely Byron's fault. Hanson in his characteristic fashion had failed to answer a single one of Byron's letters in the course of more than a year, so that his client had had no idea that his property was not sold, and that Scrope was still in desperate straits. In repentant mood he wrote on 26 November 1810 to Hobhouse, who had arrived back in England on 16 October:

> Tell Davies, in a very few months I shall be at home to relieve him from his responsibility which he would never have incurred so long, had I been aware 'of the law's delay' and the (not Insolence) but 'Indolence of office'. – I presume he is very wroth and in that mood, to use his frequent quotation, in which the 'Dove would peck the *Es*tridge.'

It seems that Scrope was driven to contemplate desperate remedies for his financial condition, for later in the same letter Byron said: 'Sandford Graham . . . tells me that Davies is to be married to an

82

heiress whom he picked up at Bath'. On 10 January 1811 Byron wrote
from the Capuchin Convent at Athens '. . . present my respects to
Matthews and Davies, who is I hear about to throw himself away on a
rich wife, and none of the seemliest, according to my reporter'.
Whatever the truth of the rumour, this was the last mention of
Scrope's matrimonial venture. His morale can scarcely have been
improved, however, by a letter he received from Hanson, written on
20 February, in which that worthy revealed that 'His Lordship does
not say a word about returning Home which I am very sorry for – I am
wholly without funds to make any Payments for his Lordship . . .' By
May, however, Byron was making his way home, and wrote to
Hobhouse from Malta on the 15th '. . . as I hear nothing but
croaking from H[anson] I am hastening homeward to adjust (if
possible) my inadjustable affairs . . . Tell Davies it is with the
greatest regret I see him in such a Situation from which he shall be at
all events and at all expence relieved, for if money is not ready I will
take the securities on *myself*.'

Either the anger which Byron feared that Scrope would feel at being
so long deserted never existed, or it evaporated with their reunion.
Scrope was the first to greet him, on the evening of 14 July, the very
day that he landed at Sheerness. The next day Byron told Hobhouse 'I
dine with Davies today, he came to me *drunk* last night, and was very
friendly, and had got a new set of Jokes, but to you they are doubtless
not new'.

Financial concern was soon thrust from the minds of both Byron
and Scrope by personal tragedy. On 1 August Byron's mother died; on
5 or 6 Scrope wrote to him as follows:

My dear Byron

Matthews is no more – He was drowned on Saturday last by an
ineffectual attempt to swim through some weeds after he had been
in the Cam 3 quarters of an hour – Had you or I been there
Matthews had been now alive – Hart saw him perish – but dared
not venture to give him assistance. Had you been there – Both or
neither would have been drowned – He was indeed a man of talent
– My soul is heavy – I can do nothing – I wander about in despair – I
shall never see his like again – His body was found 12 minutes after
he had sunk – They tried every effort to restore animation but in

vain — Such was the end of the man whose mind appeared to be possessed of greater powers than the mind of any man I ever knew — God bless you —

> and believe me ever yours
> Scrope Davies

Limmer's Hotel Conduit St.
Do write to me —
You shall hear from me again when my mind becomes tranquil.

At the head of the letter Byron noted 'Received Aug" 7th at Newstead the day after I received a lively letter from the *dead* Aug" 8th 1811 B.'[12] The day he received Scrope's letter Byron replied:

My Dearest Davies, — Some curse hangs over me and mine. My mother lies a corpse in this house; one of my best friends is drowned in a ditch. What can I say, or think, or do? I received a letter from him the day before yesterday. My dear Scrope, if you can spare a moment, do come down to me — I want a friend. Matthews's last letter was written on *Friday* — on Saturday he was not. In ability, who was like Matthews? How did we all shrink before him? You do me but justice in saying, I would have risked my paltry existence to have preserved his. This very evening did I mean to write, inviting him, as I invite you, my very dear friend, to visit me. God forgive —[13] for his apathy! What will our poor Hobhouse feel? His letters breathe but of Matthews. Come to me, Scrope, I am almost desolate — left almost alone in the world — I had but you, and H., and M., and let me enjoy the survivors whilst I can. Poor M., in his letter of Friday, speaks of his intended contest for Cambridge, and a speedy journey to London. Write or come, but come if you can, or one or both.

To this in turn Scrope responded with a letter received by Byron on 11 August, as he noted on it:

12 The letter from Matthews to which Byron refers was in answer to one which Byron had written on 31 July announcing his return to England. Byron's letter, the text of which is printed in the Anthology, was found in Scrope Davies' trunk. He in turn had presumably found it in Matthews' rooms when arranging his affairs, and no doubt felt it wise to abstract it, given the indelicate nature of its contents and the reference, however oblique, to Greece and homosexuality.

13 Presumably Hart.

My dear Byron,

Heaven's vials of wrath have been poured out upon us — I this morning received a letter from Hobhouse[14] — His letter resembles a man whose speech is interrupted by his sobs — Had he felt less I had less esteemed him — It is my intention to visit Cambridge on Monday — there will I view the accursed spot where Matthews was seen to perish. The consolation, my dear Byron, which I am able to give you, must be trifling indeed — Such as it is you shall receive it — for on Wednesday or Thursday next — I hope to see you at Newstead — My destination is Scarborough — There shall I live alone unseen of any, — The world forgetting by the world forgot for three weeks — At present the utmost I can hope is to endure life — To enjoy it I despair — ⟨The conversation of Matthews had the power to render confinement delightful⟩ — I was going to say something about Matthews — I cannot. In him (a solitary instance) were combined genius to dazzle, eloquence to persuade and reason to convince — Do write an epitaph for him — You, and you alone are capable of doing him justice — I have several of his letters — declamations, and other compositions all of which claim a religious admiration — I do not speak of him in this way because 'sublatum ex oculis' — I paid tribute to him when living — whether he esteemed my intellectual powers or not, I am unable to say — that he delighted in my company — I aver with pride — and certainly never was I animated to attempt flights beyond my strength but in his presence. His admiration of you was unbounded — I shall mourn his death. Matthews 'Mors tua delenda est non nisi morte mea' The third of August shall by me be ever held as a solemn fast. γαρ γερας εσι θανοντων — My mind on that day felt an oppression and I foreboded some dreadful calamity. The genius of the mind warned me of an approaching evil. I mentioned this circumstance to a man with whom I travelled from Lord Cavan's on the morning of that day — Matthew and myself agreed to appear (if spirits do exist after that they have shaken off this mortal coil and have the power to revisit this sad vale of tears) to each other, and clear up all the doubts and uncertainties about future existence — I live in hope.

---

14 Scrope's melancholy task had not ended with Byron. Hobhouse had been compelled by his father to join the army as the price of paying his debts — the alternative had been exile in the Isle of Man — and was with his regiment in Ireland. In his diary for 7 August he wrote 'Received from S.B. Davies the fatal news of the violent death of my oldest and best friend, C.S. Matthews . . . Wrote as well as I could to S.B. Davies, to Lord Byron, and David Baillie. Alas, alas, who is there left?'

God bless you, and give you strength to overcome all your calamities.

The return of tranquility to Scrope's mind seems unfortunately to have coincided with that of hyperbole to his style. His first, brief, letter strikes the more deep-felt note of grief. Who, however, can stand comparison with Byron as a letter writer? To them the tragedy seemed all the greater because they had foreseen that it might happen. As Byron wrote to John Murray:

> . . . One of Matthews's passions was 'the fancy'; and he sparred uncommonly well. But he always got beaten in rows, or combats with the bare fist. In swimming, too, he swam well; but with *effort* and *labour*, and *too high* out of the water; so that Scrope Davies and myself, of whom he was therein somewhat emulous, always told him that he would be drowned if ever he came to a difficult pass in the water. He was so; but surely Scrope and myself would have been most heartily glad that
> > 'the Dean had lived,
> > And our prediction proved a lie' . . .

Scrope was as good as his word, and passed four or five days with Byron at Newstead. On the 22nd Byron wrote to Francis Hodgson 'Davies has been here, and has invited me to Cambridge for a week in October, so that, peradventure, we may encounter glass to glass. His gaiety (death cannot mar it) has done me service; but, after all, ours was a hollow laughter.' Scrope must have discussed with Byron business as well as the lamented Matthews, for he wrote from Harrogate 'Do come to Harrowgate — Here I am — and here I shall be till the 20th of September — At all events let me hear from you — God bless you and yours — Scrope Davies'. In a postscript he added 'An Uncle of Ackers tells me that your property at Rochdale is *very valuable* — so do not be hasty —'. To this encouraging piece of information Byron replied on September 2nd:

> I am detained here by the Ins. no — the Indolence of 'Office' (an Attorney's) and the 'Law's' or rather the Lawyer's 'delay' [Byron never believed in wasting a good joke by confining its use to one correspondent only] for my worldly Director will not come before 14th and I must be patient, for I like *fair* means as well as any body when *foul* are not likely to be so useful as they are always agreeable.

— I shall attend to your hint in the Postscript, but what can I do ? You might as well preach moderation to the mad or maudlin, as caution to an embarrassed man. — You know my situation, indeed you have a right to know it, you know too how completely I am in trammels, and all the advantage I am ever likely to derive from that property, is the sad satisfaction of knowing it to be lucrative, and never being able to make it so. — If my affairs are not in some order very soon I have made up my mind to the step I shall take, what that is, I think you will guess, and all things considered it would not be the worst.

The veiled threat in the last sentence appears to be Byron's first mention in his correspondence of the idea of suicide. It was an idea that fascinated both of them, as it did so many of their contemporaries. In Scrope Byron felt he had a sympathetic confidant.

The succession of deaths — to those of his mother and Matthews was added that of his school friend Wingfield in the Peninsula — brought home to Byron the sense of his own mortality, and he resolved to make a new will. On 12 August he wrote to Samuel Bolton, his mother's lawyer in Nottingham, enclosing the draft. Among other provisions, including the entail of Newstead on his cousin George Anson Byron, and legacies to various servants, was a clause 'The claims of S.B. Davies, Esq., to be satisfied on proving the amount of the same', and another leaving his 'Library and furniture of every description to my friends Jn. Cam Hobhouse, Esq. and S.B. Davies, Esq., my executors'. Bolton was unhappy about a possible conflict of interest, and wrote 'If Mr. Davies has any unsettled claims upon Lord Byron, that circumstance is a reason for his not being appointed executor; each executor having an opportunity of paying himself his own debt without consulting his co-executors'. To this Byron made the lordly rejoinder 'So much the better — if possible, let him be an executor. B'.

By 10 October Byron had returned from Rochdale, his 'everlasting agent [Hanson, who put] off his coming like the accomplishment of a prophecy' having at last made the journey North. He was free to take up Scrope Davies' invitation to visit him at Cambridge, and on 22 October he reported their proceedings to Hobhouse:

I write from Scrope's rooms, whom I have just assisted to put to bed in a state of *outrageous* intoxication. — I think I never saw him so bad before. — We dined at Mr. Caldwell's of Jesus Coll: where we met

Dr. Clarke and others of the Gown, and Scrope finished himself as usual. — He has been in a similar state every evening since my arrival here a few days ago. — We are to dine at Dr. Clarke's on Thursday . . . I like him much, though Scrope says *we* talkèd so bitterly that he (the Said Scrope) lost his listeners . . . Every body here is very polite and hospitable, my friend Scrope particularly. I wish to God he would grow sober, as I much fear no constitution can long support his excesses. — If I lose him and you, what am I? . . . — Excuse this dirty paper, it is of Scrope's best.

Drunkenness was certainly one of Scrope's besetting sins, though it was one he shared with a good number of his contemporaries. That he lived to the age of sixty-nine suggests that he had indeed a remarkable constitution. Perhaps there is no need to attribute his excesses to more than the *mores* of his time and some inborn predisposition to dependence on alcohol. In exile he was proud that he had been able to wean himself from it. One is driven to wonder, however, whether the strain of his existence did not drive him to seek oblivion in drink. He was chronically in debt, and he had no resources save what he could win by gambling. What was more, as a dandy, a wit, a 'diner-out', he had a reputation to maintain. Hobhouse noted in his diary on more than one occasion that if Scrope could not dominate a conversation, or at least play the part of a leading protagonist, he would relapse into silent discomfiture. Byron's account of his conversation with Dr. Clarke is another instance. There was no lack of competition, and in particular Scrope must surely have realised that while he himself had merely talent, Byron had something more. There is no evidence that Scrope felt jealousy of Byron, and indeed, as we have seen, Byron was always anxious to value his friend highly, but there was in the trunk one small item which may suggest that from time to time Scrope had brought home to him the consciousness of their disparate status. The item is a note[15] from Spencer Perceval of Trinity College, son of the ill-fated Prime Minister, declining an invitation to meet Lord Byron in Scrope's rooms, since he was 'unfortunately engaged in such a manner that [he could not] possibly make [his] escape.' At the head of the note Scrope himself has written 'Byron dined with me on this day and blazed forth with genius. I am unhappy.'

15 The note is undated, but since Perceval matriculated in October 1813, it must refer to one of the two visits to Cambridge which Byron made in 1814, for they were his last.

Some six months after Byron's return from Greece Scrope's financial burden had still not been removed. On his arrival in London from Newstead on 13 January 1812 Byron must have found a somewhat peremptory letter from Scrope, for he wrote the next day from his lodgings at 8 St James's St:

Dear Davies, On arriving in town last night I found your letter and immediately set off to my solicitors' with it, who will take measures accordingly and write to you today as I left a frank for that purpose. — I have been doing everything to raise money by mortgage on Newstead for these last three months to no purpose. I have been disappointed in every expectation and as these people will not allow time, we must have recourse to legal measures. — If they thought proper to wait a little longer until my arrangements could be completed, this might have been avoided, but as the business now stands, there is no other course. — For me to take the annuities on myself as they now stand would be madness, when they only require exposure to be quashed, but if the parties would accept proper interest and fair terms I should have no objection to the measure. — You will recollect that the money was paid in my presence to me and the disputes I had with Riley and Thomas at their house on their own exorbitant charges for the papers, I am sure I was present at the payment of *all* either at Thomas's or my lodgings in Brompton, this you can prove without difficulty. — My Solicitor will explain more fully the course to be taken, it is an unpleasant one but, unless they will give time, the only means of extrication at present. — Nothing has been wanting on my part to hasten the arrangement. I have returned to England, journeyed here and there, and suffered every possible anxiety on this subject, and I still hope to adjust it, without much delay. — To yourself on my own part I am at a loss how to express myself, your friendship has been put to so severe a test; I wish to preserve it if possible and at all events can never be your enemy, you can have no conception how I am harrassed, pray let me hear from you immediately; and believe me

Yrs. very truly
Byron

Byron's reference to his lodgings in Brompton is further evidence that the loan in question was arranged in the Spring of 1808. The legal course which was being planned was to repudiate the debts on the ground of their being incurred by a minor. For this purpose it was important to be able to show that the loan had actually been made to Byron himself. Two days after he wrote to Scrope Byron sent Hanson a memorandum on the subject. Part of its significance has been obscured by the fact that Marchand in his edition of Byron's Letters has tentatively expanded Byron's 'Mr. D' to 'Mr. Dorant', whereas in the light of the letter just cited it is clearly intended to stand for Mr. Davies. In the memorandum, among other matters, Byron stated that:

> In 1807. Ld. B. through the means of a Mr. Carpentiere or Carpenter then living at Dorant's hotel as manager of the York under Dorant, was made acquainted with Messrs. Thomas & Riley *who declined advancing money on* Mrs. & Miss M[assingberd]'s security without the addition of another. — Mr. D. on Ld. B's *application* consented to lend his name. — The papers were signed by Mr. D. in Ld. B's *presence* at *Mr Thomas's* in Hanover Street, *Ld. B. received* [two words illegible] *paid for the papers after some dispute* on the exorbitancy of the charges, and lodged certain sums with Mr. D. for the payment of Interest. — Afterwards *proceeded* to the Insurance office in the Strand. — Ld. B. has frequently seen Messrs Thomas and Riley before and since the transaction, at their house, at Brompton, and in St. James's Street. — They perfectly understood at the time, the annuities were taken up by him. — Recollects Riley pointed out *one of the parties* at Mr. T[homas]'s saying with a smile, 'this man wishes to see how his money is paid himself.' —

Byron gives the date of his first acquaintance with Messrs Thomas and Riley as 1807. It is, however, by no means unlikely that he had to wait until the spring of 1808 before he saw his loan.

By August 1812 Byron had decided that Newstead would have to go. It was offered for sale by auction on 14 August, but despite heroic efforts by the penniless Hobhouse to run up the bidding, failed to reach its reserve. The next day, however, a Mr Claughton of Lancashire, possibly acting as agent for another, made a private offer of £140,000. By rights Byron's, and with him Scrope's, troubles should have been over. With that scarcely credible bad luck, however, that seemed to dog Byron's business affairs – perhaps the name of that bad luck was Hanson – he proved to have closed with a bad lot. Perhaps Claughton never had the money to pay in the first place, perhaps he or his principal repented of his purchase, but at all events he began a campaign of prevarication and evasion that was to bring Byron to the verge of insanity, and to contribute substantially to the break-up of his subsequent marriage. In the meantime it was Scrope who was to be the first victim of Claughton's want of honesty.

The sale of Newstead over, there was nothing further to detain Byron in a London where the season had finished, and he proceeded to Cheltenham, arriving there by 23 August at the latest. He was accompanied for part of the time by Scrope. Writing to Byron in July 1817 to give him the latest news of society, Scrope was reminded of their time there together, and wrote '. . . your favourite Miss Rawdon is affianced to Lord W. Russell – the brother of Lord Tavistock – Miss R. is not what she was when you and I some six years since attended her to the theatre at Cheltenham to witness the performance of that Lout the Young Roscius,[16] in the Tragedy of Douglas 'by command of Lord Byron' –'. Elizabeth Anne Rawdon was the daughter of John Rawdon, brother of the first Marquess of Hastings. Scrope did not in his memory exaggerate his friend's partiality for her, for Byron had written to Lady Melbourne in September 1812 'Miss R. has always been a mighty favourite with me, because she is unaffected, very accomplished, and lived amongst the Greeks of Venice and Trieste . . .; I moreover think her very pretty though not at all in the style of beauty which I admire most'.

Confident that Claughton would by then have paid his deposit, Byron entered into another characteristically complicated deal with Scrope Davies. In a letter dated 27 October 1812 written from Mrs Bones's at Newmarket – the call of the turf was more compelling than that of Cheltenham waters – Scrope set out the transaction and its unforeseen result:

16 William Betty, the 'Young' or 'Infant Roscius', was a striking symptom of the decline of the English stage. He first appeared in London on 1 December 1804 at the age of thirteen, and for a year swept all other actors out of the public notice. The House of Commons was even adjourned early so that Members could see him act. His last appearance as a boy actor was in 1808, but he still appeared from time to time until he retired on 9 August 1824. In later life he freely admitted that the enthusiasm of his admirers had been misplaced.

Dear Byron,

In a conversation which took place between us on the eve of my departure from Cheltenham I expressed a wish that you would honor a Draft on you for 1500£ should circumstances render such a proceeding on my part necessary – From my having advanced 1500£ on your account to Capt. Agar and from having experienced of late a series of losses, I was obliged to give a Draft on you for the above sum – I was sorry to find however that either from negligence or inability you had given no instructions about the payment of the above sum.

I am at present in serious distress from want of money, and shall be obliged in the course of the next week to pay all the remaining sum due on my bond given to Capt. Agar – I do therefore hope and trust that you will give directions about the sum of 1500£ being immediately paid into the hands of Sir James Esdaile and Co. on my account – and I will send your Bond to you or to any person whom you may appoint – Pray write to me by return of post and believe me

Yrs
Scrope Davies

I hope Mr. Claughton has not failed to stick to his bargain – I also hope that the Bankers of Cheltenham have explained to you how perfectly innocent I was of the delay on the part of the Bankers in London honouring my Draft of 100£

Byron was embarrassed that, as we would put it in modern parlance, his cheque had bounced. On 31st he fired off two letters to Hanson from Eywood where he was staying with Lady Oxford, in the first of which he enclosed the offending bill – the bill itself is preserved together with Scrope's letter –, and in the second the letter itself. The first letter read 'Dear Sir – The inclosed bill will convince you how anxious I must be for the payment of Claughton's first instalment, though it has been sent in without due notice *I cannot blame Mr. Davies who must feel very anxious to get rid of the business* – Press C[laughton] & let me have an answer whenever you can to this Place' and the second 'Dear Sir – *Do pray press Claughton as Mr. D's business must be settled at all events – I send you his letter & I am more uncomfortable than I can possibly express myself upon the subject – pray* [act?].' At last on 8 November,

Claughton having paid over £5,000 on the fifth, he was able to make the order for payment 'Dear Sir — Not being able (& today being sunday also) to procure a stamp as the Post town is very remote, *I must request this letter to be considered as an Order for paying fifteen hundred pds. to S.B. Davies Esqre. & the same sum to your own account for the Tythe purchase — Mr. D's receipt can be indorsed on the bond*.'

The long, long tale of Scrope's guarantee and loan had almost another two years to run, and when it ended it is hard to see why it did so then rather than at another time. On 24 March 1814 Byron wrote Scrope a formal letter, asking him to state the amount of the debt. To this Scrope replied in a manner equally formal:

My dear Lord	
The bond debt is	4633
Seven months interest	135- 2-0
	4768- 2-0
Deduct Property Tax	13-10-0
	4754-12-0
There is also due on the last bond	50-00-0
	4804-12-0

Before your Lordship shall leave England, I should wish to have an interview with your Lordship —

> I remain
> your L^d^ship's
> Obd^t^ Servant
> Scrope Davies

Scrope's calculations reveal that he charged Byron interest at five per cent. A letter written by Byron some three years later, on 8 July 1817, to Kinnaird who by then had taken over the management of his finances, not only further confirms that Scrope's guarantee was made before Byron came of age in January 1809 but also reveals that at a later date Scrope took over the debt and discharged it himself. Thus is explained the apparently puzzling contradiction whereby Scrope initially guaranteed a loan, but was finally repaid an actual sum of money. The letter reads as follows:

> My dear Kinnaird/ — On reconsidering your transcription of Mr.
> Hanson's statement — I perceive — or imagine that he states the
> principal of the Jewish annuities at £9000. — This is wrong —
> because altogether they did not amount to much more originally —
> *& six thousand pounds have been paid off which were originally guaranteed*
> *by Scrope Davies to whom I reimbursed the money which he had himself*
> *discharged a few years ago*. — Since I came of age I raised only one sum
> between two & three thousand pounds principal — and subse-
> quently another of six or seven *hundred pounds* — & of these I paid off
> just before leaving England most of the interest & *one principal* sum
> of 600 pds. redeeming the annuity thereof of which Mr.
> H[anson] has the restored papers — The sum therefore to the Jews
> cannot by any means be so much — unless he includes *Sawbridge's*
> annuity which is not a Jewish transaction. — There were some
> others for which a Mrs. Massingberd (since dead) was security — but
> for these time can be taken because they cannot come upon the
> legality of the transaction being during minority — & though I shall
> give them their *principal* & *legal* interest — yet I am not so far
> prepossessed by the treatment I have had from these gentry as to
> liquidate that claim — until *all* the others — contract debts & all —
> are discharged & liquidated. —

Why Byron chose the Spring of 1814 to discharge a debt which had
dragged on for six years is hard to say. Probably he thought that at last
Claughton was about to complete, and he would be able to depart on
that journey to the East for which he had been making elaborate
preparations since the preceding summer. Scrope's reference to Byron
leaving England suggests that this was so. At all events Byron wasted
no time in paying the money over. On Friday 25 March he wrote:

> My dear Scrope —
>
> My Bankers (Messrs Hoares) will discount some bills of Mr.
> Claughton's today to the amount required & I *peremptorily* hope the
> whole will be adjusted tomorrow & transferred to you. — Hobhouse
> has informed me of some unintentional sin of omission on my part
> towards you in regard to an appointment made to meet Col.
> Matthews the brother of our late friend — I can only say — that the
> whole thing had entirely escaped my memory — and I trust it will

not live in yours; had I been at all aware that you had been in the least annoyed by this or any other apparent negligence on my part I should long ago have said – what I say now – that I am sorry for it. – In the ignorance of my innocence – I had imputed this estrangement to any cause but the real one – I thought that a sudden passion for ye Prince Regent – the columns of the Courier – or – to be serious – pleasanter pursuits than visiting an abstemious friend might have made this hitch in our acquaintance – but of any real cause of difference between us I had as little suspicion – as I now have hesitation in saying that I wish I had known it before. – Hobhouse & I have a kind of a dual: Club once a week at the Cocoa – to which we are allowed to ask one visitor – who must be a Coc*o*an – will you dine with us on Monday next? at 6. – We are restricted to fish all the year except Lent when *flesh* is strictly enjoined – the season is luckily in your favour for greater variety of viands as a guest – pray come. –

> ever yrs very affectly
> Biron

The mention of discounting Claughton's bills shows that part at least of his payments to Byron must have been made in the form of post-dated bills of exchange. That Byron asked his bankers to discount them, that is, to pay less than their face value in advance of their date of expiry, again seems to show that he was in a hurry to settle with Scrope, perhaps because of an intended departure. The reference to a hitch in their acquaintance suggests that it was not Scrope who had sought out Byron. The next day, the 26th, Byron was able to write:

My dear Scrope – The bills are discounted & I have sent a draft on Hoares for the whole sum to your bankers – I trust tonight – or tomorrow will apprize you of the receipt of the same. – I shall merely add that I by no means consider the obligation cancelled with the bond – though I much regret [first page of MS. cut off here] Tomorrow at 6 – the *Cocoa* – shall you order? or shall *I* – remember *fish* – and what meats you please. –

> ever yrs. most truly –
> Byron

The engagement for Monday night had been brought forward to Sunday, and Hobhouse was no longer to be one of the party. In his Journal entry for 28 March Byron reveals that the dinner became something of a celebration:

> 'Yesterday, dined *tête-a-tête* at the Cocoa with Scrope Davies — sat from six till midnight — drank between us one bottle of champagne and six of claret, neither of which wines ever affect me. Offered to take Scrope home in my carriage; but he was tipsy and pious, and I was obliged to leave him on his knees praying to I know not what purpose or pagod. No headache, nor sickness, that night nor to-day. Got up, if any thing, earlier than usual — sparred with Jackson *ad sudorem*, and have been much better in health than for many days. I have heard nothing more from Scrope. Yesterday paid him four thousand eight hundred pounds, a debt of some standing, and which I wished to have paid before. My mind is much relieved by the removal of that *debit*.'

In fact the money had been paid a day earlier than Byron thought. In Scrope's bank-book from Messrs. Biddulph, Cocks and Ridge — found in his trunk and now volume 17 in the Scrope Davies Papers — there is an entry on the credit side for 26 March 1814 which reads 'Lord Byron £4804-12-4'. Five shillings were deducted for the stamp, and Scrope was left with £4804-7-4. Thus ended, on a note of drunken hilarity, a long drawn out affair in the course of which Scrope displayed the most exemplary patience and forbearance, a fact which Byron did not fail to acknowledge on many occasions.

Scrope Davies may not have made Byron the immediate loan which enabled him to go to Greece (the honour belongs to the unsung Colonel Sawbridge), but he did, at the cost of an anxiety which sometimes bordered on despair, perform for six long years the less romantic but vital service of fending off the ever more peremptory demands of the money-lenders. Perhaps, by consenting to hold a severely undergunned financial fort during Byron's travels it was he, after all, who made it possible for the poet to leave, and to make the most of his formative voyage to the East.

4

The Go-between:
Piccadilly and Geneva

The next few years were not easy ones for Byron, and they culminated in a crisis which tested to the full the loyalty, courage and judgement of Scrope Davies, Hobhouse and Kinnaird. Byron was unable to go abroad owing to the impossibility of completing the sale of New-stead, and he drifted into various loves and ever deepening debt. His tumultuous affair with Lady Caroline Lamb was succeeded by a period of calm passed with the Countess of Oxford. Lady Oxford went abroad in June 1813, and Byron then began the notorious relationship with his half-sister Augusta, wife of Colonel Leigh. Scrope, although he was later to be astonished when it was rumoured that the affair had reached the point of incest, could not but become involved even though on the sidelines.[1] He had known Augusta at least since 1811, in which year he must have made a maladroit attempt to please her, for Byron wrote her a letter on 30 August saying 'I don't know what Scrope Davies meant by telling you I liked Children. I abominate the sight of them so much that I have always had the greatest respect for the character of Herod'. The proximity of Cambridge to Six Mile Bottom, Colonel Leigh's country house, meant that Scrope was available to give support when Byron's predicament became too much for him. One such occasion was the visit that Byron paid to Six Mile

---

1 It has been suggested that two passages in Hobhouse's diary, to wit 'Today I discover a frightful sign of what I yet know not' in the entry for 16 May 1814 and 'Kinnaird and I walked home together — We made mutual confessions of frightful suspicions' in that for 19 May, are an indication that Hobhouse and Kinnaird at least suspected that Byron had committed incest with Augusta. A passage in the entry for 20 May, however, shows that their fears were of a more personal nature. It reads 'I walked to Pearson's in Golden Square — but he was not at home — at six o'clock I called on him again — he examined and pronounced nothing the matter'. George Pearson was a distinguished physician. His diagnosis proved correct. No more is heard of suspicions in Hobhouse's diary.

Piccadilly and Geneva

Bottom between 10 and 13 September 1813. It seems to have been then that he and Augusta decided that they could not go abroad together. In his perturbation Byron descended on Scrope. As he wrote to Augusta 'I joined my friend Scrope about 8 and before eleven we had swallowed six bottles of his burgundy and Claret – which left him very unwell and me rather feverish – we were tete a tete. I remained with him next day and set off last night for London which I reached at three in the morning.'

The same day, 15 September, Byron wrote to Murray asking him to 'enquire after any ship with a convoy *taking passengers* and get me one if possible'. His first reaction to a crisis was, as ever, to escape abroad. That solution being rendered impossible by Claughton's prevarications, the affair with Augusta continued for the rest of that year and the next. Eventually it was decided between Augusta, Byron and his confidante, Lady Melbourne, that marriage was the only way to break the fatal bond. He allowed himself to become engaged to Lady Melbourne's niece, Anne Isabella Milbanke, a girl who had piqued his interest two years before by the old device of refusing him.

The unhappy story of Byron's marriage has been often told, and there is no need to rehearse it in detail here. The apportionment of blame aroused fierce passions at the time, and has continued to do so ever since.

Strange as it must seem, the one redeeming feature of Lady Byron's married life was the presence for two prolonged periods at No. 13 Piccadilly Terrace, the Byrons' London house, of Augusta Leigh. She was there from the end of April to the end of June 1815, and from 15 November 1815 until 3 April 1816. She had put her affair with Byron behind her, even if Byron had not, and was determined that his marriage should work. She showed an unbiassed devotion to both of them, and stood up bravely to Byron on behalf of Annabella and her family. Her account of that sad period is the only one which seems not at all to be *parti pris*.

If Annabella was fond of Augusta, and grateful to her for her support, far otherwise was her attitude to Byron's male friends. She regarded them as an unmitigatedly bad influence, leading him into drunkenness, and encouraging him in atheism and other noxious views. She dated the period of a serious increase in Byron's drunkenness and ill behaviour from the time of Hobhouse's return from France in July 1815. In fact, this was hardly just, since Hobhouse's diaries reveal that after 21 August he did not see Byron again until half way through November. Annabella was not alone, however, in mistrusting Hobhouse. Augusta too at that time regarded him as an unworthy companion. Hobhouse, for his part, in his *Narrative of the Separation of Lord and Lady Byron*, gave the other side of the story. He wrote concerning the relations between Byron's bachelor friends, that is to say, himself, Scrope Davies and Douglas Kinnaird, and Lady Byron as follows:

> It may be permitted to say that her ladyship had formed an incorrect judgement not only of his Lordship, but of his Lordship's friends, who, from not exactly bearing that cast of character which she might have been accustomed to regard as necessary for the communion of married men, she was induced to look upon as the associates of wickedness, rather than as the votaries and encouragers of a steady and honourable attachment to the companion of many years. She was unwilling to believe that any principle could be found in men *not* belonging to a certain school; and more especially in those belonging to that pernicious persuasion [scepticism in matters of religion] of which she unfortunately fancied that her husband was the very Coryphoeus, founding her opinions upon sundry playful paradoxes, of which *a total inapprehension of irony and of humour* of any kind prevented her from appreciating the true value.

The truth, it may be presumed, lay, as so often, somewhere between the two points of view. Few brides approve of their new husband's rackety bachelor friends, those reminders of freedom lost, and most endeavour to see them off. In upper class circles of the period, however, husband and wife customarily each went their own way, and so far from Byron exceeding what was usual it was remarked at the time that he and Lady Byron spent an uncommon amount of time together. That his friends knew nothing of Byron's treatment of his wife, and therefore can not be accused of encouraging him in it, is a reasonable deduction from their reaction to the separation when it came. Indeed, after it was all over Scrope conveyed to Lady Byron his assurance that he had never been her enemy – an assurance which she received with scorn. By the end of 1815 the constant infestation of No. 13 by bailiffs – in addition to the fact that no rent had yet been paid on the house – convinced even Byron that it must be given up.

After a blazing row in Annabella's bedroom on 3 January 1816, it was agreed between them that she and the baby should go down to her parents' house in Leicestershire. Byron would close down the establishment in Piccadilly, and after an interval follow her.

After Annabella's departure Augusta Leigh and their cousin George Byron remained at Piccadilly in order to keep an eye on Byron, whose conduct had led Augusta to conclude that he must be mad. She had, for a time at least, persuaded Annabella to the same opinion. The madman, however, felt an immediate weight lifted from his shoulders with the departure of his wife, and set about enjoying his newly recovered freedom. Augusta allotted herself the unenviable task of weaning him from the brandy, and establishing a more regular and healthy routine. In this it is ironic to find that she had an ally in Scrope Davies, while Hobhouse, preacher of homilies, threatened to set her efforts at nought. On the evening of Annabella's departure on 15 January, Augusta, Byron, George Byron and Scrope went together to Drury Lane. Augusta reported to Annabella:

> The Play last night affected him [Byron] much even to tears, but G said it was nothing to ye last time. He appeared very odd all the time there and I am perfectly sure that Scrope D remarked it from his looks and manner. B. set him down on our way home and proposed a *supper at Watier's* which made me shake, but ye other scarcely answered and most determinedly held off from everything of the sort.

The next night, Tuesday 16, Byron went to the play with Scrope again, but Augusta was able to record that he had come home early. So far he had drunk no brandy, and was 'very tractable' with the doctor. On Wednesday night all was upset. Byron proceeded with Hobhouse to a dinner given by James Perry, the editor of the *Morning Chronicle*. Augusta was enraged at Hobhouse's irresponsibility. To Annabella she wrote:

> B returned between 12 & 1 this Mng with Hobhouse — both drunk — sent me & George to bed, & call'd for Brandy! Fletcher says H. drank none but B replied to his declarations to that effect 'So much the better — there will be the more for me' — & drank two glasses — would not take his Calomel & in short so far so bad! One comfort is *H* looks really dying — God forgive me, I hope He will take him to a better world — but however B. frown'd to such a degree at me to go

100

away that this dear friend (I mean fiend) either was or pretended to
be quite shock'd – said he wd go – & when B pursued me out of the
room to apologise for his frowns (when by the bye he tumbled flat
on his face up the staircase) H said to George all sorts of *tendresses* of
course to be repeated to me – I was *all the Angels* in ye world &
fortunate for him I was married! Fletcher has just informed me he
left the house door open at 3 o clock in ye morn'g & 'lucky we had
not all our throats cut!'

Even as Augusta wrote this letter her chances of saving Byron's
marriage were being destroyed. Annabella received a letter from her
friend Selina Doyle whom she had consulted about the advisability of
seeking a separation. Probably her mother saw the letter, in which
reference was made to Byron's conduct. At all events an extremely
unattractive cat was now out of the bag. Annabella's parents had
hitherto remained in ignorance of Byron's behaviour towards their
daughter. Few young wives are eager to confess that their marriage is
not a success. Lady Noel, as Annabella's mother was now called, had
never liked Byron, and she was determined that her daughter should
not return under that monster's roof. She departed at once for London
to seek advice.

The interview which Lady Noel had with Dr. Stephen Lushington,
an eminent Civilian, or advocate in the ecclesiastical courts, was most
encouraging, and dissolved her fears of failure or of Annabella's losing
custody of the child. Lushington even added a further lurid reason
why Annabella should never return to her husband. Byron's affair
with one particular actress might well expose her to the risk of
venereal disease. What was more, like so many divorce lawyers to this
day, Lushington proved an immovable opponent to reconciliation.
Annabella's descendents considered him the driving force behind the
separation. At all events, it was agreed that the first move be taken by
her father, and Lushington drafted a letter for him to copy. All this
activity was unsuspected by Byron, who was accordingly dumb-
founded when on Friday 2 February he received the following:

My Lord, However painful it may be to me, I find myself compelled by every feeling as a parent, and principle as a man, to
address your Lordship on a subject which I hardly suppose will be
any surprise to you. *Very recently,* circumstances have come to my
knowledge, which convince me, that with your opinions it cannot

tend to your happiness to continue to live with Lady Byron, and I am yet more forcibly convinced that after her dismissal from your house, and the treatment she experienced whilst in it, those on whose protection she has the strongest natural claims, could not feel themselves justified in permitting her return thither.

Byron could not believe that Annabella had concurred in this action, and considered that she must be acting under her parents' compulsion. He replied the same day, stating that her departure had been by agreement, and was the result of financial embarrassment. He concluded by asking for proof that Annabella had sanctioned her father's proceedings. At the same time Augusta wrote:

> My dearest Annabella
>
> I am desired by B. to write you a line and ask whether the separation between you (proposed this day by your Father) is *your* wish — and if so, he will acquiesce, and that you need not be under any apprehension of intemperate feelings or conduct on his part towards those belonging to you.

Byron had conceded a vital principle. If Annabella could convince him that it was her decision, and hers alone, she was free to go.

The next day Byron wrote to Annabella saying that he must hear directly from her what it was she wanted, and asking if the separation proceedings had her sanction. He asked her, as he had asked her father, what were the specific accusations made against him. Once again he conceded 'I shall eventually abide by your decision — but I request you most earnestly to weigh well the probable consequences'. That same day Annabella wrote to Augusta 'You are desired by your brother to ask if my father has acted with my concurrence in proposing a separation. He has'.

By Monday 5 February Byron himself had received no reply from either father or daughter. Hobhouse, who had no suspicion of what was going forward, found when he called that day at Piccadilly Terrace 'Lord Byron exceedingly depressed, more so than in an intimacy of eleven years he had ever seen. Lord B. at first seemed unwilling to mention the cause of his dejection; but, at last, with tears in his eyes, and in an agitation which scarcely allowed him to speak, mentioned the proposition he had received from Sir Ralph

Noel'. It was a time when loyal friends were needed, and when to be such a friend called for courage in the face of society's hostility. Scrope Davies, Douglas Kinnaird, and Hobhouse did not fail him and their devotion Byron never forgot. Writing to Scrope on 7 December 1818 – the letter was found in Scrope's trunk – to decline returning to England in order to assist Hobhouse in his electioneering, Byron protested:

> You can hardly have forgotten the circumstances under which I quitted England, nor the rumours of which I was the Subject – if they were *true* I was unfit for England, if *false* England is unfit for me. You recollect that with the exception of a few friends – (yourself among the foremost of those who staid by me) I was deserted & blackened by all – that even my relations (except my Sister) with that wretched Coxcomb Wilmot[2] and the able-bodied Seaman George,[3] at their head, despaired of or abandoned me – that even Hobhouse thought the tide so strong against me – that he imagined I should be '*assassinated*'; – I am not & never was apprehensive on that point – but I am not at all sure that I should not be tempted to assassinate some of the wretched woman's instruments, at least in an honourable way – (Hobhouse's parliamentary predecessor,[4] one of them, having already proved the existence of Nemesis by cutting his own throat) and this might not much forward his Election.

When it became clear how much Byron would need the support and advice of his friends, Hobhouse moved up to London. His diary entry for 28 February reads: 'Went to London. Put up at 11 Gt. Ryder Street the lodging of S.B. Davies Esqre'. The next night he and Scrope dined with Byron at Watiers, on which occasion the deserted husband appeared quite merry. Maintaining his friend's spirits could not, however, detain Scrope long from the serious business of life. 'After dinner', wrote Hobhouse, 'I went to the Cocoa and sat up – in the play room where S.B.D. lost his money'. From then until 18 March when

2 Robert Wilmot, Byron's cousin.

3 George Byron, a Captain in the Navy, and another cousin of Byron's.

4 Sir Samuel Romilly, who despite a general retainer from Byron accepted Lady Byron as his client. He committed suicide in November 1818 after the death of his wife.

Hobhouse left for Whitton, his father's house outside London, it appears from his diary that the three friends saw each other constantly. How did Scrope, Hobhouse and Kinnaird feel able to support a man who had been guilty of most reprehensible behaviour? There seem to be two answers to that question. One is the unquestioning loyalty felt by three men, all of them unmarried, for a friend of some nine years standing who had fallen foul of his wife and his in-laws. The other is that Byron was less than frank with his friends. On 9 February he told Hobhouse that 'he never lifted up a finger against her – the harshest thing he ever said was that she was in his way'. Hobhouse commented 'He told me and told me again and again that he had told me *all*. The matter continued inexplicable'. On the 12, however, Hobhouse learnt from Augusta and George Byron 'what I fear is the real truth that B has been guilty of very great tyranny – menaces – furies – neglects and even real injuries such as telling his wife he was *living* with another woman – and actually in *fact* turning her out of the house . . . locking doors, showing pistols – frowning at her in bed – reproaches, everything – he seems, to believe them, to have been guilty of'. Hobhouse was astounded. 'I found it difficult to account for his wishing to deceive me', he wrote in the same diary entry. Later that day he taxed Byron with the accusations. 'I got him to own much of what I had been told in the morning – he was dreadfully agitated – said he was ruined and would blow out his brains – he is indignant but yet terrified . . .' By that stage Byron's friends could hardly desert him.

The first problem to be confronted was how to reply to Annabella's request for an 'amicable separation'. Byron was disinclined to grant this until convinced that she was not influenced by her parents and her friends. A letter from her lady's maid, the wife of Byron's valet, most unfortunately gave the impression that she was. In reality, what the maid saw was probably the anguish of indecision – Annabella had in fact written her husband two affectionate letters soon after leaving London – rather than the result of coercion. Furthermore, Byron demanded to know the specific charges made against him. These Annabella's advisors were unwilling to reveal no doubt because of the weakness of her case in an age when such concepts as 'mental cruelty' could scarcely be said to exist. Another reason for Byron's refusal, Hobhouse related, was originally suggested by his immediate friends; who, when they heard the most positive assertions that the cause of the impending separation was an addiction on the part of Lord Byron to vices of the most disgraceful and abominable nature, were obliged to communicate the intelligence, painful as it was, to his Lordship, and to advise the only denial of such charges then in his power, namely, a decided resolution to come to no *private* arrangement, which might compromise his character, by the supposition that he was *afraid* of the disclosures of a public court of law.

The rumours which circulated concerning the reason for Lord and Lady Byron's separation played an important part in the whole affair, and, as the letter from Byron to Scrope quoted earlier shows, continued to cause the former much bitterness. They started innocently enough, not long after Annabella's departure, with the belief that Lord Byron was mad, and had sent his wife away to the country. His conduct at the theatre was enough to fuel such ideas. The silence on the part of Annabella and her advisors as to the nature of her accusations against Byron was, however, a fertile seedbed wherein strange plants might grow. Two monstrous growths were sown by Lady Caroline Lamb, who saw there an ideal opportunity for revenge. Byron had left a hostage to fortune by telling her, a woman whom he knew to be unbalanced, of his homosexual adventures, and of his affair with Augusta Leigh. For his folly he was to pay dearly. On 9 February Hobhouse recorded:

> D[ouglas] K[innaird] told me this morning that the Melbournes are in arms against Lady B. G[eorge] L[amb] called her a d'd fool, but added that C[aroline] L[amb] accused B of — poor fellow, the plot thickens against him. He is depressed most dreadfully, yet still laughs as usual & says he shall 'go to Court to be presented on his separation'.

Throughout the various documents connected with the separation the long dash appears always to stand for sodomy. Three weeks later incest too made its appearance in the scandalous reports. The longer Augusta remained at Piccadilly after Annabella's departure the greater the danger to her reputation. This was pointed out to her, but as long as she felt she might be of service to her brother, Augusta stayed beside him. On 29 February Hobhouse noted 'Mrs Leigh has been forbid all intercourse with her [Annabella] at her lawyer's request. A story has now got abroad against *her* (Mrs. L) *and* B!!!'

Meanwhile Byron continued to oppose a separation. By 22 February he felt himself driven into a corner by the double threat of legal action and continuing rumours and this confirmed him in his obstinacy. Annabella wrote that day to her mother 'Ld B. now says the reports are so bad that nothing worse can be produced against him in Court – and therefore he does not care what he is accused of . . .' To Lord Holland, who had been asked by Lushington to mediate between the parties, as a last expedient before going to court, Byron wrote 'In short – they are violent – and I am stubborn – and in these amiable tempers matters stand at present. – They think to drive me by menacing with legal measures – let them go into court – they shall be met there'. He nevertheless allowed Lord Holland to show him an offer made by the other side. Annabella was by this time very despondent as to her chances of being allowed to keep her child. She decided that the best hope was to buy Byron off. As she told her mother 'Half the Noel Property was offered, and only £200 per ann asked at present' – in other words, Byron was to have half the property which Annabella would eventually inherit from her mother, and she would resign to him all save £200 of the £1,000 a year payable by her family under the marriage settlement. Byron saw straight through this appeal to his supposed mercenary instincts. Hobhouse recalled that 'His Lordship was overwhelmed with indignation at this, which appeared to him a studied insult, but which his friends presumed to have been the technical language of Lady Byron's lawyers. He rejected the terms at once'. His friends were wrong. Annabella assured him that the 'Matter and Manner' of her offer 'were dictated and approved by me'. She did, however, 'disclaim all design of Insult or offence . . .'

Impasse had now been reached. Both sides were ready for a legal battle, and prepared their ammunition. Byron's camp, still not convinced that Annabella was acting of her own free will, pondered the feasibility of prosecuting her family for conspiracy or detainer. Hobhouse argued the case for this with Hanson on 4 March, and they decided to put it to the experts at Doctors' Commons, as the building housing the ecclesiastical courts was called.

The next day, Tuesday 5 March, saw the turning point of the whole affair. It was a day characterised by intense activity on the part of almost everyone concerned. Annabella began by writing Byron a letter, drafted for her by Lushington, in which among other things she said 'Most calmly and repeatedly have I weighed all that has passed, and after the maturest deliberation the result is a firm conviction that a separation is indispensable. This resolution is not formed under the impulse or at the suggestion of others; it is mine, and mine only, and for the consequences I alone am responsible'. She went on to claim the performance of the promise which Byron had made in his first letter to her, 'And after your repeated assertions that when convinced my conduct had not been influenced by others, you should not oppose my wishes, I am yet disposed to hope those assertions will be realised'. Later, despite Lushington's injunctions to the contrary, she had a meeting with Augusta. Recounting the meeting to Lushington, she said, 'My Interview with Mrs Leigh has made the desired impression. My Maid had offered to take her oath that I was detained at Kirkby *against my will* – on this false ground the family have been acting'. Her assessment of the interview was correct. Despite the fact that she had once again urged Annabella to return, Augusta was finally impressed by her determination not to do so. To Byron's friend Francis Hodgson she wrote, 'I see and am convinced she will not be Shaken. What then is left but for B to consent to amicable arrangement! and I *fear* there are many who will persuade him to the contrary.

In accordance with her new conviction, Augusta wrote to Robert Wilmot, a cousin of Byron and herself. She told him that Byron wanted to see him, and went on:

> I fancy the object of this interview is for you to go with a message from him to Lady B. being determined to write no more – and I have *some* hopes that in the hands of so tact [*sic*] a person as you, *legal measures* MAY be avoided. I have been giving him my opinions on this subject, and have reason (from experience in *past* cases) to think it just possible they may have weight tho' *at first* they appear to be rejected.

Wilmot for his part had already arranged to see Annabella that evening, telling her in his letter that he thought Byron would settle, and offering his services as mediator.

Meanwhile Hobhouse had been engaged in the fruitless task of addressing a further appeal to Annabella couched in the most pompous terms, offering guarantees for Byron's future conduct if she would only return to him. He took the letter with him to Doctors' Commons when he, Byron, Hanson and, it appears, Scrope repaired there in search of advice. The Doctors gave it as their opinion that Byron should not cite, but that he had a good defendant's case. Hobhouse showed his letter to Byron, who approved, and then to Scrope, who also approved. To round off a busy day Hobhouse and Scrope then dined with two noted pugilists, John Jackson and Tom Cribb. Hobhouse admired the manners and tact of 'Gentleman' John, but could not feel the same about the 'stupid beast' Cribb.

Hobhouse's letter, which would in any case have been counter-productive, was already too late. It, and the opinion of the learned Doctors, had been superseded as a result of Annabella's interview and letter. The following day, Wednesday 6, meeting Wilmot on the way to Byron, Hobhouse was still arguing for taking the case to court, but when he saw Annabella's letter, and heard from Byron the admission that he had said she was free to go if she could prove she desired it of her own free will, he too agreed that Byron ought to do as she wished. At long last, therefore, Byron himself consented to a separation. He sent Annabella a proposal whereby he would give up all the £1,000 per annum income to her, but would make no arrangement in advance about the property which would come to him for life, as Annabella's husband, at Lady Noel's death.

No whit abashed by the failure of his two preceding schemes, Hobhouse now came up with a new idea. He 'spoke to Mrs Leigh and asked her if she did not think L^d B and his friends had a right to demand previous to any separation a positive disavowal of all the heinous charges made against Ld B. as making any part of her charges. She said yes.' The next morning, Thursday 7 March, Hobhouse drew up a declaration by which Lady Byron would disavow 'cruelty systematic unremitted neglect gross and repeated infidelities – incest and––.' At two o'clock he and Scrope took the paper round to Byron. Opinions differed. 'B. and D. seemed to think those things had better not be put on record, and certainly not on the same paper with the separation as that would make the disavowal seem like the price of separation.' At this point Wilmot arrived, and Byron and Scrope Davies withdrew. Wilmot read Hobhouse's letter, and agreed to take it to Lady Byron. Scrope and Byron entered the room again while they were talking, and, as Hobhouse put it 'seemed afraid of my compromising the matter'. The account in his diary continues 'D. urged the necessity of Lady B's disavowal being previous to and altogether unconnected with the separation — it was agreed she should be asked by Wilmot to write a letter tantamount to my declaration'. Hobhouse drew up a memorandum based on his letter, and the party broke up, agreeing to meet again at two o'clock the next day. That night Scrope Davies, Hobhouse and Solomon Norton dined together at the Piazza. Hobhouse wrote that Scrope's 'fun and Norton's good humour and anecdote made the evening pleasant', but no doubt the eight bottles of claret and one of sherry which they consumed made their contribution also.

The forebodings of Scrope Davies and Byron were, as it proved, justified. Annabella wrote to Lushington 'I enclose for your previous consideration a paper which I am required to sign as the preliminary of any Separation — I never will'. The next day, Friday 8, Wilmot met Scrope and Hobhouse at Byron's. Wilmot took Hobhouse into another room, told him 'that Byron was mad and that something horrid would be proved against him' if he went to court, and gave him a letter from himself to Hobhouse. In it he stated that Annabella had specified 'certain terms of arrangement'. One was that she would take only £200 per annum of her fortune, plus her 'pin-money' of £300 per annum. As Mrs. Clermont put it in a letter to Lady Noel 'Lord B: offered the whole of her present fortune but that is not thought right to take he having so little'. The second was that Byron should stipulate in legal form that when she inherited the Noel property he would do what he thought just. The third was that arbitrators should be appointed at once to arrange the separation privately. In either of those two cases she would make the following declaration: 'Lady B. positively affirms that she has not at any time spread reports injurious to Lord Byron's character and conduct, nor have any such reports been sanctioned by her, or by those most nearly connected with her'.

Having read this letter Byron and his two friends unanimously 'exclaimed that the disavowal was there made clearly the bribe for separation and would be thought so by the whole world'. Hobhouse gave an account of the discussion which followed:

> I said the disavowal was in itself not sufficient. Lady B. must not only disavow the rumours having been spread but that the specific charges — that is incest and — made no part of her charges. We agreed to give up the cruelty and adultery in her own house — as to

the first W. told me he knew Lady B would not consent to disavow that – but it was agreed that Wilmot should actually specify the two grosser enormities . . . We broke up thinking Lady B. would not consent.

That night Hobhouse and Scrope dined together at George's Coffee House, where they had a good dinner for fourteen shillings.

Wilmot reported back to Annabella, and Lushington drafted a revised declaration. Annabella then emended the draft so as to avoid saying that no reports injurious to Byron had been spread by her friends, since they had in fact all asserted that his ill-conduct caused the separation, but she did declare that she did not consider herself in any way responsible for the rumours, and that 'two Reports Specifically mentioned by Mr. Wilmot' would not have formed part of her charges should the case have come to court. The declaration was only to take effect when the separation was concluded by consent.

The following day, Saturday 9 March, the four men were to meet again. Hobhouse arrived first, and found Wilmot showing something to Byron. Wilmot and Hobhouse then retired together, and the declaration was read out to Hobhouse. When Hobhouse agreed that the declaration would be satisfactory if signed by Annabella and witnessed by Wilmot, the latter showed him that it was. Wilmot then showed Hobhouse a second paper, which he entitled a principle of separation, and which was in fact the same as the 'certain terms of arrangement' which they had all discussed the day before, except that instead of Byron being called on to stipulate that he would do what he thought just when the Noel property fell in, he was in this paper required to 'make an arrangement with respect to it on fair terms of arbitration'. In answer to Wilmot Hobhouse said that he saw no objection at all to the principle, provided it was understood to have nothing to do with the disavowal. The two of them then went back into the other room, and Hobhouse told Byron that he thought both papers satisfactory. Byron. 'as it appeared to [Hobhouse] assented'.

At this point Scrope Davies came in, and there occurred the incident which was to lead to no end of trouble, and indeed, nearly to bloodshed. Many of the details of the crisis have become more clear thanks to the papers left in his trunk by Scrope who was, after all, one of the leading protagonists. Hobhouse continues his account:

Wilmot withdrew with him and when the two came back S.B.D.
said he thought the business also satisfactory — W. read over the
disavowal paper in my presence and then put it into his pocket to
keep it until the affair should be concluded — he took his leave in
spirits — we all thought — at least I thought the affair concluded —
S.B.D. and I walked home — dress' d Ld B. called in his carriage and
took us to Drury Lane . . . Coming to Wattiers we dined at 10
o'clock — good dinner and wines light.

The more relaxed mood in which the three friends at last found
themselves was to be shortlived. The next day, Sunday 10, the
intervention of another advisor set their achievement at nought.
When Hobhouse arrived at Byron's he 'found S.B.D. and Kinnaird
with him — and the whole house in rumpus . . . Kinnaird was
violently against the last article of the Principle [that concerning the
Noel property] and to my surprise Davies said he had never seen that
paper and would not presume to give any advice on money matters
which a lawyer should decide'. Hobhouse, less cautious, stuck to his
view that the principle as to the Noel property was equitable, and bet
Kinnaird ten guineas that Sir Samuel Romilly would agree with him.
Byron for his part declared that he was in no way bound by the paper
of the day before. He regarded it as a memorandum to be put into his
lawyers' hands for discussion. Hobhouse and Scrope then left, and
despite their misunderstanding rode together in the Park. Hobhouse
later set out for his father's house at Whitton.

To Augusta fell the unenviable task of telling Wilmot that his
mediation had fallen through. On Monday morning she wrote to
inform him that Byron had consulted Hanson, who agreed with
Kinnaird. She herself feared that Hanson and others were 'driving B.
on to destruction', but in reply to her arguments Byron asked 'am I
to give these men an advantage over me as long as I live? by saying I've
been bullied into terms'. Wilmot, a vain and pompous individual, was
enraged at the set-back to his endeavours, and fired off peremptory
remonstrances in all directions. To Byron he wrote on 11 March
requesting to be informed whether his Lordship:

> did not hear the paper read, which *Mr. Hobhouse copied*, and whether
> he did not distinctly assent to it, *after hearing* that Lady Byron's
> declaration was satisfactory to his friends Messrs. Hobhouse and
> Davies?

2ndly. Whether it was not sent to Mr. Hanson by his Lordship's authority?

3rdly. Whether his Lordship did not say that they had better make haste and get the instrument ready for his signature, or that he might be off for Dalmatia, or words to that effect.

4thly. Whether his Lordship does not recollect Mr. Hobhouse's shaking hands with Mr. Wilmot, and wishing him joy on the success of his mediation.

5thly. If, as Lord Byron asserts, Mr. Wilmot's negotiation was confined to the recognition of a *mere principle* of separation *independent of terms*, why was Mr. Wilmot sent to Lady Byron, at Lord Byron's *especial* request, with a distinct proposition from himself relative to terms?

6thly. Whether the proposition with respect to the Noel property contained in the paper copied by Mr. Hobhouse was not Lord Byron's *own* proposition, with this exception, that Lord Byron proposed *a written promise*, and that Lady Byron insisted upon *a legal instrument*, to which alteration Mr. Wilmot *positively asserts* that Lord Byron and his friends Messrs. Hobhouse and Davies gave their unqualified assent.

To Hobhouse and Scrope Davies he sent letters addressed to Piccadilly Terrace and identical except in one or two words. That received by Scrope read as follows:

Dear Sir

It is with feelings infinitely stronger than astonishment that *I hear* that Lord Byron has refused to assent to the principle of Separation, which was agreed upon last Saturday *in your presence, under your sanction*, and *with your approbation* and which I *conceive* that Lord Byron was bound *in honour to me*, as *well as to yourselves*, to carry into effect.

You will oblige me by an immediate answer *in writing* to inform me if your opinion coincides with mine.

Yours very truly
R Wilmot

23, Montague Square
Monday [11 March 1816]

Scrope sent his groom down to Whitton with Hobhouse's copy, enclosing a card saying 'I think it advisable you should come to town immediately'. Perhaps understandably, since it was already seven o'clock in the evening, Hobhouse sent back a note saying he would come up the next day. When the family were gone to bed he began to consider Wilmot's letter. He though it provocative, and wrote several letters to that effect which he tore up. Nevertheless, he recorded, 'I certainly did assent myself. I certainly thought Byron had and as certainly that Davies had. I thought therefore that the objection could no longer come from Byron although it might from his lawyers'. Hobhouse then came to the melancholy conclusion that he must either persuade Byron to comply, or 'give Mr. W. satisfaction' – that is, agree to fight a duel. The next day, as he wrote in his journal,

> very unwilling I rode up to town – not knowing what to make of the matter, – and thinking there must be some fighting . . . I found there had been queries put in an angry tone both to him [Byron] and Davies – which he had answered as rudely and D. mildly through Mr. Ridley Colborne . . . I told B. my mind distinctly that I thought he was wrong – but he was positive – and I then sat down and wrote to Wilmot in the spirit of last night which as Davies said it would not do I threw into the fire. B. wanted to write a violent note which we threw into the fire – it was agreed that I should call on Wilmot.

Byron's rude, and Scrope Davies' mild reply both survive. The former, in the parts where it answers Wilmot's abrupt enquiry, reads:

Ld. Byron presents his compliments to Mr. Wilmot. Lord Byron assented to the *principle* of a separation. Lord Byron himself submitted the paper to Mr. Hanson for consideration after having previously discussed the points it contained with his friends – but having come to no definitive conclusion upon them. – Lord Byron did say to Mr. Wilmot that dispatch was desirable – but never entertained an idea that an instrument was to be drawn up & signed without further consideration with friends or legal advisers. – Ld. Byron saw Mr. Wilmot (he believes) shake hands with Mr. H[obhouse] – or Mr. H[obhouse] with him – and Lord Byron did speak of an intention of visiting Greece by way of Dalmatia – but does not understand that this was to be a part of the articles of separation. – Mr. Wilmot was requested by Lord Byron to wait on

Lady Byron with a view to comply with her wish to open a negotiation – & he was selected from a wish to consult her feelings as being at the same time a relative of Ld. B's and a person who was more likely to be impartial & agreeable to herself & friends than other & more intimate connections of Ld. Byron's – Lord Byron's 'own proposition' was a promise (which he has no objection to renew) to do what should be deemed fair and liberal by Lady B – in the event of the Noel property falling in – Lady B – may insist on what 'legal instrument' she pleases – that was a subject for *consideration* – & Ld. B. – neither did – could – would – nor will give unqualified assent to any such proposition – either from Lady B – or any person or persons whatsoever. Ld. B. – is surprised that Mr. W. should describe Mr. Davies as giving 'assent' on questions of property as Mr. D. always declined giving an opinion upon such points at all. –

Interestingly enough, in view of the fact that Hobhouse found this answer rude, a draft in Scrope Davies' hand of the first part, down to 'agreeable to herself and friends', was found in his trunk. Either Scrope drafted the letter for Byron, or, more probably, they worked on it together. At all events he must have consented to Byron sending it off, whereas he joined with Hobhouse in consigning the violent note to the flames. At the same time he composed a letter of his own— the unfinished draft was also in the trunk. It is written on the back of a letter which he had received from Nicholas Ridley Colborne, afterwards Lord Colborne, a friend of Annabella's family who was later appointed one of the trustees to the separation. Colborne's letter, in which he asks for a meeting with Scrope to discuss the separation, is dated merely 'Tuesday', but given the contents of Scrope's letter this was clearly Tuesday 12 March. Colborne's letter having been delivered by hand, Scrope's letter was no doubt written the same day.[5] It reads:

Dear Sir,

The only writing submitted to my inspection on Saturday last was Lady B's Declaration.

I have neither sanctioned nor approved of any mode of arranging

---

5 The next day Scrope drafted another letter to Wilmot, setting out at greater length his recollection of the negotiations. The text of this letter is printed in the Anthology.

the distribution of property but have studiously avoided even the hearing any such discussion.

The only manner in which I have interfered in this affair has been in desiring B. not to enter into any negotiation previous to Lady B. having signed such a Decl.^{n} as that you showed me, and in cautioning against making too liberal concessions lest a miscon-struction might be placed on his conduct, and lest that might be attributed to fear which in reality was an act of kindness.

What took place between Mr. Hobhouse and yourself previous to my arrival I cannot say — this I can say [end of draft].

As agreed, Hobhouse at once set off to find Wilmot, but being unable to do so, returned to Byron's. There Byron assured him that he did not want him or Scrope Davies to quarrel — that is, fight a duel — with Wilmot. If there was to be fighting he would do it himself. Byron did however promise not to send any notes to Wilmot. With this assurance Hobhouse went back to Scrope's lodgings, dressed, and together they dined at the St James's Coffee House. After dinner Hobhouse returned to Byron's, picked up his carriage, and went round to Wilmot's house in Montague Square.

Hobhouse conducted himself in the lion's den with great skill. As a result of his conciliatory behaviour the very real danger of a duel receded. He stated that he had himself been convinced that both Byron and Scrope Davies had assented to the 'principle of separation', but that he had since been assured by Byron that that was never his intention, and by Scrope that he had never even seen it. He obtained from Wilmot an expression of his perfect satisfaction with Hob-house's conduct, and furthermore 'stated to him the necessity of his making some apology to S.B.D. he (W) having in that case misunder-stood Mr. D — W. agreed to call and recall'. When it came to asking Wilmot 'to call on Byron and throw Lady Byron's disavowal in the fire and finish his mediation', however, Hobhouse was not so successful. It appeared that Byron had after all sent his violent note,[6] 'so that W. had made up his mind to have done with his cosen'. Hobhouse accordingly returned alone to Byron's, where he 'received congratula-tions from Scrope Davies etc'.

6 The violent note complained of Wilmot's language, and made it clear that if there was to be any fighting it was to be, as Byron had insisted to Hobhouse, between Byron and Wilmot, and not between Wilmot and either of the other two.

Byron's camp was now divided against itself, with Hobhouse and Augusta in favour of his making the legal commitment at once, Kinnaird and Hanson opposed, and Scrope refusing to have anything to do with the question. Court action appeared inevitable, and Annabella's side renewed their hints of revelations to be made that would destroy Byron for ever. Byron became once more depressed and suicidal, and for the first time began to say that he must have been mad during periods of his marriage. Scrope and Hobhouse, however, remained unable to divine what his dreadful crime could have been. On Thursday 14 Augusta wrote to Hodgson 'What this mysterious charge can be is beyond ye utmost stretch of my imagination to guess. He *vows* HE knows not – and when I have implored Mr. Hobhouse and Mr Davies to pause well before they advise, they answer "Can we doubt his word? he has assured us he knows of nothing".' On the Tuesday Hobhouse had recorded: 'B own'd to S.B.D. and me at last, that he may have been *bereav'd of reason* during his paroxysms with his wife – it appears to me he has made some confession. I am still however in the dark utterly'. In the dark they were both to remain. By the Friday of that week Byron had repented of his attitude, and agreed to accept arbitration as to whether he should at once make the legal stipulation concerning the division of the Noel property. There was no hearing in court, and no revelations were made.

It was to be more than a month, such were Hanson's delaying tactics, before Byron finally put his signature to the deed of separation. It was not an easy period for him nor for his friends. The business of preparing for departure abroad was a distraction, but he was still harrassed by duns, depressed by the separation, and made the object of scandalous gossip. Towards the end of March, when Hobhouse and Scrope had been out of London for a few days, Augusta wrote to the former 'Do not forsake your most unfortunate friend – if you do, he is lost – he has so few *sincere* friends and well judging ones'. Annabella, writing to tell her mother of the famous incident at Lady Jersey's on 8 April when Byron and Augusta were cut by several of their acquaintance, named some of her supporters, and concluded 'Indeed I don't know any body except the Piccadilly crew of blackguards who is avowedly against me . . .' In their isolation the 'blackguards' were often together. On 3 April Hobhouse, who had left Scrope's lodgings on 18 March to go down to Whitton, moved into No 13 with Byron, and that night Scrope Davies and Leigh Hunt dined with them. It appears that two men of creative talent being of the party, Scrope felt cut out, and consoled himself with wine. Hobhouse wrote that 'D. said he could not get in a word between the *two* authors – he fell down in B's room'. The underlining of 'two' suggests that Hobhouse, in his turn, was offended by Scrope's remark. He would have considered that there were three authors present. Hunt later wrote of that period 'The adherence of his old friends was also touching. I saw Mr. Hobhouse and Mr. Scrope Davies (college friends of his) almost every time I called'. On the 9th Scrope gave a dinner at the Clarendon for Hobhouse, Byron, Douglas Kinnaird and Sir Francis Burdett. At midnight Hobhouse went to the Duchess of Somerset's, and when he returned with Lord Kinnaird, found 'the party still at it – broiled bones, punch, and a fracas succeeded which I need not set down'. That night they sat up until six in the morning. On the 11th the same party dined at the Clarendon again. On that occasion, according to Hobhouse, they 'had a pleasant day – though Davies was obliged to walk off – he went to bed, got up again went to the Union and won 3700£'. Scrope thereupon departed to Newmarket, leaving Hobhouse to pursue the thankless role of mediator between Byron's and Lady Byron's parties. They were both successful. Scrope was enjoying a winning streak, and at last, on the 21st April, the deed was signed. Byron was free to leave.

The signing was followed by a 'session', at which the two Kinnairds, Byron, Hobhouse, Samuel Rogers, and Scrope were present. The wit must have flowed as freely as the wine, for 'Rogers was afraid to leave the room and his character behind him –'. In his Journal Hobhouse recorded the events of Byron's last days in England:

April 22 . . . dined at home – everything prepared for Byron's departure – all his papers put into my hands – he received a visit from Mr and Mrs Kinnaird at night who brought him a cake and two bottles of champagne. Dr. Polidori did not go to bed; I did . . .

April 23 – Up at six – breakfasted – but not off until half-past nine – Polidori and I went in S.B. Davies's chaise – B and S.B.D. in Byron's new Napoleonic carriage – built by Baxter for £500 – there was a crowd about the door – when we got some way I looked back and not seeing B's carriage conjur'd up all sorts of accidents in my fancy – at last, however, it came along – with Fletcher and Bob

> Rushton . . . Arrived at Dover by half past 8 – dined at the Ship and took *light French wines*.

Hobhouse can not have been pleased to be assigned the company of Dr John Polidori, whom he considered 'an odd dog', and whose appointment as Byron's medical attendant he had not approved. Polidori, the son of an Italian settled in England and his English wife, was vain and unstable. At the age of twenty-six he committed suicide, but his share of immortality has been assured by his being Byron's doctor, Dante Gabriel Rossetti's uncle, and the eponym of one of the characters in Mary Shelley's *Frankenstein*.

The next day the weather prevented Byron from sailing, and the friends had to amuse themselves at Dover as best they might. Hobhouse went on:

> Dined at five, walked in the evening to the Church to see Churchill's tomb. The old sexton took us to an open spot or churchyard without a church, and showed us a green sod with a common head stone . . . Byron lay down on his grave and gave the man a crown to fresh turf it . . .

> Polidori committed a strange solecism to-night . . . his attachment to reputation and his three *tragedies* is most singular and ridiculous. B. says he shall have the reputation of having made a sober common place fellow quite mad.

Polidori gave his own account of that evening in a journal which he had begun the previous day, John Murray having offered him £500 for a record of Byron's travels.

> We then returned [from the graveyard] home, where, having delivered my play into their hands, I had to hear it laughed at – (an author has always a salvo) partly, I think, from the way in which it was read. One of the party, however, – to smoothe, I suppose, my ruffled spirits – took up my play, and apparently read part with great attention, drawing applause from those who before had laughed. He read on with so much attention that the others declared he had never been so attentive before.

To judge by Polidori's other productions his play must have been quite absurd. It is tempting to see Scrope Davies, of whose kindheartedness there is so much evidence, in the role of the attentive reader. He is certainly a more likely candidate than the disapproving Hobhouse or than Byron, whose name Polidori would surely have given with pride. At all events, that evening was by no means an abstemious occasion. Writing from Ostend on 26 April 1816 to report the safe arrival of himself and his attendants Byron told Hobhouse:

> . . . we were landed at least ten hours sooner than expected — and our Inn (the 'Cure imperial' as Fletcher calls it —) [Cour Impériale] furnished us with beds and a 'flaggon of Rhenish' — which by the blessing of Scrope's absence — the only blessing his absence could confer — was not indulged in to the extent of the 'light wine' of our parting potations.

With the morning of 25 April came the chance of sailing, though the wind continued contrary and fresh. Hobhouse continued:

> Up at 8, breakfasted, all on board except the company. The Captain said he could not wait, and B. could not get up a moment sooner — even the serenity of Scrope was perturbed — however after some bustle out came Byron, and, taking my arm, walked down to the quay . . . the bustle kept B. in spirits — but he looked affected when the packet glided off. I ran to the end of the wooden pier, and as the vessel toss'd by as through a rough sea and contrary wind saw him again — the dear fellow pulled off his cap and wav'd it to me . . . He . . . told me he felt a presentiment that his absence would be long. S.B. Davies said the same thing — but I told both that I had always had the same presentiment on leaving England.

Byron had escaped abroad. Scrope and Hobhouse had to return to London, where scandal and rumour raged unabated. Hobhouse wrote in his Journal:

> Davies and I took a turn on the pier — came back, paid a 20£ bill at Wright's and got into S.B.D.'s chaise for London — where we arrived by eight o'clock — we sent to Kinnaird to tell him we were coming to dine with him, when, lo and behold came Mrs K. in the Carriage saying there was a row expected at the Theatre, K. having received 15 anonymous letters stating that Mrs. Mardyn would be hissed on Byron's account. She wanted us to repair thither forthwith, but we dressed, dined with K. no disturbance at Drury Lane; the fifteen letters two or three . . .

119

The opprobrium which Byron's friends had earned by their loyalty to him was not long in manifesting itself. On 7 May Hobhouse 'found S.B.D. had been blackballed at Brooks's, notwithstanding I had written positively to D[ouglas] K[innaird] stating that I would not be put up and that he should not put up S.B.D. without asking him'. Consolation was, however, possible. 'A committee of 7 are to choose a 100 new members'. On that occasion Scrope was, it is pleasant to note, successful.

Meanwhile there were some happier matters to occupy the thoughts of Byron's friends. Hobhouse had always intended to follow him abroad after two or three months, and it appears that Scrope too must have promised to come out. In a letter to Hobhouse written on 26 May Byron said '. . . I trust to see you and the "forefender"[7] Scrope according to compact'. Ten days earlier he had written to Hobhouse 'If Scrope comes out – tell him there are some "light wines" which will bring to his recollection "the day of Pentecost" and other branches of his vinous thirty nine articles.[8] – I have solaced myself moderately with such "flaggons of Rhenish" as have fallen in my way – but without our Yorick they are nothing.' In what was proving to be the somewhat trying company of 'Dr. Pollydolly', Byron was missing Scrope, both as a drinking companion and as 'a fellow of infinite jest'. The doctor himself said in a letter to Hobhouse 'You and his other friend Scrope Davies form a great subject of conversation'.

At last, on 8 June Hobhouse was able to announce 'Scrope *will* come. He has reduced his body pecuniary of late at the Union, "sleek as he came he must go out", and he has brought himself round to the point whence he started this season. However, he comes in search of you and light French wines.' To this Byron replied on the 23rd 'I await your arrival – with that of Scrope – whose pocket appears (by your late letter of revolutions at the Union) to have become as "light" as his "wines" – though I suppose on the whole he is still worth at least 50-000 pds – being what is called here a "Millionaire" that is in Francs and such Lilliputian coinage'. He then went on to say that he had taken 'a very pretty villa in a vineyard . . . called Diodati,' and

7 'Forefender' no doubt refers to the joke quoted in the previous chapter about Scrope's amorous exploits at Brighton.

8 The significance of this joke, which Byron recalled several times, is by no means clear. Perhaps it is a blasphemous pun referring to the gift of the Holy Spirit.

instructed his friend that he was not to go to an inn, but to 'come on to head-quarters – where I have rooms ready for you – and Scrope – and all "appliances and means to boot" '. Diodati was at Cologny, a suburb of Geneva, overlooking the lake. He also announced that he had a third Canto of *Childe Harold* finished – the longest of the three – being one hundred and eleven stanzas – which he would send to Murray by the first plausible conveyance.

On 29 July, at half-past-eight in the morning, Hobhouse and Scrope, with their servants, set out in Scrope's carriage for Dover. They did not ship the carriage, but on arrival at Calais picked up one of Hobhouse's which he had left there the year before. In the course of the crossing on the 'Flora' packet, Hobhouse 'supported' a pretty Miss Loveday, who was feeling unwell. This was not the last service he did her. At the end of his journal entry for that day he wrote 'displaced a waiter who was looking at my girl undressing'. Whether on this occasion displacement had its usual implication of substitution we shall never know.

Calais had recently acquired a distinguished resident well known to both of them, and that night they 'supped with the banished Beau Brummell'. He regaled them with a scandalous tale about Sheridan, whose funeral Scrope and Hobhouse had attended together two weeks before, and how he had raped Lady Bessborough. Hobhouse 'could hardly believe [his] eyes, seeing Brummell in a greatcoat drinking punch in a little room . . .'

The friends, perhaps guessing that Byron would have recorded his journey in the lines of *Childe Harold*, had determined to follow in his footsteps, and accordingly set out across what is now Belgium, but was then part of the Kingdom of the Netherlands. Byron had chosen not to cross Restoration France and indeed, in his travelling carriage modelled closely on Napoleon's, he would have been conspicuous to say the least. The carriage has been represented as a mere example of insensate extravagance, but it was more, a deliberate and provocative political gesture. He had originally not even wished to visit 'the deadly Waterloo', that field which enclosed 'an Empire's dust'. Scrope and Hobhouse, who shared Byron's admiration for Napoleon, did actually refrain from visiting the scene of a battle both recent and catastrophic. In every other respect, however, they were the most insatiable of tourists. The wars with France had closed the Continent to Englishmen for a generation, and for Scrope at least this was his first trip abroad. Scarcely a church escaped inspection, and it is interesting to learn how many of the pictures they admired had but recently returned from Paris. Napoleon had pursued a policy of looting art treasures such as was to be repeated in the next century by the Nazis. They were favourably impressed by the cleanliness of the King of the Netherlands' domains, and by the well-being of his subjects — with the exception, that is, of Liège, whose inhabitants were all drunk, and where even Scrope's 'dandy impassivity' was destroyed when he saw a girl knocked down by a drunken postilion.

From the Netherlands they passed into Prussian territory, and made their way up the Rhine. At Koblenz they narrowly missed the ferry on their way back from a visit to the Ehrenbreitstein. This incident, slight in itself, led Scrope to remark that it summed up the whole story of his life — a joke which, perhaps, revealed the emptiness behind the jester's mask. Hobhouse, at least, thought it worth recording. By 12 August they had reached Offenburg, and Hobhouse wrote to Byron

> We are so far on our way to join you at your godsend villa; and I put these few lines in activity to give you that important intelligence . . . I would thank you to give me one line . . . letting us know . . . which side of the lake you have immortalised. Scrope is with me, and only Scrope; you who know him want no other. Unfortunately Newmarket speculations call him homewards by certain days not recognised in our calendar. He has ninths and twenty-fifths and the Lord knows what other epochs unknown to baser matter. He is eager to see you . . .

Hobhouse was looking forward to exploring Switzerland and Italy in company with Byron. For Scrope, however, always more independent than Hobhouse, the turf was paramount. The concatenation of circumstances which was to deposit Byron's and Shelley's manuscripts in Scrope's trunk for 156 years was being joined link by link. From Offenburg they went to Schaffhausen, inspected the Rhine Falls, visited Zurich, which they found 'crammed with English', passed through Lucerne and came to Berne, in whose 'broad streets . . . with [their] colonnaded houses [they] recognised something superior to whatever [they] had before seen in Switzerland', and, with an enthusiasm which we can still share, they 'hailed the capital of the wisest Government in Europe'. At last, on 26 August, they 'set off to

Sécheron, along the finest road in the world'. They 'went on to Nyon, Coppet, Gentoo' and 'came over in a boat to the vineyard below the villa Diodati. Went up and found Byron in a delightful house and spot.'

That same day Scrope and Hobhouse met Shelley, who came to spend the evening at Diodati. Byron and Shelley had met for the first time towards the end of May at the Hotel d'Angleterre in Sécheron, the village next to Cologny. They had been brought together by the machinations of Claire Clairmont, who had succeeded in making herself Byron's mistress shortly before his departure from England. She was the step-sister of Mary Godwin, who in turn was the mistress, and later the wife, of Shelley. As Polidori succinctly put it in his record of the meeting: 'P.S., the author of *Queen Mab* came: bashful, shy, consumptive, twenty-six: separated from his wife; keeps the two daughters of Godwin, who practise his theories; one L.B.'s.' During the first weeks of June the Shelley party installed themselves in the Maison Chappuis, near the shores of the Lake of Geneva, while Byron took the Villa Diodati, a few hundred yards inland but raised on a hill. There followed a summer fruitful for English poetry. Byron and Shelley were impressed by each other, and met almost every day. They shared a love of sailing, and were happy to make two excursions a day in the boat which they had bought together. A longer voyage round the Lake, in the course of which they visited the scenes made sacred by Rousseau and Gibbon, gave the world Byron's *The Prisoner of Chillon*, more stanzas for his Third Canto of *Childe Harold*, and Shelley's 'Hymn to Intellectual Beauty'. Later that summer, towards the end of July, Shelley and the two young women made an excursion to Chamonix. The great mountain and its surroundings inspired in him the poem called 'Mont Blanc', one of his most ambitious and difficult productions. Shelley's account of his expedition no doubt reinforced Byron in his desire to see those scenes for himself, but he wished to do so in the company of his friends. In his letter of 26 May to Hobhouse he had said that he did not like to begin his Alpine scrambles without them. At all events, the day after the arrival of Scrope and Hobhouse, while they were exploring Geneva, an ugly town according to the latter, Byron wrote to Augusta, informing her 'I am going to Chamouni (to leave my card with Mont Blanc) and I mean to buy some pretty granite and spar playthings for children (which abound there) for my daughter – and my nieces – you will forward what I select to little Da – and divide the rest among your own. I shall send them by Scrope.' The next day Hobhouse and Scrope, indefatigable sightseers as ever, seized the opportunity of going to Ferney to worship at the shrine of Voltaire. An old man who showed them the church remembered the great man, and described him as wearing an embroidered coat, and a wig which covered his shoulders. He had been tall, and very thin. Shelley spent each evening at Diodati, and on the 27th they all went out a short time on the water.

On 29 August there was much activity. Shelley and his party were returning to England, and left Geneva at nine in the morning. With him Shelley took a notebook containing Claire's transcripts of Canto III of *Childe Harold* and *The Prisoner of Chillon*, together with several other short poems written by Byron during that summer. This MS., together with a covering letter which Byron had written on the 28th, Shelley delivered to the publisher John Murray in London on 11 September. In the letter Byron said that he hoped Thomas Moore or Shelley would oversee publication of the poems, and that he wished Augusta Leigh to be consulted before publication of the 'Epistle to Augusta'. Of Canto III of *Childe Harold* Byron kept with him his draft, a fair copy in his own hand, and another transcript, this time in Mary Godwin's hand. This, until the discovery of Scrope's trunk, was all that we knew. It was presumed possible that he had kept with him the drafts of *The Prisoner of Chillon* and some at least of the other poems.

The same day that Shelley departed, Byron, Scrope, Hobhouse and the egregious doctor set out for Chamonix. They took two carriages, and three servants. Unfortunately, at starting, the postilion, who was a butcher, was found not to be able to ride. With more caution than courage, Byron and Scrope left the carriage abandoning Polidori and Hobhouse to their fate. The party dined at Bonneville, and started out once more for Sallanches where they planned to sleep. They proceeded up the ever narrowing valley of the Arve, and as evening fell Hobhouse got down to walk. This proved a wise decision, for not long after the butcher nearly upset the Doctor and the landaulet. The next day they set off for Chamonix, in two charabancs according to the Doctor, according to Hobhouse in three. They made a detour in order to walk across the glacier of Bossons, finding some difficulty in descending from it, especially Byron, who was not helped by his lame leg. On arrival at Chamonix they dined, and went off again in their charabancs to see the source of the Arveiron. This was the foot of a glacier descending from the famous *Mer de Glace*. They were told that it was extremely dangerous to go under the ice whence the river gushed forth, since the glacier was constantly breaking up, but Scrope nevertheless 'picked his way over the torrent to the fountain, and we all adventurously followed, and put our heads under the overarching ice, and saw the rushing fountains below for a moment'. What a debt would posterity not have owed to Scrope if he had contrived to get Byron killed before he had ever written *Don Juan*? He was not, however, as foolhardy as 'two Hollanders', about whom their guide had told Shelley and his companions, 'who went without any guide into a cavern of the Glacier and fired a pistol there which drew down a large piece on them'.

The next day, Saturday 31 August, the weather was so bad that they set off for home, not, however, before Byron had bought from a 'marchand naturaliste' various presents for his female relations. He wrote to Augusta to tell her that Scrope was bringing them back to England, and was also to give her an account of the trip. 'To Scrope I leave the details of Chamouni and the Glaciers and the sources of the Aveiron.' At three p.m. they stopped for the night at Sallanches. Scrope and Hobhouse went for a walk about the town in the rain. Drawn to a billiard room, they found that workmen were the players, while a woman acted as marker. They also noticed the great prevalence of goitre among the population. The cause, they were assured by the Doctor, was not the water but the air. In consequence of this, the women, being sedentary, suffered more frequently than the men.

With their return the next day to Diodati there was leisure to read Byron's latest poems, and to discuss his affairs. Hobhouse recorded 'Byron had given me before another Canto of Childe Harold to read'. He thought it very fine in parts, but was not sure he liked it as much as the preceding cantos. There was an air of mystery and metaphysics about it. By that date Hobhouse had not yet, however, read *The Prisoner of Chillon*.

The next day Byron gave Scrope the fair copy in his own hand of the new canto, written in a red morocco bound quarto notebook. Scrope proudly inscribed the volume 'This M.S. was given by Lord Byron to Scrope Davies at Geneva September 2^d – 1816'. Byron intended that Scrope should take the volume home and show it to Murray, for use in comparison with Claire's transcript 'in such parts as it may chance to be difficult to decypher'. He had already attached a note to the transcript to this effect. At the same time, or in the course of the next few days, Scrope acquired two other MS. volumes, whose very existence remained unsuspected until the opening of his trunk. They were octavo notebooks with marbled orange, black and blue paper covers, very similar in appearance but not in fact identical. One contained a transcript of Byron's *The Prisoner of Chillon* in Mary Godwin's hand, with extensive additions and emendations made by Byron. The notebooks being of a kind known to have been used by Shelley, but not by Byron, it would appear that Shelley supplied Mary with one so that she could copy the poems for Byron down at the Maison Chappuis. Claire once suggested to Byron that he could pretext copying as an excuse for her to come up to Diodati. Mary, while undoubtedly attracted by Byron, was more discreet.

The contents of the other notebook were far more surprising to the openers of Scrope's trunk. They were a fair copy in Mary Godwin's hand of Shelley's 'Hymn to Intellectual Beauty', a fair copy in Shelley's own hand of his 'Mont Blanc', and two entirely unknown sonnets, by Shelley, but in Mary's hand. That the *Childe Harold* MS. had once existed, and had been in Scrope's possession, had always been known, even if its location had not. That an unrecorded MS. of Byron's other major composition of that summer should emerge from the trunk was exciting, but understandable, and indeed, as we shall see, its existence could have been deduced from evidence in the Public Record Office. That Scrope should have been possessed of a MS. of Shelley, on the other hand, was both unexpected and inexplicable. For one thing, Shelley had no need of a courier, since he had only just left for England himself. For another, there was no reason why he should give one of his MSS. to a man whom he scarcely knew. Third, and most important, it was not a MS. with which Shelley could dispense. Comparison of the fair copies of the two major poems as found in the new notebook with the drafts of those poems in another notebook, now in the Bodleian Library, and with the first printings, reveals the important place filled by the new notebook in the textual history of the poems. The 'Hymn' and the two sonnets are, as we have seen, in Mary's hand. She must therefore have been supplied by Shelley with a reasonably fair copy in order to transcribe them. 'Mont Blanc', however, is in Shelley's hand, and is likely therefore to have been transcribed by him from a draft, presumably that in the Bodleian notebook, which is heavily revised, but virtually complete. The draft of the 'Hymn' in the same notebook is not, however, complete, which is a further reason for supposing that Mary worked from an intermediate copy made by Shelley. The subsequent history of the poems bears out this hypothesis. Soon after Shelley returned to England he sent 'one or two specimens' of verse to Leigh Hunt, who acknowledged them in the *Examiner* of 6 October, but confessed in the number for 1 December that he had no sooner received them than they were 'unfortunately mislaid'. One of the 'specimens' was the 'Hymn to Intellectual Beauty', in the form, it would appear, of Shelley's intermediate copy, and it may well have been accompanied by the two sonnets, also in the copies from which Mary had transcribed them. If this was so, then Shelley, having now lost both the Scrope Davies notebook and his own intermediate copies, must have decided, wisely perhaps, given that the sonnets were occasional poems of no very great merit, to abandon them, and for the next one hundred and sixty years they were heard of no more. The text of the two sonnets is printed in the Anthology. He did, however, reconstruct the 'Hymn', and it was printed in the *Examiner* for 19 January 1819. The many differences between the printed text and that found in the Scrope Davies notebook reinforce the conclusion that Shelley had lost his intermediate copy and returned once more to his original draft, with which indeed the *Examiner* text frequently agrees in opposition to the notebook.

To go on and reconstruct 'Mont Blanc', of which Shelley had had no fair copy other than that in the Scrope Davies notebook, and which he had not therefore been able to offer to Leigh Hunt, must have seemed too disheartening. And in effect, it was not until October 1817 that he found the impetus to undertake the task, when Mary decided to collect together for publication the journals of their Continental tours of 1814 and 1816. The poem was published in *History of a Six Weeks Tour*, 1817, immediately following Shelley's letters describing the same scenes. Comparison of the Bodleian draft, the text in the Scrope Davies notebook, and the printed version make it clear that in this case too, Shelley returned to his draft, but often chose a different word or phrase from among two or more alternative or even cancelled possibilities. The fair copy in the Scrope Davies notebook was made within a month of the composition of the poem, while the text as printed was reconstructed fourteen months later. One was made while the scenes and the emotions they had evoked were still fresh in

Shelley's mind, the other at a time when they could be recollected in tranquillity. 'Mont Blanc' is a great poem, and has long been considered a difficult one. The new version confronts us with fewer problems, and in a few places, after comparison with the draft, reveals what must surely be errors in the first printed text. It would be wrong, however, to assume that additional difficulties encountered in the printed text are all the result of error. Most were the deliberate intention of the poet. By the same token, it is fruitless to debate which version of 'Mont Blanc' is preferable to the other. They are different, that is all. Thanks to a possibly unique set of circumstances, Shelley's loss has been our gain.

What was the explanation of that loss? There are several possibilities, but whether any one of them is correct can not be said in the present state of our knowledge. That Scrope Davies stole the notebook can be discounted straight away. It would have been a wholly uncharacteristic act, and moreover literary MSS. did not have the commercial value which we nowadays attach to them. The great similarity between the two notebooks with marbled covers suggests that they may have been picked up together in error when that containing the 'Prisoner' was taken up to Diodati. Alternatively, Shelley may have left his notebook at Diodati, either by mistake, or so that Byron could study it or have it copied. Scrope Davies may have been charged by Byron with returning it to Shelley in England, but may equally have been unable to find him. Shelley and Scrope moved in very different circles, Shelley did not live in London after his return to England, and in those days, being estranged from his father, would have been difficult to trace. There is no mention of the loss in any of Shelley's, Mary's or Claire's extant letters, which suggests that Shelley had no idea where it had gone, nor to whom to apply for its recovery. Finally, it may be worth noting that although Scrope signed his name in the 'Prisoner' notebook, he made no such claim to ownership in that used by Shelley.

The last few days that Scrope would ever pass in Byron's company were employed in excursions either on foot or by boat to Geneva, while after dinner they would sit up until midnight discussing Byron's writings and affairs. On Tuesday 3 September Polidori missed his appointment at the boat, and Hobhouse walked back to Diodati. Scrope, however, always kinder to the trying doctor, waited for him, so that the four of them 'din'd after waiting for the Dr and D.

much to B's horror'. On the Wednesday, wrote Hobhouse, Scrope, whose athletic prowess had become known even in Geneva, 'went to play tennis with the marker . . . a match which brought Professor Pichet who, amongst his other pursuits, is manager of the tennis court and has written a treatise on it, to the place and other 20, who had not seen such an amateur for a long time!' Hobhouse went on to note that the court had no dedans, a structural feature of the royal game normally regarded as essential, although this would have cost only 20 Napoleons more on top of the 170 needed for the rest — 'from this may be judged the spirit of the Genevese'. The expectations of the local fans were fulfilled by a hard match, but Scrope was nevertheless 'beat three sets even by the marker'. That night Scrope bade farewell to Byron for the last time, though neither of them knew it. The next morning he was called at half past three, and accompanied by the loyal Hobhouse, and by Byron's page Rushton, whom he was escorting back to England, walked through the dark to Geneva. There they were kept at the gates which should have opened at half past four until past five. Happily the *diligence* which should have left at five did not do so until six. 'So much for Geneva discipline' wrote Hobhouse, going on to remark 'took leave of my friend and fellow traveller with whom I have not had even a bickering upon our six weeks tour — good fortune attend him.'

Scrope's kindness in undertaking the various errands with which he was entrusted by Byron has hitherto been ill rewarded. All that was known of the business was a series of letters from Byron to Murray enquiring on a mounting note of concern whether he had ever received the *Childe Harold* MS. The final one, written from Venice on 4 December, stated:

> There are some things I wanted and want to know — viz whether Mr. Davies of inaccurate memory had or had *not* delivered the M.S. as delivered *to* him — because if he has not — you will find that he will bountifully bestow extracts and transcriptions to all the curious of his acquaintance — in which case you may possibly find your publication anticipated by the 'Cambridge' or other Chronicles.

This letter, together with the fact that the whereabouts of the MS. remained unknown, led students of Byron to conclude that Scrope, so far from faithfully delivering the MS. to Murray, had never been near him either through dishonesty or incompetence, and had kept it for himself. This view was reinforced by the knowledge that Murray had cannily stipulated with Byron that he should receive all of the poet's MSS. The explanation, however, is contained in the first sentence of that same letter from Byron. He wrote: 'I have written to you so frequently of late – that you will think me a bore – as I think you a very impolite person for not answering my letters – from Switzerland – Milan – Verona – and Venice'. The fact was that Byron had not been kept up to date with events. As he said later in the same letter 'From England I hear nothing – and know nothing of any thing or any body'. In reality Scrope had not only taken the MS. to Murray, but had remained in constant touch with him while together they defended Byron's interests. The clue which led to the revelation of Scrope's true conduct was a passage in a letter from Byron to Douglas Kinnaird, written on 12 January 1817:

> He [Murray] tells me of a row with an Impostor – a book seller who has been *injunctioned* – by the aid of an Oath from Scrope Davies – I would give a trifle to see Scrope's affidavit – and to have heard half the good things he has said upon the subject. – 'Hath he laid perjury upon his Soul?' – no doubt he will say so – as he always adds his sins to the other obligations he has conferred upon me.

Mr. Martin Davies, a collateral descendant of Scrope Davies, feeling that he too 'would give a trifle to see Scrope's affidavit', sought it out in the Public Record Office. The case was one brought in Byron's name by Murray against one James Johnston, bookseller of Cheapside and Oxford Street, seeking to restrain Johnston from publishing certain poems which he had advertised as being by Lord Byron, but which were in fact completely spurious. The case was heard by the Lord Chancellor on 28 November, and the injunction was granted. On 25 November Scrope had sworn his affidavit, while Murray had sworn one two days previously. Scrope made oath, and said:

> That he [was] intimately acquainted with the said Complainant Lord Byron [and that] on or about the latter end of August or the beginning of September last parted from the said Complainant near Geneva and brought from the said Complainant to John Murray . . . two of the last new Poems written by the said Complainant being the Third Canto of Childe Harold and the Prisoner of Chillon . . . and that these poems were totally distinct from the spurious works.

Scrope later went on to aver that he had 'been long in the habit of conversing and corresponding with the said Complainant and [had] lately had frequent conversations with him on his Poetical Works in the most confidential manner' and that he had never heard Byron mention any of the spurious poems. What was more, he had 'frequently conversed with the said Complainant on the Monies' which he had received for the copyright of his poems, and 'never heard him mention that he received any sum of money from the said Defendant'.

It clearly appears, therefore, that Scrope did faithfully discharge his commission from Byron, and take both the MSS. to Murray. By the time he arrived, however, the poems were set up in print and Murray, having no use for them, returned the MSS. to Scrope. Indeed Murray had no claim to them, for it was only in a letter of 12 September 1816 that he wrote to Byron 'I would venture to submit as a mark of your favour, that you would present to me the original MSS. with every scrap belonging to it'. Scrope had left Geneva in possession of the MSS. on the fifth, and if his inscription is to be believed, the *Childe Harold* MS. at least had been presented to him on the second. Byron, writing to Murray on 9 October 1816, said 'Mr Davies I hear is arrived – he brings the original M.S. which you wished to see' – 'see,' not 'have'. Murray himself obviously did not feel that Scrope had in any way cheated him. Not only did the two of them combine to defeat the rogue Johnston, but Murray's letters to Byron throughout the succeeding months are full of references to visits made to him by Scrope. On 25 March he wrote: 'Mr Davies came in soon after the arrival of the Second Act [of *Manfred*] and read me a portion [of] a Letter to himself written in spirits sufficient to satisfy me that you were better . . . Mr D has borrowed the 1st and 2nd Act for three hours –' while on 15 August he reported: 'Mr Davies was with me yesterday (wch I shall not forget as he promised me a Dozen of extraordinary Burgundy) and swore that he would bring me a long letter for your Lordship tomorrow – he is not very well – but in no worse spirits –'.

Nor was Scrope Davies less punctual in his other commissions. On Sunday 29 September 1816 Augusta Leigh wrote to Lady Byron:

I have seen Mr. D yesterday – he very kindly came over from Cambge ye day after his arrival. I have got some of the Cargo from Mont Blanc and shall take ye first opportunity of sending what is for Ada to Town to be forwarded to you. Mr D. gave me much ye

131

same acct as H[obhouse] [that Byron had reformed and was calm and sober] but added 'they *found* him very gloomy.' He had improved in spirits since they had been there. He most *positively* and *upon his honour* denies the truth of every thing we have heard reported [that Byron was living a promiscuous existence at Geneva], and says that whatever may have been at first ye English are now anxious to be invited to his house, but that he does not like seeing people. He thinks he does not like *Dr. P*[olidori] and that the first convenient opportunity he will be dismissed.

The delivery to her of Byron's trinkets was by no means the last service which Scrope did Augusta. She was under constant pressure from Lady Byron who hoped to use her as a tool in her strategy for retaining custody of Byron's daughter, and from Byron himself, who kept urging her to join him abroad, or failing that, suggested that he might return to England to see her. On top of that she was afraid that the publication of two poems which Byron had written to her while at Geneva would fuel the rumours concerning their incest, rumours which her resumed friendship with Lady Byron was designed to allay. In her alarm she turned to Scrope for advice.

Augusta Leigh's letters to Lady Byron reveal how constantly he was with her. At first the subjects of their discussions were the possibility of Byron's return, and the rumours concerning Byron's sexual malpractices which were still circulating in London. Scrope told her that he had traced the latter to their source, and from something he said she suspected it was Caroline Lamb. On the other topic his remarks were less satisfactory. He said that he thought Byron would return to England, and indeed

> that *he* intended going over to him in Spring and bringing him back if he could. But dearest A [wrote Augusta to Lady Byron] do you think *if* all these things are true — I mean *de l'hyver passé* — that *his* friends CAN possibly *remain* in ignorance! It is impossible for *me* to speak of them of course . . . Do you think an *anonymous* letter to S.D. would do good — in short can you think of anything!

Augusta's concern, groundless as it proved, that Byron might return was soon overshadowed by a more immediate problem, that of the possible publication of the two poems Byron had addressed to her. The fact that there were two caused a certain amount of confusion among those who were working for their suppression, and indeed, has continued to do so among those who have tried to interpret the references in various letters from different correspondents. The earlier poem – the MS. is dated 24 July 1816 – was that known as 'Stanzas to Augusta', and beginning 'Though the day of my destiny's over'. To the modern reader it seems very innocent, as does even the other poem, written about a month later, the 'Epistle to Augusta', which begins 'My sister! my sweet sister! if a name', and which is more explicit in its expression of Byron's love for his sister. Nevertheless, despite the fact that he had already begun *Manfred*, in which he defiantly chose incest as one of its themes, Byron was not unaware that such effusions could well cause annoyance and harm to Augusta, who, as well as being open to personal embarrassment, was dependent on her position at court for the support of her family. He accordingly wrote to Murray on 28 August 1816, speaking of the manuscript consigned to the care of his friend Mr. Shelley 'P.S. There is in the volume – an epistle to Mrs. Leigh – on which I should wish to have her opinion consulted – before the publication – if she objects – of course – *omit* it!

That Murray obeyed his behest is proved by a letter from Byron to him written on 5 October: 'I have received a letter from Mrs L[eigh] in which she tells me that she has decided on the omission of the lines entitled 'an Epistle &c.'. – Upon this point – her option will be followed. – You will of course remember that these lines are the only ones in the volume which I will allow to be omitted . . .' In the face of this injunction Murray did not see any object in showing the remaining poems to Augusta. Confusion and consternation were therefore caused by letters to both Augusta and Lady Byron from Mrs. Villiers, a friend who aided and abetted the latter in her persecution of the former. Writing on 20 October, Mrs. Villiers said that a friend of hers had asked her if she had seen the new poems of Lord Byron which were to come out at the same time as *Childe Harold*, saying at the same time that *The Prisoner of Chillon* is 'beautiful, and so are the stanzas to Mrs. Leigh, but well may you and her friends be in a passion now – these stanzas are so very atrocious, and it is *so* evident that he wishes by them to confirm the abominable report of last year'.

Imagining that this description must refer to the already suppressed 'Epistle', Mrs. Villiers suspected Murray of treachery. Augusta wrote to him at once, and at the same time consulted Scrope Davies. That it was the 'Epistle' which they all feared was about to be published is proved by the letter which Scrope wrote to Murray on 25 October:

> I was this morning at Six mile Bottom and saw Mrs Leigh in considerable perturbation about some reports that have reached her of the publication of the Lines addressed to her, beginning 'My Sister'. Pray write to her and allay her apprehensions — If by any accident they should have been sent to the press, at all events prevent their publication — How any body could have seen them appears to me very strange, as I am not aware of the existence of any other copy than that now in Mrs. Leigh's possession — Should you hear that Mr Shelly [*sic*], or any other person is possessed of a copy you will perhaps be so good as to request them not to hand it about among friends and acquaintance —
>
> Yours truly
Scrope Davies
>
> When will the Canto come forth? I beg to have a copy sent here as soon as possible — Excuse this scrawl which I am obliged to write in bed —

Augusta had asked Scrope if Shelley might not have copies, and had been little comforted by his reply '*most probably* for he knew THE Lady had *written out* the ms'. Murray wrote to Augusta 'disclaiming vehemently any and every share of *his*', whereupon Augusta was upset to think that she might have offended him. In the end the mystery was cleared up by Mrs. Villiers sending Augusta Margaret Mercer Elphinstone's copy of the offending stanzas. On 2 November Augusta wrote to Lady Byron:

> After all, *the* lines (which I enclose) are totally different from those we thought of. I never saw, heard or knew of their existence till Mrs. V sent me ye copy obtained from Miss E, and indeed dear A, had I read them first in print, I should not have *determined* in my own mind that they *were* addressed to the Person to whom they are attributed.

Nevertheless, she went on to say, if anyone did do so that was sufficient reason for suppression. Murray, having Byron's explicit instructions before him, naturally thought otherwise. Once again Scrope was consulted, in the hope that he might take upon him the suppression. He, however, wisely took Murray's view, the more so since he could imagine the effect on Byron that a gratuitous suppression might bring about. On 7 November Augusta reported Scrope's views to Lady Byron:

> *As I expected*, he treats ye subject exactly as [Murray] does – says he has carefully read over the lines and cannot imagine any thing in them that I could wish otherwise. He is going to Town tomorrow and will see and talk to M. But *we* both think if 5000 are printed must they not be circulated? and if these lines are omitted in the rest, will it not be said, Why? and then S.D. says as I think, may ye omission not cause him, B, to write something else, considering me as a Victim to Slander &c &c and full of bitterness towards you and yours.

In the event wiser counsels prevailed, and Augusta came to consider that Mrs. Villiers had greatly exaggerated matters. She wrote to Lady Byron on 12 November: '. . . I wrote to M[urray] to say that I thought the *least evil* was *to* publish, and have begged him to be silent on what I have said on the subject of *not* publishing. So, as far as *that* goes, c'est finie.'

With Byron's arrival in Venice on 10 November 1816 the years of his obsession with Augusta were drawing to their close. Although he remained devoted to her, by the 17th he could tell Tom Moore that he was in love with Marianna Segati, and from then on a series of Italian mistresses served to distract him. A letter to Augusta dated 1 October 1816 ends 'Believe me ever and truly my own dearest Sis. most affectionately and entirely yours'. A letter written on 13 January 1817 ends 'Ever yrs'. They had been three turbulent years, and the connection with Augusta had led to a disastrous marriage, to scandal, ostracism and exile. Throughout them Scrope Davies had exhibited that exemplary loyalty which was one of his most attractive features. His calm and good judgement had soothed and guided both Byron and his sister, and he had placed his time very largely at their disposal. Neither of them forgot the unselfseeking devotion of a friend who had faced the fury of society to support one who from being famous had become notorious, and who considered that the day of his destiny was over, and that the star of his fate had declined.

It had been on 5 October 1816 that Byron and Hobhouse left Diodati, and set out for Milan and Venice. From Italy they both wrote to Scrope and he, infrequently, wrote to them. Their letters were preserved in Scrope's trunk. On 7 November Hobhouse sent from Verona an account of their journeyings in which he told, among other things, how Byron had dismissed Polidori, and how in Milan they had 'passed three weeks very agreably there amongst the discontented who, I dare say, you agree with us in thinking the only passable company in all countries. It would do your heart good to hear the complaints of the Italians against the present state of things . . .'[9] Hobhouse went on to say, with remarkable lack of prophetic power, that he doubted whether Venice would please either of them.

On 16 February 1817 Hobhouse wrote to Scrope from Rome. He was impressed by the relics of antiquity, but not by the Romans, who 'are the most wretched and ignorant and insolent of all the Italians I have seen and do everything they can to render the monuments of their former glory inaccessible by dead cats and rotten eggs and cabbage tops and cinder and human ordure'. The next despatch was written by Byron at Venice on 7 March:

> My dear Scrope — Though I regard your not writing as a baseness — yet I cannot longer refrain from enquiring how you are — in health and fortunes — and whether you have yet seen a 'Boa Constrictor' . . . Dr Polidori — as you know was congeded by me previous to passing the Alps — and you may have probably heard that he was subsequently forwarded to Florence by the Milan government for a squabble with a Hungarian man of war. — He wrote to me lately from Pisa — his present project is — to go [to] the Brazils to teach (not 'the Dutch English') but the Portuguese — Medicine which they are fond of to distraction.

A little over a month later Byron wrote a further account of the delinquent doctor:

Venice — April 10th 1817

> My dear Scrope — The Doctor Polidori is here on his way to England with the present Lord Guilford — having actually embowelled the last at Pisa & spiced & pickled him for his rancid ancestors. — The said Doctor has had several invalids under his proscriptions — but has now no more patients — because his patients are no more — the following is the Gazette extraordinary according to his last *dispatches;*

9 After the fall of Napoleon the provinces of Lombardy and Venetia had been given to Austria.

Piccadilly and Geneva

⟨*Officers* ⟩

Ld.Guilford	– killed	– inflammation of bowels –
Mr.Horner	– killed	– diseased Lungs –
Mr Js Hope's son	– killed	– Scarlet fever –

Rank & file – killed – 45 paupers of Pisa – wounded & missing (the last supposed to be dissected) 18 in the hospitals of that city. –

Wounded

Lady Westmoreland – incurable – her disease not defined. But the Doctor himself is alive & well & still bent upon the Brazils – Frederic North that was & the disconsolate widow of his embalmed brother – have bodkined him homewards; – & I shall advise him to pay his court to the jointure. – He brings me news from Rome of Hobhouse & Bailey – who are as inseparable as their exceeding disproportion will admit. – Hobhouse's brother's wife has brought forth a son – Hobhouse himself is several months gone with book[10] but has probably felt fewer qualms than his future readers. – Polidori left him over Dionysius of Halicarnassus[11] – & other folios which he must read (at least the tops of the pages) with a ladder . . .

Polidori has put me out of humour with a parcel of rumours – much the same as those of last year from Geneva – about harlotry women – which were rife among the dirty English at Rome & Florence – it is very odd that they will not let me alone – I see none of them – I harm nobody – I make love but with one woman at a time – & as quietly as possible – & they lie through thick & thin – & invent every kind of absurdity – and all about 'PP Clerk of this parish'.

Murray tells me that you carried off two acts of 'Manfred' which I think would suit you admirably – he being something like your favourite 'Boa Co⌊n⌋strictor' – to be sure – I must have been mad when it was written – but you & I are so now & then.

Is it serious that you and Kinnaird are out-coming? is it true that W. Webster is writing upon the suspension of the 'Habeas corpus'?

10 A projected work on the antiquities of Rome the materials for which were later incorporated into Hobhouse's *Historical Illustrations of the Fourth Canto of Childe Harold*, 1818.

11 Dionysius of Halicarnassus was the author of a work known as the *Archaeologia Romana* or *Roman Antiquities*.

137

— and Jackson — how is Jacky? 'before G—d Sir' — I hear that the fancy has had a sad reality in somebody being killed in a fight — which will turn the pugilistic uniform to Sackcloth.

When shall you & I at two in the morning (or it may be-*three*) sit in fierce defiance of imploring friends — & insist upon another bottle (or bowl — with broiled bones-) & nap over the woes of humanity — & the shameful disbelief in the 'day of Pentecost.'? — The wines of these parts might do very well for the Gauls & Teutones & Cimbri — who knew no better — but one bottle from your binn is worth all the vineyards from hence to Otranto.

Sometime towards the end of May Scrope bestirred himself into writing a letter to Byron. Though characteristically undated, it is dateable by the reference to the Harrow Speeches, which that year were held on 5 June. A letter from Henry Drury inviting Scrope to attend is dated 17 May. Drury added, revealing that the dinner was to be quite an occasion, 'I lay for 100.'

My dear Byron,

Silence procreates itself — I omitted to write — and afterwards omitted to write because I had omitted to write — Forgive me . . . Moore's new poem[12] has not yet appeared — I doubt his success in anything else than trifles. He is an elegant shrub — as Wellington in a Ball Room has been compared to an Oak in a hot-house.

A decent Epigram has lately appeared on a gentleman here who objected to [?Chalk Farm][13] because he had a wife and a daughter —

> Our heroes abhorrent of slaughter
> Have improved on the Jewish Command
> And honour their wife and their daughter
> That their days may be long in the land.

I see Mrs Leigh most days — she is in good health and spirits, as is Georgiana who sends her love to you. — Mrs L. like myself thinks your miniatures hideous — have you had a paralytic stroke? or are you represented as being in the House of Lords? with the mouth all on one side? They are positively hideous and I need not add, very

12 *Lalla Rookh*.

13 A traditional venue for duels.

unlike the original. Holmes will not proceed to his engraving of them till he again hears from you.[14]

In some of your letters you give us hopes of seeing you in England this year – in others you make us despair – What are your intentions? . . . Kinnaird and myself intend to be at the Harrow Speeches. Think of us on that day as we shall think of you and drink to you in Drury's [?hottest] Port. I shall not fail to go to the Church yard and to ascend the tower where as the Devil tempted God, you tempted me to fall down and slay myself – but I was then not as I now am sick of life.

Your Witch Drama[15] is in some parts divine 'Colouring the clouds that shut me out from Heaven' 'Carnation'd like a sleeping infant's cheek Hush'd by the beating of her mother's heart' – and some other passages are worthy –

Scrope's judgement of Moore was sound. Although out of friendship Byron praised *Lalla Rookh* in public, Hobhouse wrote in the margin of his copy of Moore's biography 'Nevertheless I have heard him express a very different opinion of Tommy's [Turkish?] tale'.

Before he had received Scrope's letter Byron wrote again, on 6 June. The middle of the letter is taken up with instructions to Scrope and Kinnaird concerning the sale of Newstead and of Rochdale. The beginning and end are as follows:

My dear Scrope. Many prodigies besides your own promise have announced a letter from you – but it tarries like the wheels of Sisera's chariot – howbeit I make great allowances for the meetings & other interruptions to your intentions if you ever had any. – From Hodgson I received not long ago a diuretic letter of the most urinary tenderness – which I by no means propose as a model for yours; – after describing his insipid happiness in a Derbyshire vicarage – he exclaims 'Oh! my Friend! inveni *portum*' – which being interpreted I presume to mean *port-wine* – that being the only port at least which I ever knew him to find or seek in the course of

---

14 The miniatures had been painted by Prepiani in Venice, and taken back to England by Polidori. Byron, though saddened by Scrope's and Augusta's reaction, bowed to their judgement. On 19 June he wrote to Augusta 'Since the pictures are so bad – they need not be copied – the poor painter seems to have been ignorant of the art of flattery'.

15 *Manfred*.

the last twelve twelve-months. — I am just returned from Rome where I went to see the Pope and Hobhouse; — of things remarkable in Rome I can tell you nothing not described elsewhere — except that we saw three delinquents guillotined a short time before leaving the city . . . If you ask me my plans I can only say that I have *none* — except *not* to reside in England; — I am perfectly serious — & have been so much more happy & tranquil since I passed the Alps — that you need hardly wonder at a resolution justified by experience; — & when you recollect what I have encountered since my funeral with Miss Milbanke & in consequence of that interment you will perhaps be disposed to commend my intention. — There is one motive which might & may bring me to England — but as it is purely personal — I regard it less seriously. — [remainder of page erased] All this erasure & blotting will puzzle you but it alluded to a subject which — as I shall have to take your opinion & advice upon it when we meet — I shall not anticipate — because what I have to do — will probably require to be done in your presence, *at any rate at present* I will postpone what I meant to say. —

> Yours ever truly
> & affectly
> [scrawl]

The erasure and blotting did indeed puzzle Scrope, and they continue to puzzle us as well, so thoroughly were they done. The reference to something being 'done in your presence' suggests a duel, Scrope having ever been Byron's first choice as a second. With the benefit of hindsight we can deduce that the deleted passage set out a scheme for returning to England, or at least to Calais, and challenging the detested Brougham. In a letter to Augusta written on 11 May he had said: 'I was not till lately aware of all *the things* he B [*rougha*]*m* has *said* and *done* — but being now aware of them depend upon it — he shall answer it'. At the time, however, Scrope was not able to make that deduction. He eventually replied some time in August:

My dear Byron

'No turnspit gets into his wheel with more reluctance than I sit down to write; yet no dog ever loved the roast meat he turns better than I do him I now address'. So said Oliver Goldsmith to Robert

Brianton, so says Scrope Davies to Baron Byron. I dare not attempt to vindicate my past shameful silence, tho' I might call up a thousand excuses, many true and more false – I plead not for justice, but implore mercy – forgive me my trespasses, as I do not forgive them that trespass against me.

I have not heard from or of Hobhouse for the last three months. Where is he? Did he conceive at Rome? and when will his nine months (years it ought to be) have expired? When I left you both on the banks of the Lake of Geneva last year multum gemens, Hobhouse threatened another expedition to Albania, not a secret expedition as you may suppose, but one to be published. Does he persist in this resolve? I trust not. The plague is raging throughout the whole of that country, and we have to dread one of two evils – either the plague will carry off Hobhouse, or Hobhouse will carry off the plague from Albania and deposit it at Ridgways in the shape of a thick Quarto tome. May he live to write a thousand years – may he never write to live, for our friend loves the comforts of life.

I am frequently asked about your health, your place of residence, your present occupation, and your future intentions. I give the most satisfactory replies to all enquirers, and as I do not like to say the same thing twice, I give each person a different answer. They all suppose you to be dégouté, and many look among the deaths in the daily papers and are surprised not to see yours. They little know that you dare not to die, which is the case, for Hobhouse would immediately write your life . . .

Now that Kinnaird is gone, the only person with whom I live in intimacy is Burdett.[16] Burdett like yourself, and some three others perhaps, I can meet day after day, and year after year, without being palled. I never had many friends, – and of those few death and absence have almost deprived me – but I can find no new substitutes: – The more I live, the more I am convinced friendship ought to be and must be limited to a very few – the fountain plays higher by the aperture being diminished. Burdett sends you his kindest regards.

16 Kinnaird had left for Italy on a long planned visit to Byron. On 20 June Byron had written to Hobhouse 'Kinnaird . . . threatens to come out directly – and to drag the Boa Constrictor [Scrope] with him an it be possible.' Sir Francis Burdett was an important figure in the political and social lives of Scrope and his friends. A fuller account of him is given in the next Chapter. Scrope seems to have been on very good terms with Burdett in 1817. Two letters in his trunk reveal that he lent Burdett his travelling carriage for an excursion to Ireland. It broke down, and had to be returned on a waggon.

There is little new in the political literary moral or immoral world: – The Whigs not only wish but hope for place – their love of place like other love is blind. Twenty years since, Burke declared the impossibility of the Whigs ever coming into power, and his prophecy has been as far as it could be, fulfilled . . .

An embargo has been laid on my gymnastics for the last three weeks by an infernal — I am even confined to my bed weakened as my body is my mind more so.

Should a gentleman of the name of Joy come across you, pray treat him with kindness. He respects my virtues, and admires your writings. Against whom do you meditate revenge? Let me not burst in ignorance. 'Vengeance is mine, and I will repay saith the Lord.' In God's name mention the object of your resentment . . .

When I recover my health, I will write to you soberly and seriously; in the mean time send me an account of you and yours. God bless you – you shall hear from me after the putting up of Newstead on the 26th.

His curiosity whetted by the mystery of Byron's unknown enemy, Scrope became a slightly more assiduous correspondent. Sometime in September he wrote again, and even apologised for the delay:

My dear Byron

I delayed writing, not so much from indolence, as because I wished to be able to communicate to you something definitive respecting the fate of Newstead. Kinnaird however will satisfy your most eager curiosity on this subject.

Frere, Gifford, John Smyth (Member for Hobhouse's University) and I [?] applaud Manfred to the very Echo. There are parts which I confess, I wish had been omitted – Lallah Rooke [*sic*] is esteemed as it ought to be – a trifling production of a trifling mind.

I have heard nothing of Hobhouse for many months – Where is he? at Rome, at Naples or at Florence? Pray tell him (what in my last letter I desired you to tell him) that his Albania has risen in value – waste paper never was so dear in England as it now is. I languish to see the author. Against whom Byron do you mutter vengeance? – Vengeance is mine and I will repay saith the Lord. There is no one just cause why I should be in spirits, and yet I am scarcely depressed. My friends are all either out of the King's Dominions or in the King's Bench.[17] Fortune has frowned upon me and steeped me in poverty to the very lips. I am miserable as have no one to whom I may communicate my sorrow — With all this I laugh and have no hope.[18] I have lately lived with Burdett — his simplicity charms me, as my admiration of him has increased is increasing and cannot be diminished either by his public enemies or private friends.

Kinnaird is kind and benevolent as ever — I would have accompanied him to Venice . . . sed Diis aliter visum est. Instead of lounging on the Rialto, I must content myself with viewing the [?] Bridge at Cambridge, and instead of enjoying your society, I must endure the mawkish stupidity of College fellows, and the quiet ugliness of the Cam (not H).[19]

Whether in high or low spirits whether fortunate or wretched, my esteem for you will ever remain unaltered and unalterable.

> Adieu
> God bless you
> and believe me
> Yrs most truly
> Scrope Davies

Write to me, and quickly and copiously — and the more you say about yourself the better.

No reply to this letter was found in Scrope's trunk, but he was soon to have first hand news of his friends. Hobhouse's long stay in Italy was drawing to a close, and on 8 January 1818 he left Venice to make his way home.

17 The King's Bench Prison for Debtors.

18 A reference to one of Byron's favourite quotations. In his note to line 382 of *Hints from Horace*, referring to Charles Simeon the evangelical, he wrote 'Mr Simeon is the very bully of beliefs, and castigator of 'good works'. He is ably supported by John Stickles, a labourer in the same vineyard: — but I say no more, for, according to Johnny in full congregation, '*No hopes for them as laughs.'* In a letter to Augusta Leigh written on 19 December 1816 Byron identified Stickles as 'a methodist preacher who [made his immortal pronouncement] on perceiving a profane grin on the faces of part of his congregation'.

19 Hobhouse's middle name inspired in Scrope an infinity of puns.

5

Radicalism and Flight

The last two years that Scrope Davies was to pass in his native land were to a great extent occupied by electioneering. Until the discovery of his trunk few indeed would have associated the dandy and the gambler with the inner councils of Radical Reform, yet once again Scrope proves to have possessed unexpected qualities. His closest friends, Byron, Hobhouse, Matthews and Kinnaird had of course an intense interest in politics. Byron himself was possibly the most political of all English poets, and the beliefs for which he is famous — libertarian, anti-monarchical and free-thinking — united them all, for it is hard to be truly intimate with a man whose political convictions one does not share.

Political life during the years of Scrope Davies's childhood and adolescence was dominated by the French Revolution. The Bastille was stormed when he was six, and when he was ten the war against the ideological armies of revolutionary France began — a war which with two brief intermissions was to last for twenty-two long years. As the war continued advocacy of reform at home came to be equated in the public mind with support for France abroad. The result was political stagnation. With the exception of his first year, and an interval of some eighteen months in 1806 and 1807, the whole of Scrope's life in England was passed under a Tory government.

It was not altogether surprising therefore that Scrope and his friends were as young men to be found in the ranks of the Whigs, and as supporters moreover until his death in 1806 of Charles James Fox, leader of the Reform, or left wing Whigs. Fox it had been whose enthusiasm for Napoleon had earned reform a bad name, and it was an enthusiasm shared by Scrope and his friends. In their eyes a government ever more oppressive at home opposed abroad the Corsican titan who had torn down the ancient tyrannies and was engaged in ushering in a new age of freedom and justice. However false that belief, the friends kept faith with Napoleon, and their reaction to Waterloo was very different from that of the vast majority of their countrymen.

It was not only a spirit of opposition natural and indeed desirable in young men which governed the political notions of Scrope Davies and his friends. There was also the appeal of glamour — 'radical chic' is the name that has been given to it in our day. It must have seemed so much more exciting to be associated with Charles James Fox — he who made the marriage between reform politics and gambling, a marriage surely most attractive to Scrope Davies — than with Spencer Perceval; so much more elegant to mix with the Dukes of Bedford and of Devonshire than with the dull old King and stuffy Tory squires. Hobhouse noted with pride in his diary, after he and Scrope Davies had dined with the exiled leader of the dandies, 'Brummell said the Regent owned the Whigs kept the best company'. Scrope Davies, Hobhouse, even Byron — despite his title he had only his poverty-stricken childhood in Aberdeen behind him, and no ready-made contacts in high society — had their way to make in the world, and it was in the salons of the great Whig hostesses that wit, talent and style could take a man to the top.

In the case of Scrope's friends, if not in his own, there was also the part played by family tradition. The ambitious were moved by more than filial piety. To gain a seat in the unreformed — as in the reformed — House of Commons was a matter of knowing the right people, and this was not to be achieved by scorning family alliance. Byron had a truly Whig pride in the antiquity of his title, and his guardian, the Earl of Carlisle, had been a follower of Fox, only parting from him in 1794, while his wife had been one of that bevy of beauties who bought votes for Fox with their smiles. Kinnaird, too, came of a Whig family. His father and brother were each for a time Scottish representative peers, and his brother was an M.P., in that interest. Hobhouse's father was for many years a Whig M.P., his enthusiasm for moderate reform being sustained by his conversion to Unitarianism after his first marriage. Not only did this make him eager to see the civil disabilities suffered by dissenters removed, but he was also swayed by the typically Unitarian commitment to free speech. Later, however, disillusioned by the turn matters were taking in France, he went so far as to take office under Addington in 1803, and later still to accept not only a place but also a title from the Tory government — indeed, his distress at the assassination of Spencer Perceval was chiefly occasioned by the jeopardy in which that unlooked-for event had placed his impending baronetcy. Nevertheless the Unitarian atmosphere in which the younger Hobhouse grew up implanted in him his humanitarianism and his hatred of religious intolerance. Scrope alone had no tradition on which to draw, and as it proved he was the only one who never made an attempt to enter Parliament. Lack of influence and of fortune no doubt combined to prevent it, together with his dependence on gambling which reduced the time and energy available for other matters.

Scrope Davies, needless to say, had a facetious explanation for Byron's attachment to the Whigs. In 1841 he informed Thomas Raikes, a fellow-exile in France, that

> Byron was a Whig, because he fell into the society of young Whigs at Cambridge, who established a Whig club, and dined together. Byron went for the sake of the dinner. He used to tell an anecdote, which he always prefaced by saying, 'It must be allowed they were well read in history'. At one of these dinners, the present Duke of Devonshire presided, and rose up to give a toast. 'Gentlemen,' said he, 'I will give you the noble cause for which' (here he turned round to Hobhouse, and asked in a whisper, 'Which of them died on the field?' And not getting an answer, he continued) 'for which Sydney died on the field, and Hampden on the scaffold.'

So much of Scrope's account is true as that Byron and Hobhouse were while at Cambridge certainly both members of a Whig club founded, according to Byron, by Hobhouse, who however in later years denied the honour and ceded it to Lord Tavistock. The membership was typically whig, being involved in a net-work of inter-related families, but with a strong Foxite flavour. Neither Scrope Davies nor Charles Skinner Matthews are to be found among the members. Matthews was probably felt to be too radical, while Scrope was excluded by his lack of social status and family connection.

Byron was the first among the friends to enter Parliament, since as a peer he did not have to face the hurdle of election, but his career was brief. Nevertheless it resulted in new contacts which were to have a very great influence on both the social and political lives of his immediate friends. He took his seat in the House of Lords on 13 March 1809, but did not enter the chamber again before going abroad. When Parliament assembled in January 1812 he began to attend. On 27 February he made his famous maiden speech opposing a government measure to introduce the death penalty for Luddites convicted of smashing the newly introduced wide frames for knitting – an innovation that had caused widespread unemployment and distress. The chief centre of the industry was Nottingham, the nearest town to Newstead. Lord Holland, who was not only the Recorder of Nottingham but the nephew and heir of Charles James Fox, could be relied upon to oppose the bill, and Byron sought his advice and alliance. Among those who congratulated him on his speech, 'probably from a fellow feeling in ye sentiments', was Sir Francis Burdett.

Burdett was an immensely rich landowner of ancient family who had, without much enthusiasm, entered Parliament in 1796 when his father-in-law the banker Thomas Coutts bought for him one of the two seats returned by the rotten borough of Boroughbridge. Once in Parliament he had supported with fervour the attacks of the Foxites on the war and on repression at home. He had never been a Whig but if anything, as he once confided to Hobhouse, a Tory. Burdett's enemy was the 'system' whereby, as he believed, Whigs and Tories, both equally corrupt, were interested in nothing but fighting each other for the spoils of office. His rank and wealth allowed him the independence to pursue a natural inclination to assist the oppressed unfettered by the practical considerations of party politics.

At the time when Byron and his friends first met him in 1812 Burdett had been one of the two independent reform members for Westminster for five years. He had been disillusioned by the performance of the Whig 'Ministry of All the Talents' in 1806–1807, had attacked both them and the Tories at the general election which followed the death of Fox in September 1806, and without Whig help had finished bottom of the poll for Middlesex. In March 1807 the Whig administration fell, and another general election ensued. Burdett had had no desire to stand again, but had been approached by a committee of reformers from Westminster, one of the few seats where anything resembling a free election could be held. He had agreed to accept the seat if he were to be elected without any interference on his own part. In the event he was elected with a large majority at an expense of £780 to which he had contributed nothing.

Burdett had once been the lover of the Countess of Oxford, and he and the Oxfords were constantly together. Perhaps it was because of him that Hobhouse found himself at Lady Oxford's ball on 22 June, and at dinner with the Oxfords on the 24th. In his account of the evening Hobhouse gave his impression of Lady Oxford, and of one of her daughters, Lady Jane:

> Lady Jane Harley a delightful creature but un peu libre . . . Lady
> O. most uncommon in her talk and licentious – uncommonly civil
> – made a push to get me into the Hampden Club – for the first time
> in my life knew how to put off a question and civilly say no.

The Hampden Club, named for the opponent of Charles I, had just
been founded by Burdett and Major Cartwright as an aristocratic
political club whose purpose was to provide leaders for the reform
movement.[1] Lady Oxford was in some ways the movement's chief
recruiting officer – on occasion recruiting the same members to it and
to her bed.

Byron was to find himself among that number. By 4 November
1812 he could write that he was 'deeply and seriously engaged'. Lady
Oxford remained his mistress until June 1813. During that time she
drew him, for a time at least, into the radical camp, and kept him up
to the mark. When noting in his journal for 1 December 1813 that he
had declined to present a petition on behalf of one Baldwin, a debtor,
he wrote

> Now, had [Lady Oxford] been here, she would have made me do it.
> There is a woman, who, amid all her fascination, always urged a
> man to usefulness or glory. Had she remained, she had been my
> tutelar genius . . . Here I cannot stimulate myself to a speech for
> the sake of these unfortunates, and three words and half a smile [of
> Lady Oxford] had she been here to urge it (and urge it she infallibly
> would – at least, she always pressed me on senatorial duties, and
> particularly in the cause of weakness) would have made me an
> advocate, if not an orator.

Without her to encourage him Byron grew 'sick of parliamentary
mummeries'. 'The fact is', he wrote, 'riches are power, and poverty is
slavery all over the earth, and one sort of establishment is no better
nor worse, for a *people* than another.' At the same time, he resolved to
adhere to the Whigs, 'because it would not be honourable to act
otherwise'.

---

1 The qualifications for membership were the same as for the House of Commons, that is to say
an income of £300 a year from landed property. Scrope Davies would therefore have been
excluded. It was intended to act as a bridge between the Reform Whigs and the Radical
Reformers, but in the event, and perhaps inevitably, its life was not long.

Disillusioned by party politics at home, Byron transferred his enthusiasm to following the fate of Napoleon, who since the failure of his Russian expedition was being relentlessly pressed back on all fronts by the united forces of reaction. On 17 November 1813 he wrote in his journal 'Buonaparte! Ever since I defended my bust of him at Harrow against the rascally time-servers, when the war broke out in 1803, he has been a 'Héros de Roman' of mine – on the continent; I don't want him here!' This was an attitude which united him with Hobhouse and Scrope Davies, but Hobhouse, at least, felt that there should be limits. In his diary for 10 February 1814 he wrote that at Lord Holland's 'the news of the day was the defeat of the French . . . which hardly pleased them – now this seemed to me carrying the feelings of domestic politics too far'. Nevertheless, when next day he dined with the Hollands, he found his lordship 'the most delightful man alive'. At that time Hobhouse was, like Byron, on good terms both with the Burdettites and the Foxites. Douglas Kinnaird, too, was a regular diner at Holland House. It was a time of truce, if not of alliance, between the moderate and the radical reformers.

From the evidence of Hobhouse's diary, and the Holland House Dinner Books, Scrope Davies does not at that time seem to have belonged to either clique. It is very probable that he met the Oxfords at Cheltenham when he was there with Byron in the autumn of 1812, for he certainly met the Rawdons, the other family which Byron mentioned in the same breath. Whenever Hobhouse met Scrope, however, whether it was at Cambridge whither they all went on 18 November 1812 to vote against an anti-Catholic petition, or in London, it was always in the company of the Kinnairds. When Scrope's friendship with the Harley family, and his intimacy with Lady Oxford began it is impossible to say. Perhaps it was in the course of the year 1817 when, as we saw in the last chapter, he spent a good deal of time in the company of Burdett.

The intermingling of political and social life was made strikingly evident by the crisis over Byron's separation from his wife. Those who gave dinners for Byron during his last days in England, those who came to bid him farewell, were drawn from the same familiar group of Reformers, Burdett, the Kinnairds, Hobhouse and Scrope Davies. One perceives yet again how narrow had been the foundation of even Byron's social success, how the politics of himself and his closest friends had confined their circle to that small group of free-thinking,

149

free-living, almost raffish Reform Whig and Radical aristocrats, the scandal ridden world of Lady Oxford and her Harleian Miscellany, of Lady Bessborough and Sheridan, of Lady Caroline Lamb, so different from the world of Jane Austen, so at odds with the rising tide of Methodism and Evangelicalism that was foreshadowing the Victorian age. Consciousness that he had not been accepted by his class as a whole contributed to the rancour against England which gnawed at Byron during his years of exile.

It was not only in their sexual laxity that Byron's friends were unusual. In the whole of Europe their class alone possessed a relatively large degree of political freedom. Only as a member of his class and country could Byron have written as he did. Even the terms of imprisonment suffered at various times by Burdett and Hobhouse were limited by the life of Parliament – they were in no danger of disappearing for life into some dreadful dungeon. The ruling class held back from more than petty persecution of their own.

On 2 February 1818 Hobhouse arrived back in England after an absence of a year and a half. As a result we can once more employ his diaries to learn about the activities of his friends. Hobhouse himself, it appears, lost no time in seeking out his confederates. On the 5th he 'called on D. Kinnaird – saw him, he will be member for Bishop's Castle in the next parliament it seems – S.B.D. has partially recovered himself. I dined with D.K. met S.B.D. and embraced'. On the 13th Hobhouse dined at Brooks's with Scrope Davies and Burdett. The latter seemed to Hobhouse, who at this stage was still a Whig, if a Reform one, to be 'as lively as ever about politics'.

One detects a note of chagrin in Hobhouse's reaction to Kinnaird's good fortune. Hobhouse had long nourished parliamentary ambitions, and between him and Kinnaird there had been an element of rivalry and suspicion for some time. Four years earlier, with the encouragement and help of Scrope Davies and Kinnaird, he had had designs upon one of the two Cambridge University seats. In the early part of 1814 it was rumoured that Lord Palmerston, the Secretary at War, who being an Irish peer could sit in the House of Commons and was one of the University members, might accept a United Kingdom peerage and move to the Upper House. This would bring about a bye-election, and Hobhouse began to form the ambition to stand as an opposition candidate. In the early days of April he saw Scrope Davies several times – on one occasion the two of them, together with Byron and Douglas Kinnaird, dined at the Cocoa Tree and 'sat until 4 concluding by a supper of grilled and punch of champagne and green tea and rum' –, and on the fifth he set off to Cambridge in the 'Telegraph' coach to stay with him. The next day Hobhouse 'called on a variety of [his] senior acquaintance – having in view the possibility of coming upon them for a favour in future times'. That afternoon he and Scrope 'dined in King's hall at 4 on a noble cod's head sent down by Stepney for Davies – afterwards [they] took wine in K's combination room . . . the Vice provost in the chair a complete collegian – he talked of butter'd muffins in silver covers and laid out the bill of fare at an inn with the most painful minuteness'.

The next morning Scrope came into Hobhouse's room with the *Star* newspaper in his hand, and exclaimed 'It is all over Hobhouse – *Buonaparte is dethroned*.' On 11 April Hobhouse left for London, determined to make the best of his way to Paris 'whilst yet any part of the Napoleon vestiges [might] remain'. He did not return to England until 8 May. On the 24th of that month he taught himself to waltz, but by 5 June he had returned to more serious matters and wrote a philippic against the Prince Regent which was published anonymously in Leigh Hunt's *Examiner* under the title of 'Vox Populi'. On the 16th Scrope Davies called with the unwelcome news that 'Vox Populi' was to be 'pursued by the King's Attorney General'. At the same time, as Hobhouse noted 'He made me take a resolution of standing for the University of Cambridge in the event of Palmerston's being made a Peer. Come what will come what may, I am determined to try and have accordingly commenced operations.'

The University electors – that is to say the Doctors and Masters of Arts, some five hundred in all, – were as venial as the electors in any other constituency. Nothing daunted, as Hobhouse recorded, on 2 July 'S B Davies and myself set off at 3. in his carriage and four horses to Cambridge and arrived there by $\frac{1}{2}$ past nine. I went down to the Commencement to see how the land lies for my attempt.' The next day Hobhouse became agreeably aware of what an influential figure his supporter was: 'The popularity of my friend S.B. Davies is encreasing every day at Cambridge – such is the power of talent – he began with nothing – not even a character – and although he has risen entirely as far as his means are concerned by gambling – has a respectability and power equal to any individual I know of his age'. For the next few days Hobhouse, Scrope Davies and Douglas Kinnaird were busy canvassing in various colleges. On the fifth, however, all Hobhouse's plans were set at nought. Lord Palmerston made a speech in St. John's College declaring that he was not to be made a peer. The next day Byron arrived from Six Mile Bottom, the house of Augusta Leigh, and dined with Scrope. The following afternoon they all set off in Byron's coach for London. In the evening they dined at the Cocoa Tree and Hobhouse discovered that Kinnaird had told Byron that he must have 'lost his senses to think of standing for Cambridge – so there is no faith in man – K being one of my chief advisors, but I will not reproach him – and in spite of all – I will come in for the University'. He never did.

It was not long after Hobhouse's return from Italy in 1818 that he, Scrope Davies and a few others gave their friendship and the compatibility, if not identity of their political views, institutional form by the foundation of a Club. The minutes of the first meeting, kept by Hobhouse, reveal that the '–Society'— it had yet to receive a name – was instituted, and held its first meeting at the Piazza Coffee House on 21 February 1818. Present were 'Sir Francis Burdett, Sir Robert Wilson,[2] Scrope Beardmore Davies, John Cam Hobhouse and the Hon[ble] Douglas Kinnaird'. The only absent members were Lord Byron and Henry Bickersteth.[3] The rules provided, among other things, that the society should meet every Saturday during the sitting of Parliament, unless another day was appointed, and that members were to pay ten shillings and six pence per meeting. Hobhouse was to be secretary. The minutes conclude with a list of books given to the society by the members. Scrope gave 'Bacon's Essay and Hall's Apology for the freedom of the Press', Burdett 'Milton's Works', Wilson

2 Major General Sir Robert Wilson, son of the artist Benjamin Wilson, was as colourful as any of Scrope's friends. He fought in Flanders, Holland, South Africa, Egypt, Poland, Portugal, Spain, Russia and Germany. He witnessed the burning of Moscow, took part with Michael Bruce in the rescue of the Marquis de Lavallette, and in 1821 was dismissed from the army for inciting the Household Cavalry to mutiny at the funeral of Queen Caroline. He was more remarkable for impetuosity than judgement, and was described by the Duke of Wellington as 'a very slippery fellow' who had not 'the talent of being able to speak the truth upon any subject'.

3 Bickersteth was a young lawyer and fellow of Caius College Cambridge. From 1803–5 he had been medical attendant to the Earl of Oxford, a post which it is supposed he combined with that of lover to the Countess. He certainly imbibed her radical views, and his legal career was for some time seriously impeded by his friendship with the Burdett – Oxford set. Eventually however he became Master of the Rolls, and first and last Baron Langdale. In 1835 he married Lady Jane Harley. Hobhouse first met him in May 1811.

'Wilson's Bible', Kinnaird 'Jeremy Bentham on Reform and Juvenal', Hobhouse 'Shakespeare's Plays' and Bickersteth 'Sidney on Government'. The existence of this little library shows a properly serious spirit, and that the club was not intended to be ephemeral. Nevertheless the members did not neglect the other side of social life. Hobhouse wrote in his journal that they 'had a very jolly, but rather tipsy night'. Indeed, their tipsiness seems to have led to the adoption of a rule limiting the amount of drink to be taken. When Byron on 25 March replied to Hobhouse who had informed him of his election to the club, he wrote

> My dear Hobhouse — I protest against the 'pints' of your sober Association — . . . the restriction upon Scrope will of course have the usual effect of restrictions; — for my own part I have about the same conception of Scrope's company and a *pint* (of anything but brandy) that the close reflection of many years enables me to entertain of the Trinity; unless it be a Scotch pint — and even then it must be in the plural number. — I greatly fear that Scrope and I would very soon set up for ourselves — in case of my return like 'Marius from banishment to power'.

The club, soon to be named the 'Rota', has been represented as being an inner cabinet of gentlemen by means of which Burdett controlled and manipulated the Westminster Committee, that body of reforming tradesmen, such as Francis Place, who had ensured the election of himself and Cochrane in 1807. If this was so, then the 'Rota' was not very effective. It failed to secure the return of Kinnaird in 1818, it failed to secure the return of Hobhouse in 1819, and by 10 May 1819 Bickersteth could write to Hobhouse 'Alas poor Rota! it is surely broken up. I dined alone yesterday — and left the Bill *to be* paid.'

Two problems bedevilled the Rota, as they bedevilled the Westminster Reformers as a whole. The first was a lack of identity in their aims, and the second an ambivalence in their relations with the Whigs. Of the members whom we have named, Burdett of course had behind him a long career of independence. He had also contrived to be for some years on friendly terms with the Holland House Whigs, and he and they from time to time had tried to patch up an alliance, the short lived Hampden Club being one example. Wilson advocated radical reform at their meetings, but he had friends such as Grey on the right wing of the Whigs, and his views were to say the least unpredictable. Moreover, he intended to stand for Southwark, a plan which would naturally distract him from Westminster politics. On 5 January 1819 he asked for his name to be erased from the books of the club. Scrope's views are harder to pin down, but we may suppose from his intimacy with Burdett and Kinnaird that he was a Reformer, if one who was quite able to remain on friendly terms with Reform Whigs. His political activities seem to have been motivated chiefly by loyalty to his friends. Byron in his letters gives the impression that he considered Scrope to be more detached than the others, with ideas similar to his own. Hobhouse was at that time more a Reform Whig than a Reformer, though circumstances and opportunism were later to push him to the left.[4] Kinnaird seems to have been a Reformer – he at least found no difficulty in subscribing to Radical Reform principles when asked to stand for Westminster, and he was clearly unacceptable to the Whigs as a candidate. Bickersteth was the hard-liner of the club, implacable in his hostility to the Whigs. Byron, on the other hand, who liked reform but not reformers, stated elsewhere in his letter to Hobhouse of 25 March 'As for the Whigs *I* won't leave them though they will me'.

Several members of the club, therefore, occupied a debatable land on the borders between the Reform Whigs and the Reformers. This was made easier by the fact that at the only election held in Westminster since 1807 Burdett and Cochrane had been returned unopposed. In 1818, however, there would have to be a General Election. In those days such events still closely resembled the scenes so vividly depicted by the brush of Hogarth, or by the pen of Dickens in his account of the singular proceedings at Eatanswill. There was no secret ballot, and polling extended over several days – in Westminster, a large constituency, fifteen, Sundays excluded. The opportunities thus afforded for bribery and intimidation, riot and dirty tricks were by no means neglected.

If they were clever the Reformers might once again be able to avoid such a contest in 1818. They would, however, have to find a new candidate to replace Cochrane who in May 1817 had accepted the command of the Chilean Navy. The problem was that a candidate and a programme acceptable to the Whigs might not be acceptable to

4 Byron perceived this at the time. Writing to Hobhouse on 9 November 1820 he said of his friend's radicalism 'the *line* itself is not the true one – and was not your choice – but the result of circumstances united to a little natural impatience for having waited for an opening . . .'

their own supporters. The way was strewn with dangers, through which the 'genteel reformers' would have to pick their way with skill. On the far left were 'Orator' Hunt and William Cobbett, who had formerly supported Burdett, but had since quarrelled with him. Then there was Major Cartwright, who commanded a good deal of affection, and who considered that long service in the cause of Reform entitled him to be the Reform candidate. His eccentricity, however, told against him at the poll.[5] Lastly there were the Whigs, who might accept a Reform candidate provided they were consulted first, and provided his platform avoided such contentious policies as annual parliaments or universal suffrage. They and the Reformers were well aware that splitting the vote might let in the Tories. As if the aforementioned problems were not enough, Burdett's supporters were themselves divided into three groups. The first group consisted of Burdett himself and the Rota. Conscious of being gentlemen, and as such uniquely qualified to be in Parliament, they could be tactless in their handling both of the other groups and of the opposition. Inspired by a backward looking rather than a forward looking radicalism, they were always in danger of slipping back into Whiggery and even Toryism. The second group consisted largely of those dedicated tradesmen such as Place, Brooks and Adams who actually did the work of ensuring the return of Reform candidates, and formed the bulk of the Westminster Committee, though gentlemen such as Scrope were also members. They were opposed to any compact with the Whigs. Their radicalism looked to the future, and in this they resembled the third group, the 'philosophical radicals', exemplified by Jeremy Bentham. It was his genius that gave intellectual respectability to a movement compromised by the eccentric and undeveloped notions of such as Burdett and Cartwright. In contrast to the 'genteel reformers' Bentham envisaged for democracy a voice not equal with aristocracy but dominant. Burdett, Hobhouse, Scrope Davies and their kind were the temporary standard bearers of a movement destined to travel further than they had ever imagined, and which indeed they abandoned at a certain point.

In the meantime the club met frequently at irregular intervals, and

5 Major John Cartwright, an immensely tenacious but prodigiously tedious individual whose ardour in the cause of reform was sustained by some crack-pot notions concerning the political life of the Anglo-Saxons, had been preaching universal suffrage and annual parliaments since 1776.

in addition Hobhouse, Scrope Davies, Kinnaird and Burdett were constantly in each other's company. Hobhouse was energetic in pamphleteering against various of their enemies, and in this task he was assisted by the wit and common-sense of Scrope Davies. At last, on 23 May, it seemed as if Hobhouse was to be rewarded for his enthusiasm. Jeremy Bentham, Burdett and Bickersteth combined to ask him if he would stand as the second Reform candidate. He was required to pledge himself to work for annual parliaments and universal suffrage. In great excitement he rushed to his sponsors, and then to Kinnaird, who had had thoughts of trying himself, but who handsomely said he would not stand in Hobhouse's way. While he lost no time in giving the required pledge, Hobhouse could not help feeling that in the event Kinnaird would probably be chosen. His misgivings were justified. Three days later the Rota met, and Hobhouse's nomination was not even mentioned. The stumbling block was his father. Not only had he refused to buy Hobhouse a Whig seat, but by being a friend of the Tory government had rendered his son an object of suspicion in the only constituency which he could hope to win without purchase. On the first of June Hobhouse learnt that Kinnaird had definitely been chosen at a meeting that afternoon.

The next problem was to secure Kinnaird's nomination by the body of electors. Hobhouse generously agreed to speak on his behalf, but Sir Robert Wilson revealed a potential rift in the ranks of the Rota by declining to attend the meeting lest it prejudice his chances in Southwark. In the event the meeting was dominated by the wild men of the left such as Henry Hunt, and the Committee had perforce to retreat into an inner room. There the proponents of Kinnaird and Cartwright battled it out. The Major's party remained in the minority but nothing would shake their intention of nominating the ancient hero. Hobhouse nevertheless wrote optimistically to Byron on 5 June:

Parliament positively dissolves on Tuesday next; this is Friday, and our world here is more mad and silly than ever, 6,000 gs. given for a seat, and not one to be had for 5,000 gs. — argal I do not come in. Douglas Kinnaird was yesterday put in nomination for Westminster; his opponents are Orator Hunt and Major Cartwright, and it is my belief that he will certainly succeed. Sir R. Wilson has a very good chance for the Borough of Southwark. Here would be honours for the Club to turn out two members, one for West' and another for the Borough in six months. As to myself, it matters not — plain

156

prose must be my fate to the end of the chapter. The famous Jeremy Bentham, whom you may have read of in the 'Edinburgh Review', has engaged me to put some political work of his into English. The original gibberish is very difficult, but I shall try. Murray is to have the volume.[6]

The writing was however on the wall. Kinnaird was quite unknown, and the Whigs could see that here was an opponent far less formidable than Burdett or Cochrane. Moreover, thanks to the pertinacity of the Major's friends, the Burdettites were split in two. They had also been tactless. Hobhouse wrote that same day in his diary 'This day Mr Perry of the Chronicle and young Mr Adam the lawyer determined to get a requisition signed asking Sir S. Romilly to stand for Westminster. The Whigs are in great rage against K. for not asking leave of them and against so they pretend universal suffrage to which K. has pledged himself.' Romilly, known to the irreverent as 'Squash', could as a lawyer count on the not unimportant support of his many brethren in Westminster. Hobhouse began to foresee disaster, and by 7 June became convinced that had he followed his own devices and asked permission of the Whigs to stand, then gone to the Committee, he would have been nominated and probably elected without opposition. In this he showed, perhaps, more commitment to ambition than Reform. Nevertheless, with a commendable loyalty somewhat in contrast to that shown by Scrope who 'was appointed one of the committee for managing Dug's election at Westminster, but took a solemn oath that he was going abroad in two days', he threw himself into the work of organising the campaign. What he found was not encouraging. Romilly had accepted the invitation to stand. In despair Hobhouse wrote 'We have done nothing – if the return is lost – false confidence is the cause'. By the 10th he found that the 'vaunted Westminster Committee is dissolved in air into thin air'. He wrote that same day to Scrope at Mr Williams' Inn at Bagshot begging him to return:

My dear S.B.D. –

Come back directly – matters look very bad and black indeed – although we talk very big openly – The Whigs have had great

6 Bentham's *Book of Fallacies*, eventually published in 1824. Hobhouse abandoned the task, which was then undertaken by James Mill and Francis Place.

success in their canvas amongst the unpaid tailors — Squash triumphs and we petty men decline — I suspect that the com:^{ee} is going to the Dogs — we cannot do without you — for, incredible as it may seem, nothing as yet has been done except upon some proposals made by myself & Bruce[7] — I put us in the above order as I came to the Com^{ee} first — Place sits at home and writes — well, I own, but what is that? what does he at Charing Cross when he should be at Covent Garden?

News from B[ishop's] Castle — K says he is certain — so far good — The Major will not give in so he gives out — Hunt is vastly strong in the Blackguard[8] end of town — more so than we thought — the Major will certainly draw away the third part of heaven after him — so things look bad I say — come down — Burdett's gout confines him to his room. The P[rince] R[egent] goes down to dissolve in person — as unwieldy as life — If you do not come down I must give in — I have but Bruce to help and what is he amongst so many? Wilson had only eight men at the Surry theatre, and was obliged to pick up a riot in St George's Fields in order to get a mob and bring them to the Play — Lambton & Co use him for their mirth aye for their laughter —

Farewell and fortunate
ever your's
J.C.H.

Scrope obeyed the summons, by the 13th was in London and spent all that morning canvassing with Bruce and Hobhouse. In the meantime another candidate had started. The Tory Government, seeing the disarray in the ranks of the opposition, put up Sir Murray Maxwell, a naval hero who had recently discovered the Loo Choo Islands[9] and being subsequently wrecked in the Gaspar Straits had saved his men

---

7 Michael Bruce was a figure as romantic as any to be found at that time. In 1810 he met Lady Hester Stanhope in Malta, and with her proceeded to the Levant where they lived as lovers for four years. In 1815 he fell in love with Madame Ney, and was involved in the attempts to save the Marshal from execution. He was more successful in effecting the escape of the Marquis de Lavallette, and was jailed for his pains. In 1818 he married Lady Parker, widow of Captain Sir Peter Parker, Bt., a cousin of Byron's, to the consternation of his family and friends, among them Scrope Davies, whose papers reveal that he was much involved in the affair.

8 A term generally used by the Genteel Reformers to denote the Urban Proletariat.

9 Called nowadays the Ryukyu Islands, the best known of which is Okinawa. The Gaspar Strait is in Indonesia.

by a considerable feat of leadership from the assaults of pirates and of savages. The next day Lord Holland called Bruce and Hobhouse rats. Ever since the Whigs started their own candidate the friends had been confronted by a choice. Their continued support for Kinnaird would be tantamount to a declaration of war on the Whigs, and now the divided opposition might let in a Tory. To their credit they stuck to their guns, but it was to have a profound effect on their political and social life. The disputed election led to increasing bitterness between the Burdettites and the Whigs. Although the two groups had long been suspicious of each other this had been no bar to social intercourse. Inspection of the dinner books kept for Holland House, the headquarters of the Reform Whigs, reveals that along with such constant attenders as the various members of the Russell family, Burdett, Hobhouse and Douglas Kinnaird had dined there frequently. Even Scrope Davies received a card requesting 'the honour of his company to Dinner on Sunday the 26 of April [1818] at ¼ before 7'. Among the other guests on that occasion were Burdett, Lord and Lady Tavistock, the Duke of Leinster and Lord William Fitzgerald (nephews of that Lord Edward Fitzgerald who had died resisting arrest for plotting a rebellion in Ireland), two other Irishmen, Sir John Newport and Sir Henry Parnell, both of whom had held office under the Ministry of All the Talents, and Lord Molyneux, son of Scrope's friend Lord Sefton. After the beginning of the 1818 election the most minute search of the dinner books up to the date of Scrope's flight to the continent fails to reveal the name of Burdett, Hobhouse, Douglas Kinnaird or Scrope Davies. The doors of the Whig hostesses had begun to close against them.

Meanwhile, as Hobhouse had told Scrope, Francis Place was sulking in his tent. He had been riled by the laziness and superciliousness of the gentlemen, and resolved to organise the Committee no more. In the face of certain disaster, however, he was finally persuaded to take over the running of the campaign. On 18 June he started work, finding 'everything in the utmost confusion', and from then on worked from six in the morning until ten or eleven at night to the end of the election. On the 17th the Committee had decided that Kinnaird would have to be dropped if Burdett were to survive.[10] Burdett

10 Since Westminster returned two members, each voter had two votes. He could either vote for two different candidates, or confine himself to one, a procedure described as 'plumping'. Exercise of this choice had an important effect on the result. The recipient of a good number of second votes could beat a man who had received the majority of first votes.

was eight hundred votes behind Romilly and Maxwell, while Kinnaird had only managed to score about eighty. The only consolation was that Cartwright too had withdrawn, so that all the friends of Reform, with the exception of Orator Hunt, were united.

On Monday 22 June, the fourth day of the poll, Scrope Davies, Hobhouse and Bruce, 'the only gentlemen on the Committee' as Hobhouse put it, threw themselves energetically into canvassing, now asking for Burdett alone. It seemed to them that a weight had been removed, and they got on wonderfully. They plunged into a Public House in Chandos Street, organised a procession with band and drums, and led it by a circuitous route to Berkeley Square, across Bond Street and on to Covent Garden. When the poll closed they mounted the hustings, and Bruce was bold enough to speak.[11] Orator Hunt, as they noted with pleasure, had 'lost himself by accusing a man in the crowd of belonging to the Vine Street gang'. The mob were evidently against him or rather for Burdett. As for Sir Murray Maxwell, his fate was more awful still, as related in the bulletin which Hobhouse sent Byron on Thursday 25 June:

> On Monday, B. polled nearly 800, on Tuesday 908, on Wednesday 612, and to-day 448, which has put him on the whole 248 above Maxwell, and only 220 beneath Romilly. We hope to have him in the head of the poll by Monday. He has, however, had a terrible squeak for his life. Kinnaird is our hustings orator since his resignation, and really does admirably. He has lost Bishop's Castle as well as Westminster, but deserved both. Wilson has come in for the Borough, but has turned out to be no great things . . . I have been worn out, and do not know how I shall possibly last until the end of the poll, which Hunt swears he will keep open till the last. Scrope makes the Committee laugh, and discomposes the staid intelligent iron-mongers and curriers of our party. Captain Max-

---

11 Polling took place at a temporary structure called the 'hustings' which was erected in front of St. Paul's Church; Covent Garden. It was divided into sections corresponding to the various parishes, and in front sat the clerks who recorded the votes. When polling was finished for the day the candidates or their friends used the hustings as a platform from which to harangue the crowd. The proximity of the vegetable market could make this a hazardous procedure. The vote in Westminster was confined to those liable to pay rates. Daily and running totals of votes were computed and displayed on placards.

well's face is daily covered with saliva from the patriot mob. Scrope says it reminds him of *Spit head*!!

Hobhouse's optimism soon appeared to be misplaced. The next day Sir Murray Maxwell was violently assaulted, and this won him many votes. Byron's reaction to the news was not sympathetic. He wrote to Kinnaird:

Dear Douglas — I hear wonders of your popular eloquence and speeches to the mobility — from all quarters — and I see by the papers that Captain Lew Chew has been well nigh slain by a *potatoe* — so the Italian Gazettes have it — it serves him right— a fellow who has lost three ships — an Oran outang — a Boa Constrictor (they both died in the Passage) — and an Election . . . I hear of Scrope and his jests — and Holland and his toils; — I wish you all the pleasure such pursuits can afford — and as much success as usually attends them.

Byron indeed was quite indifferent to his friends' political endeavours. His letters home at the time were almost entirely devoted to his own financial affairs, and although his friends seem to have devoted a remarkable amount of time to them despite the life and death struggle going forward at Covent Garden, he continued to write on a mounting note of impatience.

Meanwhile Burdett continued to poll badly. By 1 July his majority over Maxwell had been reduced to 240. Hobhouse recorded 'We began to tremble. Place Adams and Henry Brookes, together with Secretary Percy and Clerk Service looked very blank upon it . . . The Maxwellites bet two to one on their chance.' Any Maxwellite who struck such a wager, however, was soon to learn the truth of the adage concerning the numbering of chickens. The next day the Patriot began to leave Maxwell further behind, and even to gain on the leader, Romilly. The other parties responded to the threat, each in their own fashion. The Whigs circulated cards tending to suggest that Romilly and Burdett were allied, in the aim of securing Burdett's second votes and discouraging plumpers. The Tories for their part had recourse to bribery, not with unqualified success, as Hobhouse was amused to notice:

As for Maxwell's people the most open bribery was resorted to — taxes paid — money given — tradesmen threatened — lords and ladies soliciting twenty times a day — breakfasts luncheons coaches and every thing provided – but all would not do and in many instances after voters, particularly Irishmen, took the bribes they came to our committee – told the story and voted for Burdett next day.

Despite the two pronged attack, the final result was Romilly 5339, Burdett 5238, Maxwell 4808 and Hunt 84. So ended Scrope's and Hobhouse's first experience of electioneering. They had not managed to get Kinnaird elected, but they had at least saved Burdett. They left Covent Garden, and returned to the more salubrious purlieus of St James's. There they 'saw Romilly's chairing – which was very elegantly attended by Whig nobles and their horses and carriages and wives – with Brooks's balcony filled with ladies etc. but very little popular applause.' [12] Some of the left-wing Whigs, such as Sir Robert Wilson, gave public demonstration of the fact that they had voted for Burdett and Romilly instead of plumping for either:

Lord Tavistock – Lord Darlington, Mr Charles Fox, Sir Robert Wilson, Lady Darlington – wore the blue with their buff and blue – I saw no other signs of coalition with the people – I had my own unmixed blue, and so had Davies, and so had Bruce and so had my brother – I saw no other except Halliday and Kinnaird – Lady Holland cut me – this is not the only sign of social proscription with which my constancy has been rewarded.

There remained only one item of unfinished business – the chairing of Burdett from Hyde Park Corner to the Crown and Anchor in the Strand due to take place on Monday 13 July. In this Scrope took an active part, though he seems to have left things somewhat to the last minute. In his trunk were found two letters from Secretary Percy, both written on the morning of Saturday 11th from the Piazza Coffee House. In the first Percy says:

I regret to say that I have not succeeded in procuring an arrangement respecting the twenty Horsemen, or how or in what way they and their horses are to be distinguished. You will much oblige me by settling the point . . . The Man who heads the 20 on Horseback, immediately behind the Car, carrying a Banner 'Radical Reform', is also desirous of receiving directions. He will plait the mane or in any other way you may instruct him at his own expence.

12 The Members were no longer literally carried on a chair, but each rode on an ornamental and allegorical car, escorted by horsemen in triumphal procession.

At present I have only ten names down as follows — Mess. S. Davies — J. Hobhouse — H. Hobhouse — Kinnaird — General Ashley — Capt.[n] Halliday — and three friends of Mr Brooks . . . but I believe Mr Adams and H. Brooks intend to make part. The list should be completed immediately, or we may be necessitated to admit improper persons — or give offence.

Later that morning Percy could reassure Scrope concerning the two sets of double harness they needed, but they were 'yet without a White Horse for the White Flag — our friends are now on the look out. Can you assist as to Man or Horse or both?' Percy went on to say that if he understood Scrope's idea correctly it was that the head pieces of the Bridles for the 20 should be bound with dark blue, with a Rosette on each side. He did however still want seven names to complete the twenty.

Despite these last minute alarms, everything was all right on the day, at least as far as the procession was concerned. On 16 July Hobhouse wrote to tell Byron:

The Chairing of Burdett on Monday last was the finest sight I ever saw; it beat the Champ de Mai hollow. It is supposed that so large and orderly a crowd were never before assembled in London. The car was Kinnaird's taste; the horses were furnished by Scrope the Great.[13] A slight confusion occurred at the dinner, by reason of want of victual; for, when the doors were opened, some two hundred and fifty guests were found already at table, very much to the detriment and disappearance of the various articles provided for the refection of the company. The question was, how and why the

13 Scrope's bill for his share in the chairing survived in his trunk:

Davies Esq to Charles Mason

July 13 1818	7 Horses for one day for chairing of Sir F Burdett	£26- 6-0
	A Hack for one of the Trumpeters	10-6
	for fetching the Car	10-0
	9 men for attending to the Car & Horses	4-14-6
	Baiting the Horses	14-0
	Turnpikes	4-0
		—————
		32-19-0

devil they got there; and our short commons were seasoned by loud shouts of 'Burdett for ever, but damn the Committee!' Standing armies never put the cause of liberty in so much danger as these forerunners of ours at the dinner table. Tranquillity was not restored in less than two hours, when we proceeded to the bad port and speeches of the day; and the sober part of the company separated about midnight.

Hobhouse was too modest in his account of the dinner, which was held at the Crown and Anchor. From his diary we learn:

> Someone got up and told Burdett – he was but a man – all was uproar – Kinnaird spoke, unavailingly – Burdett made a joke of the event, they did not take his humour – the landlord was sent for – his apology would not do – It seemed that the meeting would break up – the music was pelted off – I desired Percy our Secretary to make an apology – he hesitated – when after an hour and a half disturbance – I got on the table – and made a short loud appeal to the crowd, which, strange to say, had the desired effect – the noise subsided – the music was introduced – the toasts proceeded.

Hobhouse may not have told Byron of his exploit, but evidently someone did. On 3 August Byron wrote to Scrope, asking him to forward a letter to Hobhouse. The last-named, in the midst of all his political toils, had finally become exasperated by Byron's ceaseless importunings on the subject of his financial affairs. He had begun his letter to Byron of 16 July 'I have received a great many letters from you, all in the same strain, and requiring only one answer – namely, that what you require has been done long ago'. He had concluded with the words 'By the Lord! you are an amiable fellow, and, all things considered, want nothing but a little encouragement to complete your social qualities'. Nettled by this, Byron's covering letter to Scrope read as follows:

Venice August 3ᵈ 1818

Dear Scrope –

You are requested to read and deliver the enclosed letters to our little friend Hobhouse – who has been writing to me a smart letter – but I will give it him – although he has been speaking upon a

dinner table – like Grildrig to his Majesty[14] – I suppose you picked
him out of the butter boat in which he nearly perished. As I am not
near enough – I pray you – avenge me upon him by making him
retract 'retract Sir!' and believe me ever & most affectionately

Yours
[scrawl]

P.S. Take the Poker to him – do.

In the enclosed letter to Hobhouse Byron retorted 'As for my "social
qualities" – I will back them against yours or any of the Burdett
Committee – (except Scrope) I will drink with you – laugh with you –
or do anything except *talk* with you – for any wager in wines you
choose to name'. He then went on in a strain that showed that already
he disapproved of the political company Hobhouse and Scrope were
keeping – 'Genteel Reformers' were one thing, Radical tradesmen
like Place and Co. were quite another:

> You Monster You! – I have heard of your 'campaigning at the King
> of Bohemy' and your *speeches* which *seriously* I am told were very
> good ones – as well as Kinnaird's – throughout the election – but
> you don't shine as Purveyors – and you must have cut a queer figure
> spouting among the Decanters (most of them about the same
> height with yourself) in boots and spurs to appease the angry and
> famished ragamuffins who have been licking Lew-Chew and his
> Islanders for you.

Hobhouse was not to receive this letter until 3 September. The battle
over, the campaigners were about to seek some well earned repose in
the country. Before parting, however, they had a final dinner together
down the river, as Hobhouse recorded in his diary entry for 15 July,
giving a curious picture of contemporary notions of the picturesque.
'Went down to Blackwall with Burdett – Davies – Bruce and Kinnaird and Mr Power – dined at the Artichoak – fish – excellent view of
ships gliding up through the moonlight – gibbets – charming expedition altogether.' All of them, with the exception of Mr Power, and
Michael Bruce, who was about to marry Lady Parker, widow of the
naval hero, against his father's will – the incident caused no end of
trouble to Scrope as well as to Burdett, – had arranged to meet again

14 Grildrig, meaning 'mannikin', was the sobriquet given by the giant Brobdingnagians to
Gulliver.

in a week or so at Burdett's house at Ramsbury. They were to spend two periods there during that summer and autumn. Their exploits at Westminster had no doubt drawn them closer together still, and had also resulted in some social isolation. As Hobhouse put it in a letter to Byron dated 17 August:

> I am on the list of proscribed made out by Tierney, Brougham, and Co., and the other cubs at H. House, for my conduct at the Westminster Election, that is, for doing my little most to put Burdett at the head of the poll; they wrote ballads against us which were sung or said at Lady Jersey's. Oh! how we sighed for you. 'If B. was here,' said Scrope, 'by God he would scalp them.' The insolence of Brougham to all men, increases daily, and I foresee his want of wit will run him into a filthy puddle. He was shamefully beat in Westmoreland, and talked over the mob to be against him.

Meanwhile, such troubles could be forgotten amidst the rural delights of Ramsbury. Burdett and Hobhouse arrived there together on 22 July. Hobhouse was impressed by Ramsbury, even though he was put to sleep in a garret which Burdett had fitted up for want of rooms, but not by Lady Burdett, whose 'health being very bad and her temper . . . none of the best [did] not make the most agreable of wives or of hostesses'. The daughters seemed more promising. The 'eldest daughter Sophia is a nice good girl, the next Susan a very pretty girl rather pimply clever and accomplished rather, and given to quizzing. Joanna, Clara and Angela [the future Baroness Burdett-Coutts] all pretty girls are hardly out of the nursery — the last is a little thing, 4 years old, the pet.' Hobhouse found Burdett's behaviour towards his girls and his 'shy silent wife' truly delightful. By the 25th he was beginning to fall for Susan, and caught himself looking at her 'more than beseems'. The arrival on the 28th of Scrope Davies and Kinnaird, those men of the world, can not have been particularly welcome to him, however much it was to their host. Hobhouse sadly recorded 'Kinnaird and Davies came today to B's great delight — I suppose he found me hang heavy on hand — indeed his wife is a damper'. That night the accomplished Susan sang. For the next few days the house-party rode, fished, talked and took picnics into the forest. One day Susan quizzed Hobhouse for saying 'I beg your pardon' at every word, but nonetheless when he sat next to her at dinner on the seventh he thought that she looked beautiful. The next

166

day he left Ramsbury riding on Burdett's black pony, his groom
having gone on by mistake with both his horses. Two hours after him
Scrope left in his *dormeuse*.

One topic which had occupied the four men was a proposed dinner
to be given in honour of Major Cartwright. The question was whether
to attend. They were torn between wishing to show that the Reformers could present a united front and a desire to avoid being identified with the eccentric Major. When Kinnaird arrived back in
London — he had left Ramsbury on the 2nd — he was approached by the
organisers and asked to take the chair. His own inclination was to
accept. As he said in a letter to Hobhouse written on the 4th

> Will not the effect be good . . . to the cause of Reform . . . by thus
> shewing that there is no discord amongst the Reformers? — and that
> we let not any personal considerations interrupt out cooperating?
> . . . Let me therefore hear from you by return of Post after consult-
> ing with Burdett and Davies — You see I am inclined to do it — But I
> wait on your Judgement — If I do, I trust I shall be supported by
> some of my personal friends — But I should not *care* to be *alone*, if
> they did not think proper to attend —

It appears that the majority were opposed to thus honouring 'Old
Prosy', as Kinnaird feared they would be, but Burdett, in a letter to
Hobhouse written on the 10th, said that he was inclined to go.
Kinnaird wrote to the other gentlemen on Burdett's committee
asking for their support, but in the event he and Burdett were the only
ones to attend. Hobhouse refused, and Bruce, who in spite of all
opposition had married Lady Parker on 10 August, wrote to him on
the 19th explaining why he and Scrope had not gone:

> Kinnaird wanted me to go to the Dinner; but I told him, that it
> would be looked upon as a bad omen, if, after so recent an initiation
> into the mysteries of that holy state, I should make my appearance
> at the Horns at Kennington. The fear, or the anticipation of
> cuckoldom, would have been a slight objection — but I could not
> reconcile it to my conscience, to pay a compliment to the veteran
> Blockhead, for whose understanding and principles I entertain a
> most profound contempt. The facetious Scrope was off the Needles
> when he received Douglas's invitation, and indulging in his usual
> vein of humour, he returned for answer, that it would be as easy for
> a Camel to go through the eye of a needle as for him, the said Scrope

to attend the patriotic Dinner. He is now at, or more probably in Lady Oxford — quoting Shakespeare to the Young Ladies, and explaining the beauties of the five points.

Whatever the truth of his relations with Lady Oxford, it is clear that Scrope was a great favourite with the Harleys, and on leaving Burdett he had gone on to join them in the Isle of Wight. On 26 July Burdett had written to Scrope saying how much he hoped he was coming to Ramsbury, and enclosing a letter to him from Lady Oxford, written on 21 July from Cowes. Scrope had written her an account of the Chairing, which had evidently been full of malicious and circumstantial detail. Lady Oxford wrote:

> Your account of the Chairing of our own most exquisite Idol was to the Life, my dear Mr Davies even unto the darn in the stockings and omission of gloves . . . I hope your promise of speedily visiting this Island will not be a vain one, it was determined yesterday by acclamation that our jolly parties should be postponed till your arrival. I intended yesterday to visit Carisbrook while our minds were yet fresh in the cause of Liberty and Patriotism, but . . . we went a full hour too late, and returned as wise as we went. In our sail up the river to Newport, we descried a wretched alehouse which I am ashamed to own is to the Harley family as attractive as a Court to the royalist or an insurrection to a Patriot. We there dined upon what we could get, and what we brought, and were so exceeding jolly that we agreed, none but Sir Francis and his Council were worthy of such incomparable and agreeable society — you will be astonished to learn that we . . . never thought of the things and places every one goes to see . . . All this and more is deferred till your arrival, and I trust your society will counterbalance the attractions of the Alehouse.

At the beginning of September the friends gathered once more at Ramsbury, the pretext being the opening of the shooting season. Hobhouse and Kinnaird arrived on 31 August to be ready for the campaign against the birds on the morrow. On the 6th Kinnaird departed, and on the 7th Tom Moore arrived. He only stayed two days, but the house party was clearly the greatest success. Scrope was later able to tell Moore that Burdett often said those days were among the pleasantest of his life.[15] When Moore arrived Burdett, Hobhouse and the latter's brother were out shooting, and did not return until after dinner, when the brother departed. Scrope had been fishing, and had caught his eye with the hook. No great harm had been done, but Moore walked with him into Ramsbury to have leeches applied to the eye. They laughed together 'about Douglas Kinnaird's patriotic dinner . . . in honour of the "Father of Reform", Major Cartwright. Davies proposed calling Cartwright "the Mother of Reform" instead; he *is* a most mischievous old woman'.

That evening Scrope 'laid wait for T. Moore to sing, who at last did so — sung one or two of his own songs in his own peculiar style'. According to Moore himself he was not the only one to sing. The 'second Miss B. sung very prettily, and Davies delighted with the share he himself took in the "Waters of Babylon", a chant of Purcell's which he had given Miss B'.

The next day the four men 'walked from 12 to six in the forest', and had a delightful day. 'Moore was everything — his Irish stories kept us in a constant roar . . . — he beat all of us out of the field and I saw Scrope was envious.' That night they had music, and 'were most charmed'. Scrope's "Waters of Babylon" was again set a-going.

The following day Moore left, and the day after Scrope, thinking he was to fight a duel but with whom we know not. In a letter to Byron written on 28 September Hobhouse gave a picture of Scrope at Ramsbury:

The Scrope is well in physics, and still preserves the five points. His addresses have lately been divided between *the* Lady Anne Harley, and Miss Susannah Burdett. He makes your poeshies pimp for him, for I caught him *ventre à terre* under a beech tree expounding you to the latter; where types fail, he brings out an MS. from a scented Morocco pocket-book, and a palpable hit egad! How his concerns go on, no soul alive knows; his being in love looks suspicious, for he was never known to be so when in money. He is still, however, very grand, and will not stir without his '*dormeuse*', Sir. I have left off my wig and my Whig principles together; had I a seat in the den, I

15 Scrope's meeting and resultant friendship with Moore led to his other and somewhat lesser contribution to English literature. That autumn Moore conceived the not altogether happy idea of writing a satirical poem on the Congress of Aix-la-Chapelle in boxers' slang. It was published in 1819 as *Tom Crib's Memorial to Congress*. For background knowledge and opportunities to learn the flash cant of the Fancy Scrope was the perfect *vademecum*. He took Moore to various matches, and introduced him to a number of pugilists. A letter from Moore consulting him on an important detail concerning the poem is printed in the Anthology.

should have abjured them both by throwing the former on the table as Burke did his dagger. It is impossible to bear the arrogance, selfishness, and surliness of a party that has elected Bruffam for their bully. Lord Holland-House calls me a rat for asking for single votes for Burdett, and disregarding that charming piece of perfection, Sir S. Romilly; this is the head and front of my offending, and has put me on the proscription list. So my patriotism has brought me into a filthy puddle.

It was well that the friends had enjoyed so rustic a summer, for they were soon to be plunged once more into the turmoil of urban politics. On 3 November Hobhouse went round 'to Hanson's and there in his clerk's room saw the Chronicle with a black edged paragraph – What, the queen dead – no, "Sir Samuel Romilly has cut his throat" '. Romilly's wife, the sole confidante of a man painfully inhibited, had died three weeks before, and insomnia combined with grief had driven him to suicide. Hobhouse went round at once to see Francis Place. He was out, and when Hobhouse at length discovered him at home he found that he had already drawn out a handbill in favour of Kinnaird. Hobhouse was disappointed, but Kinnaird soon suffered several blows. Lord Tavistock told him that his father, the Duke of Bedford, would not support him, and had mentioned Tavistock's brother Lord William Russell. Perry called and left word that the Whigs would not support Kinnaird, but would support Hobhouse. When Hobhouse told this to Tavistock the latter retorted that Perry was an impudent fellow. That night, however, while Hobhouse, Scrope, and two well-known dandies, 'Kangaroo' Cooke and 'Poodle' Byng were dining with Kinnaird, word came that Tavistock wanted to see Hobhouse at the theatre. Hobhouse found him in the Duke's box at Drury Lane. Taking him into the back box, Tavistock told him the astounding news that half the Whigs would support him while the other half would remain neutral. He thought Hobhouse must be the one to tell Kinnaird. At this point Kinnaird himself came into the box. After the play, as the two friends walked home together Hobhouse broke the news. They both agreed to say and do nothing. If the Committee got wind of these transactions they would consider that Kinnaird had abandoned the cause in order to join the Whigs, and that Hobhouse was no better than a Whig nominee.

There followed several days of anxious waiting, passed by Hobhouse at Brighton. On 14 November he received a letter from

Bickersteth saying that the Committee were suspicious as to the sincerity of his support for Kinnaird, since Perry was offering to support him. Hobhouse thereupon set out at once for London. After breakfast the next morning, he hurried round to Kinnaird and found him reading Scrope a letter which he intended to send Burdett. In it Kinnaird stated that he would not be a candidate for Westminster. Later that day Scrope, who in the meantime had informed Place of Kinnaird's withdrawal, told Hobhouse that many would be glad of the change. He had told Kinnaird himself that many of the Reformers preferred Hobhouse to him – not the Whigs only. According to Scrope, this intelligence had so disgusted Kinnaird that he pronounced Westminster not worth representing.

The unhappy Kinnaird understandably dithered before formally withdrawing, but the following evening the Committee decided unanimously for Hobhouse. The next day, 17 November, was that set for the public meeting at the Crown and Anchor. Michael Bruce proposed Hobhouse, who then spoke and departed. He wandered about nervously until dark, and then made for Scrope's rooms. There he found Burdett, who offered hearty congratulations. He had been nominated almost unanimously. Cobbett had had ten hands, Lord John Russell about twenty five, and Hobhouse the remainder of the 1500 or so in the room. Orator Hunt had then withdrawn Cobbett, and Lord John's proposer had said that he would not disturb the unanimity of the meeting. Everything had concluded peacefully and triumphantly.

Hobhouse's friends set to immediately to support him. Kinnaird, with admirable generosity and forebearance, sent £100 towards campaign expenses. Scrope wrote a letter to Byron, begging him to return and lend assistance.

My dear Byron

Behold! I show you a mystery! Hobhouse is nominated by the Independent Electors of Westminster as a man well qualified to fill up the vacancy occasioned by Romilly's death – The court party support a Sir Murray Maxwell.[16] The Election will not take place before the beginning of January, a period so distant as to enable you to be an eye and ear witness of the proceedings – need I add that

16 Sir M. has lost one Election and two Ships (*Scrope's footnote*).

your presence and exertions might and certainly would contribute to H's success. H. will appear each day on the Hustings and deliver fifteen Lectures on Reform — Hear him — in mercy hear him — Leave your heavy baggage and all other baggages at Venice, and you may reach England within fourteen days after the receipt of this letter — I will provide comfortable lodgings for you, and a front place in one of the booths close to the Hustings, that not a word of our friend's eloquence may escape you — He already has a fair chance of success — your presence would ensure victory — H. is in a great fuss and fidgets and spits about like a catharine wheel[17] — In vain will you ever again look for such an opportunity to show your regard for one who is devoted to you and yours. Above all you will be amused — I have much to say to you which I dare not commit to paper — so let it rest till I see you which I hope to do in the course of six weeks — I have implored your attendance here without debating the propriety of my prayer — so great is my desire to see you, and so much is it to the interest of H. that you should be seen.

Lord Holland is now sitting at the table where I am writing this letter and desires me to make his apology for not having written to you lately — the hope of being able to tell you something better than what he at present knows makes him defer writing from day to day to the last syllable etc. etc You will not be able to give your proxy, unless you yourself shall appear and take the Oaths after the meeting of the New Parliament — Is not this a strong reason for your visiting England tho' but for a fortnight — Do in Gods name do your duty to your friend your principles and yourself — and come to England. Lord H. says the best and indeed only good argument for annual returns to parliament is that they would ensure your annual return to England. Mrs Leigh sends her love to you.

believe me my dear Byron
ever yours sincerely
Scrope Davies

Our Queen is dead[18]

11 Great Ryder St
St James'
London

Radicalism and Flight

To Scrope's plea Byron replied as follows:

Venice Dec. 7th 1818

My dear Scrope,

You forget that as a Peer I cannot directly nor indirectly interfere in an Election (unless I were proprietor of a Borough) so as to be of service to our friend Hobhouse. — You forget that my arrival would probably have the very reverse effect by reviving every species of Calumny against *me* for the Electioneering purpose of injuring *him* by the reflection, and that so far from his connection with me being of use to him on such an occasion — it may possibly even *now* be a principal cause of his failing in the attainment of his object. — I wish him every success, but the more I limit myself to wishes only — the better I shall serve him or any one else in that Country . . . With regard to my more personal & private feelings — you are well aware that there is nothing here nor elsewhere that can make me amends for the absence of the friends I had in England — that my Sister — and my daughter; — that yourself and Hobhouse and Kinnaird and others have always claims & recollections that can attach to no subsequent connections of any description — that I shall always look upon you with the greatest regard, and hear of your welfare with the proudest pleasure. — . . . Pray report to me the progress of H's contest — he is in the right to stand — as even if unsuccessful — it is something to have stood for Westminster — but I trust that he will be brought in. — I have heard from all hands that he speaks uncommonly well, Lord Lauderdale told me so in particular very recently. — He is gone to England — & has a whole Cargo of my Poesy addressed to Hobhouse's care for Murray.

This letter, found in Scrope's trunk, is the one mentioned in Byron's letters to Kinnaird of 9 December 1818 and to Hobhouse of 12

---

17 Byron too had remarked this characteristic in Hobhouse. Writing to Kinnaird on 9 December 1818 he said:

> You may depend upon it that Hobhouse has talents very much beyond his *present rate* — and even beyond his own opinion — he is too fidgetty but he has the elements of Greatness if he can but keep his nerves in order — I don't mean *courage but anxiety*.

18 Queen Charlotte died on 17 November.

December 1818 respectively where he refers them to it if they wish to know his reasons for not returning to England. Its discovery is therefore of no little interest.

The Cargo of Poesy was to bring yet further distractions for Scrope and Byron's other friends, for it contained the First Canto of *Don Juan*. Since letters to and from Italy usually took about two and a half weeks, however, Byron's reply was not received by Scrope until 24 December. In the meanwhile there were numberless alarms and excursions. Nevertheless, on Christmas day Hobhouse was able to write to Byron in confident vein:

> Davies has just shown me the kind letter you have written to him. Before this time you must have received what I said on the modest request to bring Mahomet to the mountain. The attractions of a Convent Garden hustings are not of the most alluring kind, even when one is at Hyde Park; but with Alps between!! I flatter myself, however, that your kind wishes will not be lost, for I have a sort of superstition about these things, and do think that a man is the better even for a distant inclination in his favour. Things do, I assure you, look very favourable for the present. The Whigs tried hard to bitch the business, and raise up Lord J. Russell and Sam Whitbread in succession against me. The focus of the latter job was H. House, and the chief agitator, Bennett. But it would not do. The ground was taken up, and Lord Grey set his face against the attempt. Government has not yet decidedly declared for Maxwell, nor is it certain that he will receive the full support of the Ministers. The betting is for me.

The next day Byron's poems arrived, and the morning after Scrope went round to Hobhouse for breakfast. Together they read the poems, and in a letter to Byron written on 5 January Hobhouse gave an account of the occasion.

> The first time I read your 'Don Juan,' our friend Scrope Davies was in the room, and we mutually communicated with each other from time to time on the papers before us. Every now and then on reading over the poem, both the one and the other exclaimed, '*It will be impossible to publish this*'. I need not say that these exclamations were accompanied with notes of admiration at the genius, wit, poetry, satire, and so forth, which made us both also at the same time declare that you were as superior in the burlesque as in

the heroic to all competitors, and even perhaps had found your real forte in this singular style . . .

The same day I dined with Douglas Kinnaird, and read the poem to him. He did not *then* see the objection to publishing. I told him our doubts, but said, that for me, I had not quite made up my mind what to say. I do not know whether it is worth while to tell you that I cursorily mentioned to Edward Ellice, a most stout defender of his faith towards you, that 'Don Juan' had the motto *domestica facta*, and that these domestic facts were more English than Spanish. His reply was, 'I am vastly sorry for it; he stands so well and so high now, and all is forgotten' . . . I recollect you used to object to Tom Moore, his luxuriousness, and to me, my use of gross words. Yet your scenes are one continued painting of what is most sensual, and you have one rhyme with the word, and a whole stanza on the origin of the pox . . . All the idle stories about your Venetian life will be more than confirmed . . . Almost all I have said about indecency will apply to the sneers at religion. Do think a moment, and you will find the position indefensible even by the first poet of the age. The parody on the Commandments, though one of the best things in the poem, or indeed in all that sort of poetry, is surely inadmissible: I can hardly think you meant it should stand. Notwithstanding the calumnies about Atheism, &c., which you have had to endure in common with almost every distinguished liberal writer that ever lived, you have never given a handle to such assertions before.

Lastly, the satire. Both Scrope and myself agreed that the attack on Castlereagh was much better than that on Southey (which, by the way, has the phrase 'dry-Bob!'),[19] but we both agreed that you could not publish it unless you were over here ready to fight him. However, as you have drawn your pen across those stanzas, I conclude them given up . . . Neither Southey, Wordsworth, nor

---

19 The words 'dry-Bob' are found in stanza 3 of the Dedication, where Byron addressing the poet laureate, Robert Southey, says

> And then you overstrain yourself, or so,
> And tumble downward like the flying fish
> Gasping on deck, because you soar too high, Bob,
> And fall for lack of moisture quite a dry-Bob.

The appalled Scrope and Hobhouse knew only too well that in Regency slang a dry-Bob signified coition without emission.

Coleridge have any character except with their own crazy prose-lytes, some fifty perhaps in number: so what harm can you do them, and what good can you do the world by your criticism? I have now gone through the objections, which appear so mixed up with the whole work, especially to those who are in the secret of the *domestica facta*, that I know not how any amputation will save it; more particularly as the objectionable parts are in point of wit, humour, and poetry, the very best beyond all doubt of the whole poem. This consideration, therefore, makes me sum up with strenuously advising a total suppression of 'Don Juan.' I shall take advantage of the kind permission you give me to keep back the publication until after the election in February; and this delay will allow time for your answer and decision.

To this letter Byron replied with one addressed to each of those concerned. On 25 January he wrote to Murray asking him to print fifty copies of Don Juan privately. The same day he wrote to Hob-house, adding in a postscript 'and Scrope too!*that* is the unkindest cut of all'. Byron had believed that the friend whose outlook on life was closest to his own would not have censured his poem. To Scrope himself he wrote on the 26th:

Venice. January 26th 1819

My dear Scrope —

Yesterday I received through Hobhouse the decision of your Areopagus or Apollophagus — or Phoebopagus; — and by the same post I growled back my reluctant acquiescence (for the present) of which I have repented ever since — and it is now four & twenty hours. — What I meant to call was a Jury — (not of *Matrons*) and not a Coroner's Inquest. — That Hobhouse the politician & Candidate should pause — I marvel not — his existence just now depends upon 'the breath of Occupation' — that Frere the poet and Symposiast of the Coteries should doubt was natural — but that you a man of the world — and a wit, — and Douglas Kinnaird — my friend — my Power of Attorney — and banker — should give into the atrocious cant of the day surprises me. — The motto 'domestica facta' in any case — whether fully published — or simply printed for distribution must be erased — there is no occasion for a motto at all. — What I meant by 'domestica facta' was *Common life* — & not ones' own adventures

176

— Juan's are no adventures of mine — but some that happened in Italy about seven or eight years ago — to an Italian. — If the bitch Inez resembles any other bitch — that's fair — nature is for the poet & the painter. — The lines on Castlereagh must be omitted — (as I am not now near enough to give him an exchange of shots —) & also the words *Bob* at the end of third stanza — which leave 'high & dry' decent & pointless rhymes. — I have finished another canto in 206 stanzas — with less love in it — and a good deal of Shipwreck — for which I have studied the Sea, many narratives — and some experience, at least of Gales of Wind. — If we are to yield to this sort of cant — *Johnson* is an immoral writer — for in his first imitation — *London* he has 'cures a Clap' — and again — 'swear
He gropes his breeches with a Monarch's air'. — Surely far grosser — & coarser than anything in Juan. — Consult *'London'* I will try what I can do against this disgusting affectation — and whether I succeed or not — the experiment will be made. — It is my intention to write a preface stating that the poem is printed against the opinion of all my friends and of the publisher also, — & that the whole responsibility is mine — & mine only. —

H. talks to me about the woman — & of the thing being forgotten — is it so? — *I* have *not* forgotten — nor *forgiven*. —

And Ellice talks of my standing 'well & high' — who cares how I stand — if my standing is to be shaken by the breath of a bitch — or her infamous Setters on? — If she was Scylla with all her dogs — I care not — I have swum through Charybdis already. — I write in haste and in very bad humour — but in all hurry and in every Mood always. yrs truly & affcty/ [Scrawl]

PS.
I have written in such haste as to omit the most essential of All — 'the *Monies*', — I should like to know what is to make me amends for the *'ducats'* I should have received — fairly & hardly earned — am I neither to have them nor 'my pound of flesh nearest the heart?' — I will have both. —

Take for the Motto 'No Hopes for them as laughs' — Stickles's Sermons. — You will recollect the passage. —

Even before the alarms occasioned by *Don Juan* had been allayed by Byron agreeing not to publish — a relief short-lived, for on 22 February he wrote insisting on publication — fresh perils arose on the political horizon. The Whig leaders began attacking the Radical Reformers. On 13 January, coming out of his house, Hobhouse met Scrope who told him that Maxwell had withdrawn. On the face of it this was cause for rejoicing, but in fact it removed the chief reason why the Whigs had feared to oppose him. This was made very clear the next day when he was told by a Whig at Brooks's 'Well now you have got rid of one competitor – you have only to profess yourself a rational reformer – and perhaps you may have no opposition'. Any danger that Hobhouse might have succumbed to the attractions of such a course was soon removed. Francis Place, nettled by the Whig attack, drew up a characteristically prolix Report for the General Meeting of the Committee, in which he returned their fire with interest. Hobhouse, Burdett and Scrope Davies were for using forebearance towards the Whigs, and could see no use in abusing them. Scrope went so far as to rewrite another violent effusion of Place's, in which, on behalf of the electors of St James's he called on Burdett to accompany them to the poll. Nevertheless the Report was read to the General Committee on the eighteenth. Hobhouse, not having a vote, did not attend, but Kinnaird and Scrope Davies did. The forebodings of the moderates were proved correct. Scrope considered that Place had been carried away by the desire to see his own writings published. He agreed to see him, and point out the desirability of discretion. Unfortunately, that same night a meeting was held at which Place won over the Parochial Committees to his own views. It was at least agreed that the Report should not be published until a later date, but nevertheless it remained ticking away like a time-bomb ready to destroy Hobhouse's chance.

In the last days before the election the strain of the long campaign and the uncertainty as to whether or not they would be opposed began to tell. Hobhouse wrote in his diary 'I am in a horror which nothing can equal and perhaps all about nothing – I wish this election was settled one way or the other for it paralyzes me'. He and his little group of friends, Burdett, Scrope Davies and Kinnaird, had been together every day for weeks, canvassing, attending meetings, working on the Committee, dining at the Rota, and nearly every night staying up late at Lady Oxford's, the headquarters of the 'Genteel Reformers'. At last the inevitable explosion occurred. On 26 January Hobhouse addressed the United Parishes of St Anne's, St James's and St George's at the Crown and Anchor. He considered that he had

made a *'very good* speech'. Unfortunately in the course of it he allowed
his Whig breeding to show when he referred to 'the great Mr Fox', not
a correct object for the admiration of Radical Reformers. Scrope and
Burdett had been at the meeting, and that night at Lady Oxford's they
and Bickersteth took him to task for his indiscretion. Hobhouse
attributed their critical spirit to envy, an idea in which he was
somewhat treacherously encouraged by Scrope, who told him the next
morning 'that he was sure Burdett was jealous of the success of [his]
speech last night – he had watched B's eyes – and cheek when the
applauses came . . .' Scrope went on to say that Hobhouse 'had tried
B's own way with the Electors – a story – a simile – a quotation from
Shakespeare – and all . . . excellent. It was . . . a damn'd good
speech'. Four days later, however, it was still an issue. Dining with
the Rota that night, Hobhouse was attacked by the whole party. He
rounded on Scrope and called him 'infidus scurra', that is 'treacherous
buffoon'. The words occur in one of the Epistles of Horace, in two
lines which would have been well known to all of them, and which are
sufficiently unflattering, since they may be translated 'As a matron
will be different from a whore, so will a friend be from a treacherous
buffoon'. Scrope was naturally incensed, and demanded satisfaction:

Dear Hobhouse

Do you conceive it possible that I should pass over without any
sort of notice the offensive and vulgar expressions which you made
use of to me yesterday? You were angry – and I was grieved to see
that you could not be angry without being rude. Still, your being
angry was sufficient to ensure my being cool; and I received your
insult almost without an observation – but a conduct which was
prudent then would be paltry now, and I claim reparation.

Douglas Kinnaird was appalled that his two friends should quarrel,
even more so since Scrope was an active and central figure in Hobhouse's campaign. He wrote to Scrope, trying to take the blame upon
himself:

My dear Scrope –

Hobhouse has just shewn me your letter – What he writes to you
I know not – But I tell you fairly that I have the whole day been out

179

of humour with myself for having been the Cause of a momentary combat between you and our excellent friend Hob — Upon my honor I think myself the sole cause of your having given serious thought to a *liberal Gibe* — I would rather cut off my hand than that you two should think coldly of each other for another hour — Regretting my own thick headed folly

> I am My dear Davies
> Yours ever faithfully
> Douglas Kinnaird

For his part the offending Hobhouse wrote:

Dear Davies,

I can not be less ready to give than you are to demand a reparation for any words whatever they were which may have offended you —

I did think that you must have had a previous conviction that I could never mean to offend you but since you wish an avowal to this effect you may be sure I feel no hesitation in making it — If I uttered any words unfit for you to hear they were unfit for me to use and if I have to lament a wound unintentionally inflicted on your feelings I have a still more poignant regret to encounter on my own account —

I have shown this note to Kinnaird and I wish you to show it to Bickersteth —

> Believe me very truly yours
> John Hobhouse

The manly frankness of Hobhouse's letter is only slightly marred by the entry in his diary: 'Quarrelled with Scrope Davies and called him *'infidus scurra'* which was very wrong and rude — and the more so for being true.'

It was fortunate that the quarrel was soon made up, for the hour of battle was at hand. On 5 February Brougham moved the writ for Westminster. By Tuesday 9 February, the day appointed for the reading of Place's report to the General Committee, Hobhouse was still unopposed, though there had been rumours that Orator Hunt might stand, or perhaps propose Cobbett. Even before the meeting began there occurred an event of unpromising omen. The supporters of the venerable Cartwright were to be seen distributing handbills in which Burdett was attacked for preventing the return of the Major as member. When the reading of Place's Report was begun it was found to be so intolerably wordy that it was ordered to be printed without being further heard. Scrope and Hobhouse had long dreaded the effect that the Report alone would have on the Whigs, but worse was to come. When it came to his speech Hobhouse for some unaccountable reason allowed himself to be carried away and casting all discretion to the winds roundly stated that the country was sick of 'Party', and that he would as little inscribe his name in the muster-roll of Opposition as he would partake of the coals and candles of Somerset House or the Admiralty. Nevertheless by the eve of Election Day the Whigs had still not started a candidate, though it was clear that the Major intended to stand. That night Hobhouse, Kinnaird and Scrope dined at the Piazza, and afterwards walked the few yards to the Managing Committee in King St. There they found that Place was convinced that a Whig would stand, though the others were inclined to think that they had got away with it. Hobhouse went to sleep that night 'cursing Master Place's Report'.

At seven the next morning, the blow for so long dreaded fell at last. Hobhouse was informed that an application had been made in the middle of the night to the proprietor of the Piazza to let a room for a Committee to manage the election of the Hon. George Lamb[20] – the brother-in-law of Lady Caroline. He immediately went round to tell Scrope, and they breakfasted with Burdett at Kinnaird's. By nine they were at the Committee, by half past at the temporary scaffolding in Covent Garden – the High Bailiff had thought there would be no contest, and had not thought it worth while to erect proper hustings – and at ten after the reading of the usual papers Hobhouse was proposed by Burdett and seconded by Kinnaird. He then made a speech in which, not entirely by his own fault, he contrived to get himself yet further into trouble. In response to a Whig challenge to

20 Scrope had crossed swords with Lamb before. Writing to Murray on 21 May 1819 Byron twitted him for having used an excessively oblique phrase in order to express some of his doubts about *Don Juan*, and recalled an earlier example of such language:

> You talk of 'approximations to indelicacy' – this reminds me of George Lamb's quarrel at Cambridge with Scrope Davies – 'Sir – said George – he *hinted at my illegitimacy*'. 'Yes,' said Scrope – 'I called him a damned adulterous bastard' – the approximation and the hint are not unlike.

clarify where he stood with regard to Universal Suffrage and Annual Parliaments, he read from a piece of paper a declaration which had been drafted by Kinnaird.

Hobhouse has often been blamed for this declaration but it is clear from his diary that Kinnaird was the author, and it is equally clear that albeit unintentionally the latter had done his friend a considerable disservice. In order to avoid frightening the more timid electors, he shuffled lamentably, saying that he considered extension of the suffrage far less important than uniformity, and refusing to commit himself to any precise period for the duration of Parliaments. The declaration was so tortuous and ambiguous that the Whigs offered £1,000 to anyone who could interpret it, while Cartwright's supporters declared that Hobhouse was a humbug unworthy the name of Reformer. Lady Caroline Lamb, who canvassed energetically on a horse, even managed to persuade some unwary electors that Hobhouse was the Tory candidate, while George Lamb was the Reformer. The confusion caused by the declaration led to incurable apathy on the part of Hobhouse's potential supporters, and by the third day of the poll he had only Scrope Davies and one other as canvassers. To crown it all there was a period of bad weather, ever the nightmare of those who would court the popular vote. Hobhouse was always well received when he spoke from the hustings, while George Lamb was greeted with 'Baa-ing' and cries of 'No Whig', but when it came to the actual poll his machine never gained momentum, while his opponent not unnaturally picked up the Tory as well as the Whig votes. In an atmosphere of increasing despair Hobhouse and his supporters watched Lamb draw steadily away, until by the last day of the poll he had received 4,465 votes to Hobhouse's 3,861 and Cartwright's 38.

Place's part in losing Hobhouse the election was enshrined in verse by the Whigs, who at the same time did not neglect to have a hit at the apostate Sir Benjamin:

> Old Hobhouse once had got a name,
> But lost for Place his better fame,
> So now his son, a louder railer,
> Loses his seat by Place the Tailor.
> How fatal to the Hobhouse race
> Is an excessive love of Place!

Thus ended the last election in which Scrope Davies was to take an active part. His contribution had been characteristic. He had devoted some three months to working almost constantly for his friend's success. As a member of the Rota and of the Westminster Committee he had been part of the inner councils of the Burdettite machine. His influence had always been on the side of moderation and common sense. He had not made speeches, and if others had followed his example Hobhouse might have had a better chance of success, but he had canvassed, at times almost alone, he had chaired meetings, and his tact and diplomacy had made him indispensable to Hobhouse in his attempt to reconcile the irreconcilable elements which went to make up the Westminster Reformers. When the anxieties of the campaign led to a quarrel, he was quick to forgive, and was back at his place next day. By his attachment to Hobhouse he had courted social ostracism, for the members of the Rota had not escaped the attention of the Whigs and the Whig press. Surely it was of Scrope that the Morning Chronicle was thinking, when it spoke of 'the Rump that govern Westminster in [Burdett's] name, and the little Court of Dandies that wait upon his person'.

The Rota were, however, soon to have a success, but not on their home ground. On July 15 Hobhouse wrote to Byron:

I have news for you. D. Kinnaird has beaten the boroughmongers at Bishop's Castle, and is now M.P. He gives a tureen of turtle to-day on the occasion. This is (the return of K., not the turtle) a real triumph for the Reformers, as K. has commenced by carrying the war into the very camp of the borough villains, and has disgraced Lord Powis at his very lodge gates. We expect much from your Power[21]; at least as much as an honest open spoken man can do in the den of thieves. You shall hear of his progress from time to time. As for your humble servant, I am, like the lady in the play, lying fallow — except a little pamphleteering now and then.

On 4 August Byron wrote in reply. After discussing the prospects for *Don Juan*, he went on in the flippant manner which his friends' political activities now customarily inspired:

I am surprised and pleased with the news of Dougal's election — and should have had no objection to some of that same 'turtle' swal-

---

21 Kinnaird held Byron's Power of Attorney.

lowed on his inauguration – together with the cold punch annexed.[22]

Twelve days later, on 16 August 1819, a peaceable assembly of working-class reformers gathered to hear Henry Hunt speak on Major Cartwright's plan of reform at St Peter's Fields in Manchester. This was a new phenomenon which betokened the end of the Scrope Davies era of genteel reformers, and announced the inception of a mass popular movement not for revolution but for reform. The local magistrates, however, failing to appreciate the significance of this historic moment, ordered Hunt's arrest. By the time the manoeuvre had been completed eleven people lay dead upon the ground, and many hundreds had been wounded. Such was the infamous massacre of 'Peterloo', so named in ironic reference to the battle which ended the reign of Bonaparte.

To natural sensations of indignation and disgust the Westminster Reformers united the belief that if the right of free speech were not to be lost for ever it was important to call a public meeting at once. Such a meeting was arranged for Thursday 2 September in Palace Yard. Hobhouse arrived in London on 28 August. That night he dined with Scrope, as he did each night for most of the following week. There was much to discuss. Should the meeting concern itself solely with the conduct of Government, or should the question of reform be raised? If it were left out Cartwright and his fellows would claim they had abandoned it. When Hobhouse took the draft of his address round to Burdett, he, and Scrope who was already with him, objected to the mention of reform. In the event they were over-ruled, and on the great day Burdett was flanked on the hustings by Hobhouse and the venerable Major. For a brief moment the Reformers were united. It did not last long. By 4 September Cartwright was once more offended, claiming it was an insult that he should not be on the Protest Committee. Meanwhile the Whig *Chronicle* considered that

22 In justice to Byron it must be remembered that he had had no experience of the bitterness engendered by a contested election, that during his time in politics the Whigs and the Reformers had been on good terms, and that the political landscape in 1819 would have been to him quite unfamiliar. As he remarked plaintively in a letter written to Hobhouse on 22 April 1820 'Upon reform you have long known my opinion – but *radical* is a new word since my time – it was not in the political vocabulary in 1816 – when I left England – and I don't know what it means – is it uprooting?'.

Hobhouse's reference to reform demonstrated clearly that the whole meeting had been subservient to his electioneering interests.

Byron's reaction was characterstic of his mood. In his poetry he made explicit reference to Peterloo only once, in a stanza of *Don Juan*, Canto XI, which he subsequently discarded.[23] In his letters he was facetious. To Kinnaird he wrote 'Do let me know what there will be likely to be done – that one may lend a hand. A revolutionary commission into Leicestershire would just suit me – the patriots should have a faithful account of Lady Noel's cattle – corn – and coach-horses – &c. &c. what colour is our cockade to be – and our uniform?'

In the midst of political turmoil troubles of a more personal nature had begun to oppress the unhappy Scrope. Already on 30 July Byron had written to Hobhouse:

– My Sister writes to me that 'Scrope looks ill and out of Spirits' and has not his wonted air of Prosperity – and that she fears his pursuits have not had all their former success. – Is it even so? I suppose there is no knowing, and that the only way in which his friends will be apprized will be by some confounded thing or other happening to him. – He has not written to me since the Winter, in last year's last month, – what is he about! –

On 30 August Hobhouse wrote in his diary:

Early this morning S.B. Davies burst into my room and told me he had a favour to ask – 370£ for a week – to help Bob. Bligh. I consented although I knew not what would come of it . . . But if a man is not to help his friend at a dead lift what is he good for? matters must be in a sad plight with friend Scrope – that is the first application he ever made to me since we were at College.

23 Byron's views on Peterloo are given in a letter to Hobhouse written on 22 April 1820:

I think . . . that if the Manchester Yeomanry had cut down *Hunt only* – they would have done their duty – as it was – they committed *murder* both in what they did – and what they did *not* do, – in butchering the weak instead of *piercing* the wicked, in assailing the seduced instead of the seducer – in punishing the poor starving populace, instead of that pampered and dinnered blackguard . . .

In the same letter he apologised to Hobhouse for confounding him with Hunt and Cobbett, but went on pertinently to remark 'I thought that the Manchester business had effected a reconciliation – at least you all (bating Cobbett) attended one meeting, soon after it'.

Thanks to Hobhouse Scrope was able to escape, if narrowly. In his trunk was a letter, also dated 30 August, from one Charles Thorpe, sending 'a Receipt for the Bill for £670 drawn upon Mr Bligh which when paid the Judgement upon the Warrant of Attorney to Mr Howard will cease and Mr Gibbs will then send you a discharge for the sum'. If Bligh had not been enabled to meet the Bill, Scrope could not have paid the moneylenders, and the Judgement would have taken effect. Despite his misgivings Hobhouse's loan was repaid on 4 September. Scrope had won a breathing space, but he was still hard-pressed. He must have borrowed a further £250 from Hobhouse, for in his diary for 11 October the latter noted 'Dined with my father at Holme's Coffee-House – told him of the chance of my losing 250£ by my friend Scrope Davies – whose bill for that sum has been returned to me – *no order*' Hobhouse can not have been much comforted when he received a letter from Scrope on 26 October, couched in the following terms:

Dear Hobhouse

I have been disappointed of a sum of money, my promises are broken and I am wretched – But I have taken measures to ensure a very early liquidation of your debt – No human foresight could anticipate the events which have been the cause of my failing to observe punctuality towards you – And you will I hope forgive me—

Yrs ever
Scrope Davies

Such are my embarrassments in consequence of my disappointments, that I am obliged to be in London incog: A few days will I hope enable me to shake off all my endebtedness –

Meanwhile more trouble was brewing for Hobhouse, but of a different kind. A pamphlet war with Lord Erskine, self-appointed champion of the Whigs, had sprung up, and to Hobhouse's anonymous *A Defence of the People in Reply to Lord Erskine's Two Defences of the Whigs* his Lordship had retorted with *A Preface to the Defences of the Whigs*. Hobhouse discovered this on 8 October, and he devoted the greater part of the next two days to composing a reply, entitled *A Trifling Mistake in Lord Erskine's Recent Preface*. In the course of it he asked:

What prevents the people from walking down to the House and pulling out the members by the ears, locking up their doors, and flinging the key into the Thames? Do we love them ? Not at all . . . Their true practical protectors then, the real efficient anti-Reformers, are to be found at the Horse-guards and the Knightsbridge Barracks . . .

Hobhouse gave the text to Place on 11 October and on the 13th departed for Ramsbury. For the next month he forgot about the pamphlet, and busied himself over a fruitless attempt to organise a protest meeting in Wiltshire. On 6 December, however, Place told him that Stuart Wortley, M.P. for Yorkshire, had been to the bookseller who handled *A Trifling Mistake*, had bought a copy, and told the bookseller that he would move the House against the publisher and those concerned in its production and distribution.[24] What happened next was recounted by Hobhouse to Byron in a letter headed somewhat unfashionably 'Newgate, Jan. 18 [1820]':

I suppose you have seen all the story in the papers. The long and short of it is that I wrote a pamphlet that a country gentleman, not knowing what a note of interrogation meant, went down to the House and swore the late candidate for Westminster had '*recommended* the people to pull the members of the House of Commons out by the ears.' The whole House took fire or fright; the publisher was *had* up, my name was not to the pamphlet, nor did the publisher or printer know it was mine except by hearsay. I, however, magnanimous like, desired Ellice to tell honorable House that I was the author, and wished to save publisher and printer and was ready to avow myself at the bar. But what does honorable House? Without a word more – without enquiring whether I would confirm what Ellice reported – without asking whether anything was to be said – in my absence, without citing, hearing, or seeing, they make a resolve at once that said J.C.H., Esquire, *having avowed himself author is thereby* (the very words of the resolu-

24 It has been suggested that it was not Hobhouse but Place who wrote the offending lines. In his diary for 10 December, however, before the glory of martyrdom had descended upon him, bringing with it any motive for claiming the lines, Hobhouse wrote 'So here I was likely to be sent to prison for an imputed meaning which no man in his senses could fancy I had – Indeed I had read the very passages to Burdett at Ramsbury and had asked him whether he thought they looked like incitement to violence he said *no* – and he actually revised the last proofs'.

tion) *guilty of a high contempt of the privileges of this House*, and shall be forthwith committed to His Majesty's gaol of Newgate, &c.

Byron too, had had his troubles. His affair with Teresa Guiccioli had reached a stage where she had been forced to choose between him and her husband, and Byron, with new found wisdom, had pressed her to return to the path of duty. He accordingly resolved to leave Italy. He was not sure where to settle, but determined that one thing should be done first of all. He would carry out the plan at which he had hinted in his letter to Scrope written in 1817 — to challenge Henry Brougham to a duel. He wrote to Kinnaird on 16 November:

> . . . I shall quit Italy — I have done my duty — but the Country has become sad to me, — I feel alone in it — and as I left England on account of my own wife — I now quit Italy for the wife of another.— I shall make my way to Calais — as I can without going through Paris. — I do not come to England for pleasure — but I know not where to go unless to America — tell *Scrope* Davies — I must see *him* immediately — I shall write to him from Calais — perhaps to join me there — (he will pardon me the trouble) as there is a matter which has been upon my mind these three years (ever since I knew it) that I must settle immediately on my arrival. — He will understand me — and so perhaps may you — but you are both too much men of honour (as well as Hobhouse from whom I have no secrets) to let it go further — . . .
>
> Novr. 17th. Since I wrote yesterday — I have had another attack of the tertian not violent — but very tiresome. — My daughter and her nurse are also fallen ill — so that I cannot fix any precise day for my setting out; — it would not be just on second thoughts to expect Scrope to take a winter journey to Calais to see me — but I hope to find him in town on my arrival.

As it turned out this additional burden was not to be laid on Scrope. By the time Allegra was better the winter had set in, and the journey was abandoned. Byron returned to La Guiccioli, and did not leave Italy until his fatal journey to Greece.

It had been on 14 December that Hobhouse was taken to Newgate, and on the 18th Scrope Davies went round to dine with him. Scrope's financial difficulties were becoming ever more serious, and in this last extremity that honour for which he had been a legend deserted him. Not only did Hobhouse never see his £250 again, but

Scrope was so unwise as to be less than frank with Burdett. Hobhouse's comment on his visitor was 'Scrope Davies, oh the rogue,
dined with me'. Nevertheless, he must have been glad to see him, for
on 23 December Scrope went to Newgate again, and walked with the
prisoner on the roof of the gaol, the only place where he could take
fresh air. Burdett called to take his leave of Hobhouse before going
down to Bath for Christmas, but departed without seeing him since
he 'disliked encountering Scrope'. This was a sad end to a friendship
once so warm. On the 25th Scrope, Kinnaird and another shared
Hobhouse's Christmas Dinner with him, and on the 27th Scrope
returned to dine once more. On New Year's Day 1820 he appeared yet
again at Newgate, apparently in good form. He brought Hobhouse a
pamphlet on Byron and Don Juan by one Aulton, and a copy of the
last issue of Cobbett's twopenny *Register*. Scrope also had a new joke
for Hobhouse, about a man who persisted in believing in the Devonshire ghost of whom he, Scrope, had said that he saw the man would
not give up the ghost until he died. This was the courage of despair.
The next day he came again, and Hobhouse recorded the occasion in
fitting detail:

> . . . When I came down [from the roof] Scrope Davies came – he
> told me he was come to take leave – he must leave England he had
> changed his lodgings frequently but was afraid of being dodged –
> he had just 130£ to start upon the continental world with – and no
> more – he knew not whither to go – he thought of enlisting in a
> West India regiment – I asked him to dine – he said no he could not
> bear that – he was as gay as he could be – poor fellow, and so was I,
> in order to prevent him thinking I mourned more for my 250£ than
> for the loss of my friend's company – He has been very kind to me in
> his prosperity and I should be selfish and savage indeed to nourish
> any disagreable sentiments or hostile feelings towards him,
> although the sum cuts deeply into 800£ per ann – and although
> there was a want of morality and principle in the way in which he
> took me in which must not be thought lightly of by any man
> pretending to honesty – But it is a sad finale – he tells me he was in
> 1815 worth 22,000£ and a good income besides – he did not tell
> me how much he owes – Kinnaird says 10,000£ – in this Burdett,
> Myself, D. Brown – and Kinnaird I suppose – Andrews, for a large
> sum – Atkinson his servant something, his lodgings 80£ – in short
> a complete smash – he traces all to a request made by Lord Jersey to

him to come to London instead of going to Cambridge – he went to the Union – lost 150£ – and looking after that in a few nights lost almost every thing – When he went to Switzerland with me he had 5000£ about left – he has left Byron's picture in my hands and the III^d Canto of Child Harold – MSS – in Kinnaird's – he has desired Kinnaird to take his name out of Brookes' – he tells me the chances against his return are 100 gs to a shilling – Such is the end of this man – whom I have known now for fifteen years at least – almost half of my life – he was in his day certainly the most agreable man for *every day*, in London – and was so esteemed by all who knew him – he was up to his last misfortune singularly honorable in all his dealings – and has been guilty of one or two indiscreet, that is, very generous, actions towards those with whom he played successfully – He did not know much – but what he did know he knew well and from perpetually turning over Shakespeare, and Bacon's essays, particularly, had a fund of agreable quotation and ingenious remarks ever at hand. His gambling habits left him without much real feeling – yet he was a warm assertor of his friendships – he fought a duel for Lord Lowther's honour – although for a joke he would perhaps sacrifice one friend to another – He prided himself most on keeping a secret as indeed he told me at parting – Unfortunately he kept the secret respecting his own fortunes too well – for had he been explicit and told the truth when they were on the turn – his friends would certainly have done him as much good as lay in their power –. As it was he tricked Sir F. Burdett who did not like to lose 500£ in such a way but I am sure would gladly have lent him or given him 5000£ – I should think him to be 38 years of age – but even in this particular he was so close that no one knew the fact. – I dare say that his father knows nothing about his misfortune the good parson of Tetbury has another son Tom Davies – a great rogue in the Bench, – I believe Scrope assisted him much – Scrope still says he can go into the church and get a College living from 1500 to 3000£ a year – why not do this? Heaven knows whether this is the fact – He took leave of me a little before six o'clock – A strange termination of our intercourse – he running away from England leaves me in Newgate – Byron will be sorry to hear this –

Scrope seems to have lost £17,000 between 1815 and 1816, and never to have made it up again. Legend has always had it that the final irrecoverable sum was lost at Newmarket, and that Scrope made good his escape abroad direct from Cambridge. This is clearly untrue – his fall was due not to the turf but to the baize. Since his ruin was accompanied by the first lapse from strictest honesty recorded against him, it is pleasant to observe that his equally proverbial kindness did not desert him. He had continued to visit Hobhouse while in danger of being 'dodged' – a gaol was certainly an odd place of resort for one in his position –, and on the very day that he bade Hobhouse farewell he took the time to write a letter to Edmund Byng on behalf of his youngest brother, still a Midshipman in the Navy, but longing for promotion. Thus, in Hobhouse's room at Newgate, ended an era in the eventful history of Byron and the innermost group of his friends – one dead, two exiled, one gaoled, and one in the House of Commons.

6

Exile

At the age of thirty-eight, with almost half his allotted span before him, Scrope Davies found himself banished for ever from the stage whereon he had acted so singular a part. The thread sustaining the sword had snapped, and Scrope, who had exercised his wit at the expense of Brummell was obliged like him to become an exile on the continent. Money wherewith to gamble, and society wherein to shine, had been the twin pillars of his life, and from henceforward he was to have little enough of either. His income was reduced to his annual share in the revenues of King's College — in this respect he was more fortunate than Brummell —, and his society to the occasional traveller and such expatriate English and Americans as he could find in Brussels. Brussels, not Paris, for it seems that even in calamity Scrope did not abandon his principles. Not for him a refuge in France under the restored Bourbons — the first record of his residing in that country is dated 1835, when Charles X had been gone five years. Scrope Davies made for the Kingdom of the Netherlands, which at that time included Belgium, and had a reputation for hospitality to the victims of Bourbon vengefulness. He appears at first to have gone to Bruges — such at least was the information Byron received from Douglas Kinnaird. Writing to Hobhouse from Ravenna on 3 March Byron commented on the down-fall of his friend — indeed, on the downfall of them all:

> So — Scrope is gone — down — *diddled* as Doug. K. writes it — the said Doug. being like the Man who when he lost a friend went to the St James's Coffee House and took a new one — but to you and me — the loss of Scrope is irreparable — we could have 'better spared' not only 'a better man' but the 'best of Men'. — Gone to Bruges — where he will get tipsy with Dutch beer and shoot himself the first foggy morning. — Brummell — at *Calais* — Scrope at Bruges — Buonaparte at St. Helena — you in — your new apartments — and I at Ravenna — only think so many great men! — there has been nothing like it since Themistocles at Magnesia — and Marius at Carthage.

Byron imagined that Hobhouse was still in Newgate, whereas in fact the death of George III and subsequent dissolution of Parliament had not only effected his release but also given him another opportunity, this time to be successful, of standing for the representation of Westminster. Three weeks later Byron was abreast with events, but still concerned about Scrope. He resolved to give his joke about the St James's Coffee House another airing. On 29 March he wrote to Hobhouse 'And now, my Man – my Parliament Man I hope – what is become of Scrope? is he at Bruges? or have you gone to "the St James's coffee-house to take another?" ' Hobhouse was nettled at having the joke turned on himself, and felt bound to point out that Scrope had, to some extent, placed himself beyond the pale. No doubt he still felt the loss of his £250. He replied on 21 April 'Of Scrope Davies I have heard nothing since his departure; nor have I been to the St James's Coffee House to find another friend. It is a very sad reflexion that his last moments were not regulated by that honor and fair dealing for which he was so remarkable in his former career; but, poor fellow! distress will make a man do anything.' Byron was saddened by this rejoinder, and by the fact that he was no longer sure of Scrope's fate or even whereabouts. He replied on 11 May:

> I am sorry to hear what you say of Scrope – it must have been *sore* distress – which made that man forget himself. – Poor fellow, his name seems not fortunate – there was Goose Davies, and now there is a Captain (who has planted his servant & run away for mistaking signatures) – of the same nomenclature, but what can have become of Scrope? – does nobody know? he could hardly remain at Bruges, it is sad that he should 'point a moral and adorn a tale' unless of his own telling; and his loss is the most 'ill-convenient for my Lord Castlecorner' that could have occurred – I shall never hear such jokes again; what fools we were to let him go back in 1816 – from Switzerland. – He would at least have saved his credit – & money, – and then *what* is he to do? he can't *play* – and without play – he is wretched.

The feeling that Scrope's other friends had been unduly harsh persisted, for when on 22 December Byron told Francis Hodgson of their old friend's fall he wrote: 'Our friend Scrope is dished, diddled, and done up: *what* he is our mutual friends have written to me – somewhat more coldly than I think our former connexions with him warrant:

but *where* he is I know not, for neither they nor he have informed me'. Byron's puzzlement as to Scrope's location had hardly been lessened by receiving a letter from John Murray written on 15 August in which he was informed that Lady Frances Wedderburn Webster averred that Scrope had gone to South America. The impossibility of finding him proved discouraging. From that time on he appears in the letters and journals of his friends as a memory, as one to be quoted, but no longer as an actuality. Only once was Byron able to think of Scrope in the present tense. According to Thomas Medwin, when Byron was at Pisa in 1821 and 1822 he heard a rumour, presumably false, that Scrope had been at Florence. This made him ask why Scrope had never come to see him.

It is in connection with an event catastrophic to all Byron's friends that Scrope Davies first emerges from the shadows. On 19 April 1824 in the squalid Greek town of Missolonghi the poet died. Scrope's immediate reaction to the news is unknown, but with his usual kindness he did what he could to comfort the living. He wrote to enquire if Augusta Leigh still had her copy of the miniature of Byron which late in 1815 Holmes had painted for Scrope. He also offered to give her certain of Byron's letters. Writing to her on 30 June 1824, the day after Byron's remains arrived in England, he said:

> I am delighted to hear that the Miniature is where it ought to be — in your possession — keep it as the 'apple of your eye' for it will give you consolation when nothing else can. It is my intention to have some lithographs taken from it.
>
> During the last ten days I have been very unwell and utterly incapable of writing — I will deliver into your hands all the Letters you wish to possess.

Augusta felt that Scrope's generosity should be reciprocated, and sent him some rings of Byron's as a memento. On 22 September 1824 Scrope wrote:

> My dear Mrs. Leigh
>
> I have received the rings, and shall not attempt to thank you — for I am unable to do so to my satisfaction. 'Come then expressive silence' — Nothing could add to the value of such a possession but the circumstance of you having sent it — Pray give me the history of the ring which Poor B. wore — when did he get it? what is the

Stone? — on which hand and which finger did he put it? These are all trifles, but what is not interesting about the departed when they are such as he was?

When Sir R. Wilson returns to town, I must beg you to give him an interview — he will explain more to you on the subject of the lithographic likeness from B's picture, than I can explain by letter. Besides he is a great admirer of poor B. and every thing belonging to him.

I have lately met here a Mr. Hay who was with B. in the affray with the military at Milan — He (Mr. H) is a dull but a matter-of-fact man — and as such his information is interesting — He says that the gentleman whose name is in the papers (it begins with an M.) as about to become B's Boswell, is a perfect idiot, but he suspects Mr. M. to be the stalking horse to Mrs. Shelley (Godwin's daughter), whom he describes as not perhaps incapable of the task. —

When you return to town, you will see me some dusky evening glide into your rooms at St. James's — for I am bid both by business and inclination to England. Where is Ada now? you may write to me without reserve — but I have heard strange reports of Lady B. I hope they were merely reports. Your accounts of the last moments of B. have been more interesting to me than all the letters, papers, conversations, declarations and affidavits the world has produced. Remember me affectionately to Georgiana and all the family, and I beg you to take great care of your health: for you never go through any worry unless stimulated by a fever — but in the reaction consists the danger — The descent of the balloon is most dreaded by the aeronaut.

> Adieu
> Believe me ever yours
> > sincerely
> > Scrope Davies

10 Place d'Armes
Ostende

Mr. M. was no doubt Thomas Medwin, the second edition of whose *Conversations of Lord Byron* was published in 1824. Byron's friends and relations found the question of biographies of the poet extremely alarming. As Hobhouse put it in his diary 'poor Byron — he always kept his friends in hot water during his life and it seems his concerns will be of no very easy management after his death'.

The letter reveals two interesting facts about Scrope – his address at Ostend, and that he intended to pay a visit to England. Whether or not that particular one materialised, he clearly considered that such visits, if discreet and not too extended, were practicable and safe. If we are to believe Thomas Grattan,[1] who first met him in 1827, Scrope must have moved to Ostend quite soon after his arrival in Belgium. Grattan says that when he first met Scrope he 'had for five or six years been fixed in the little town of Ostende'. A description of Scrope's abode, which may well, however, have lost nothing in the telling, is to be found in, of all unlikely places, an article on famous chairs published in the *Strand Magazine* in 1893:

> There is a story connected with Lord Byron's handsome Louis XIV chair, covered in crimson Utrecht velvet. In 1835 his intimate friend, Scrope Davies, an associate of the Byron coterie of elegant men, and a wit, had made his home in an apartment that was previously a hay-loft situated in one of the squares in Ostend, the approach to this unconventional dwelling being by means of a ladder. Scrope Davies had filled two rooms, fashioned in the loft, with relics from all the distinguished men he had known, and was visited by many eminent people as they passed through Ostend to pay their respects to King Leopold at Brussels. The father of the lady who tells the story of Davies knew how to appreciate that remarkable man who, in return, invited him to the loft, where he found a curious collection of objects.
>
> He was subsequently to do Davies 'a good turn' and this sympathy led to the gentleman one day carrying down from the ladder this same high-backed chair with cloven feet, which Byron himself had given him. It originally came from his lordship's ancestral mansion, where he used it in his library.

In his book Grattan set down a detailed account of Scrope Davies' appearance, manner and way of life as he found them in 1827:

> He was then notoriously past his prime, not in years but in power, for he had led a hard life, and had muddled away the best part of those *talens de société* to which alone he owed his reputation . . . [In

1 Thomas Colley Grattan, *Beaten Paths and Those Who Trod Them*, 1862. Grattan was a writer and journalist who spent many years in Paris and Brussels.

Ostende] as the Magnus Apollo of a confined set he had probably acquired, or was at any rate encouraged in, a rather dictatorial manner.

Davies came up occasionally to Brussels to enjoy a week's dining-out. He was always welcome and well received. It was there I met him, being invited to dine, at a late hour, for that purpose at the house of an English gentleman my near neighbour . . .

I was introduced to Scrope Davies by the master of the house and placed in a seat reserved for me by his side. He attempted to stand up to receive me with due honour, but sinking on his chair he grasped my hand, vigorously squeezed it, and addressed me in a cordial greeting garnished with two or three quotations; and clearing off the bumper which stood before him he 'filled his glass again', and dropped into a half-muttered half-maudlin rhapsody which I could scarcely comprehend.

He had in fact already followed his custom of an afternoon; but recovering himself after a while he did his best, talked fluently, quoted freely, and showed that he had read much and remembered much of what he had read. But though there was a good deal to amuse in the body of his discourse, there was no method in its details. He was too abrupt in his transitions for that easy flow which is the great charm of table-talk. He brought Byron, Porson, and others into play, not as parts of a whole, in natural sequence, but rather 'showing them up' in unconnected succession . . .

There were few men of any great renown in England whom he had not met, or heard so much of as to give him the tone of an acquaintance; and when he gave a repartee of Fox or a saying of Pitt, a tirade of Burke or a sarcasm of Sheridan, it was done with such a familiar air that one never thought of asking him, Did you hear it? Were you in the house? or at the Cocoa Tree? or wherever the scene was said to have been. You took it for granted that so good a sketcher sketched from life . . . But Davies was no mimic of voices or manner . . . There was nothing dramatic about him. His features were inexpressive, and his habits of life threw over them an unvarying flush. His close cut and grizzled hair showed a forehead of no extent or mark . . . There was nothing sonorous in Davies's voice. He spoke in a rather short and snappish way, with however a gentlemanly accent. Neither was there anything pedantic in his bearing, which was perfectly well-bred. So that although he wanted the qualifications requisite for the higher order of story-telling . . . yet he had a perfect facility for that light and easy style of table-talk, which is so agreeable in society when it is not pushed too far.

But the worst of this particular talent is the too great self-confidence which it is likely to produce. The constant habit of talking for effect, the conviction that he is expected to hold forth, generates in the professional wit an impatient sense of his importance, that makes him insensible if he cannot get the lead and despotic when he has it.

Thus far Grattan's dominant reaction seems to have been one of disappointment. He is generous enough, however, to point out that he was not seeing Scrope Davies as he had been in his great days, but 'middle-aged, bruised if not yet broken by dissipation, his expectations deceived, and the scene of his display peopled by the English settlers in a small Continental capital or a Flemish fishing town'. Nevertheless he continues in a censorious tone:

Independent of the first impression, there were some after-observations not quite favourable to him which struck me. He seemed entirely deficient in information on broad and general questions of politics and morals. He betrayed a sycophantic tendency towards place and title. His habits of life were repugnant to mine, and he assumed a depreciating tone in reference to many contemporary authors whose works he had never read. But he and I met frequently, always with pleasure on my part, for I greatly admired his conversational talents, and I steered clear of all chance of mixing in scenes which I could not enjoy. He sometimes dined with me when he came to Brussels, and the hospitality of our mutual acquaintances brought us often together.

The occasion on which I recollect having found Davies most particularly amusing was one morning at breakfast with Kit Hughes, the American minister, himself a capital specimen of Yankee vivacity. The conversation turned on life in London, and Scrope was certainly at home in the racy and graphic sketches of 'the Fancy' – Gibbons, Scroggins, Cribb, etcetera, with which he made Hughes and myself laugh immoderately.

Exile

How reminiscent are the last few lines of the account given by Trelawny of Byron at Pisa.[2]

As well as enjoying the delights of dining out with the Anglo-Saxon colony in Brussels – delights which still, as Grattan's account makes clear, imposed on him the duty of singing for his supper – Scrope diverted himself by keeping up a correspondence with many of his old friends, and, like Brummell, saw quite a number of travellers, living as he did 'between London and Paris'. In 1828 he wrote from the same address in Ostend to Francis Hodgson:

My dear Hodgson,

Your letter, having been directed to me *poste restante* did not reach me till the 16th day after its arrival in Ostend. As for Moore's letter, Heaven only knows how long it has been slumbering. We have no dead letters here . . .

For James Wedderburn [Webster], whom you must have met at Newstead, has passed a few days here, on his road to Paris. Did you ever see Lady Frances? She is the only person I ever beheld in whom was everything that the eye looks for in woman. She, and she alone of all whom I have ever seen, had the 'vultus nimium lubricus aspici', 'that beauty over which the eye glides with giddy delight, incapable of fixing upon any particular claim'. Goldsmith makes no acknowledgement to Horace, though he is indebted to the above amount.

Sir James has survived Waterloo, but he has not survived his love of writing. He makes 'born' rhyme to 'storm', and 'suspect' rhyme to 'respect'. About the latter, in vain do I assert that in English Poetry a rhyme, to be just, should not be an 'idem', but a 'simile'. He goes on rhyming and reasoning, and both with the same success. I recollect to have heard B. Craven say that he once found some lines on the breakfast table at Belvoir where 'women' was made to rhyme with 'chimney' (sic): and a Mr. Elton at Brussels, when I declared that not one word rhymed to chimney, exclaimed: 'What do you say to nimbly?' The latter is, I have no doubt, perfectly orthodox at Bristol, as the former was at Belvoir. So that a rhyme is what Voltaire said of religion, a matter of geography.

2 Quoted in Chapter 3.

Exile

Your letter has recalled to my mind scenes the recollection of which now constitutes my only delight. Bacon somewhere in his letters observes, 'Aristotle saith young men may be happy by hope, so why should not old men and sequestered men by remembrance?' The past and the future are the sole object of man's contemplation. There is no present, or if there is, it is a point on which we cannot stand. While I am now writing the future becomes the past. Happiness is then a pursuit, not an attainment. In one of those runs with the Duke of Rutland's hounds, when the fox is killed the sport is over, or to be enjoyed again only in recollection after dinner.

Will the present ministry stand?[3] Sir R. Wilson says they cannot settle into permanent power. So Eldon is extinct.[4] I cannot bear to hear his adulators talking about his giving a decision without turning to the right or to the left, whereas he looked to the right and to the left without giving a decision. But what have I to do with politics? W. Drury is doing well at Brussels. He has upwards of seventy pupils. In the Summer of last year, I encountered Polehampton at Antwerp, and with him Lewis, the fishing and shooting conduct of Eton.[5] It was amusing to observe how they viewed everything through a bad pair of English spectacles.

Adieu! and when you have nothing else to do, write to one who is out of the world.

Yours truly,
Scrope Davies

I have just escaped a duel for having written a couplet on an amateur actor

Not to be hiss'd delights the dunce,
But who can groan and hiss at once?

10 Place d'Armes, Ostende

---

3 The Duke of Wellington's Cabinet, formed January 1828. It lasted until November 1830.

4 The Earl of Eldon was not dead, but no longer Lord Chancellor after having held the office, with one short break, since 1801. Scrope's judgement of him was sound.

5 All three fellow collegers of Hodgson and Scrope at Eton.

Exile

Despite his apparent courage and resignation, however, it was not to be expected that ruin, exile apparently endless, and the consolation not so much of philosophy as of the bottle should not at times bring in their train depression and despair. A picture of Scrope Davies in one of his darker moods was painted by Thomas Raikes[6] in his journal for 25 May 1835, written in Paris:

Scrope Davies, whom I formerly knew well and intimately in London, promised to pay me a visit here tomorrow; he was apparently in good spirits when we dined together on Wednesday last: my astonishment was therefore great when I received from him last night the following letter: —

'Dear R., – When you met me at dinner on Wednesday last, you might possibly have observed a gloom about me, which the gayety even of your conversation could not dispel. This moral symptom was, as it often has been, the precursor of physical derangement. Since that period, lethargic days and sleepless nights have reduced me to a state of nervous irritability, such as forbids me to see any society. At some future period, when I am in a healthy state of mind, the perusal of your manuscripts will afford me the highest gratification. At present I must visit nobody, but must strictly follow the advice which Sir George Tuthill gave me: his words were these – 'On such occasions avoid all possible excitement, or the consequences may be most lamentable'. He then quoted what Imlac says in 'Rasselas'. 'Of all uncertainties, the uncertain continuance of reason is the most dreadful.' Such language could not be mistaken, and I have acted, and must continue to act, accordingly. I would much rather be accessory to my own death, than to my own insanity. The dead are less to be deplored than the insane. I never saw a maniac, but I found myself absorbed in a melancholy far more profound than that which I ever experienced at the death of any of my friends. Babylon in all its desolation is a sight not so awful as that of the human mind in ruins. It is a firmament without a sun, a temple without a God. I have survived most of my friends: Heaven forbid I should survive myself.'

6 A well known dandy and a diarist, a friend of Brummell, and a member of Watier's and White's, where he had been something of a butt, being known as 'Apollo', since, as one who combined the roles of city merchant and dandy, 'he rose in the east and set in the west'. In 1833 financial difficulties compelled him to live in France. He remained abroad for eight years.

The perusal of this letter gave me great uneasiness, and I could only write in return an attempt at a cheerful answer, to prove that I felt no participation in his apprehensions, and imputed his lowness of spirits to mere bodily indisposition, which, as I told him, quiet and calomel would remove . . . I fear that deadly foe to human intellect, the brandy-bottle, has much to do with the excitement.

It is not extraordinary that he should quote from 'Rasselas', when it is known that the luminous author of that work was constantly a prey all his life to those morbid apprehensions.

Wednesday 27th. – I went to Paris to inquire after my invalids; but I suppose my prescription had answered, as I found that Davies was well and gone out; but this letter, coupled with some other previous circumstances, makes me apprehensive for the future about him.

Despite Raikes' fears, a year later Scrope had not only abandoned the habits of a lifetime, but was still gaining pleasure from the attentions of old friends. John Murray had offered to give him a copy of Byron's *Works*, and Scrope accepted with gratitude. On 17 May 1836 he wrote to Murray from the Hotel Brighton in the Rue de Rivoli in Paris. Whether for political or other reasons, France was now acceptable to him, and he had given up Ostend as his permanent place of residence, dividing his time between Paris, Dunkirk, Ostend and even London. In his letter Scrope betrays a characteristic which Grattan was to remark. Like those of so many exiles, his ideas had become fixed in the form which they had assumed in the years of his prosperity. His letter reads:

My Dear Sir,

Nimrod[7] informs me that it is your wish and intention to present me with a copy of Byron's Works. I need not remark how much flattered I am by this mark of your recollection of one who has been so long and so entirely secluded from the world. The pleasure I feel too is not a little enhanced by hearing that like your compatriot the Thane of Cawdor you are a 'prosperous gentleman', and I pray that good fortune may long attend you and yours. – you deserve it – your conduct towards Byron when in the Autumn of 1816 I put the

7 C. Apperly, author of *The Turf, the Chase, and the Road*.

third Canto of Childe Harold and the Prisoner of Chillon into your hands, was noble as your previous conduct during his difficulties was beyond all praise. Does he still look down with a temperate scorn on the dissecting table of your Inquisition Chamber? Of him and many others I have some notices which I much wish you to see. They are original, and I think interesting, nor am I willing they should die with me. There was scarcely a man of any celebrity during my time, that I had not the good fortune some time or other to meet. With some of these beings of a finer mould I was on terms of friendship, with many familiar, and more or less acquainted with nearly all. Barring the Bubbles (which I read because you recommended it to Nimrod) and Washington Irvine's [*sic*] Works I know but little of modern publications, and that little causes no regret at not knowing more. I was seduced into reading Washington Irvine's by accidentally stumbling on his Stout Gentleman. The Lady Morgans, Bulwers, and Trollopes of the day have no charms for me. What is good in them is a rechauffé from others — what is their own is bad. C'est un bonheur pour la plupart des ecrivains d'aujourd'hui d'avoir la memoire, comme c'est un malheur pour leur lecteurs. Swift says, it is a great art in writing to know when to leave off, as I am sure it is to know what to leave out — to sink the Offal as the Carcase Butchers say. But these writers give you the Offal and sink the Carcase.

As you desire me to mention where you may send this splendid present of yours, I beg that it may be deposited at 47 Great Ormond St. the mansion of my good and esteemed friend Mr. John Hibbert, and if I can be of any service to you on any occasion and in any way, you may command me. I shall quit Paris in a few days for my little residence at Dunkirk — where I intend to pass the Summer. Should you visit that part of the World it would afford me much pleasure to see you chez M. Crepin — Rue de l'Eglise Dunkirk. Believe me

> Yrs most truly
> Scrope Davies

Murray and Scrope Davies had at one time seen a great deal of each other, and the former's kindness was no doubt genuine and disinterested. Nevertheless, he may well have felt that it would be a mistake not to keep in with Scrope, of whom it had long been alleged that he had written or was in the course of writing a life of Byron. He would have been unusually qualified to write such a work, at least in so far as it concerned Byron's life up to 1816, not only because he had been intimately concerned in so many of its episodes, but also because Byron knew that he could not humbug him as he humbugged those whom he suspected of recording his every word for posterity and gain. Scrope appears proudly to have told each new acquaintance of his great compilation. Grattan's cynical reaction, as recorded in August 1836, was:

> I never heard but from himself of Davies having produced anything, 'in prose or rhyme', beyond the routine compositions of his college course; but the very first evening I met him he told me he had completed a life of Lord Byron – all but the last chapter, and that Murray the publisher had offered him I forget what excessive price for it. Between nine and ten years later (that is to say the day before yesterday, Friday 19th August 1836) he repeated the same information to me, word for word. The world may therefore look forward to another biography of the great poet by one of his intimate associates, if indeed Davies has not succeeded in persuading himself, by dint of repetition, that what is but an intention exists as a fact. And from his well-known way of life and his extreme indolence this is I think the probability . . .

Grattan then went on to set down some more impressions of Scrope's behaviour, behaviour which he found remarkable, but which is shared by many exiles:

> One thing very remarkable in Davies is that while he retains perfectly his recollection of all the old stories, stale jokes, and trite quotations which formed the stock-in-trade of his conversation so many years ago, he positively has not added the most trifling acquisition to it during the whole time that has since elapsed. It would seem that his brain was full and that memory could hold no more. The University, Parliament, the Turf, the 'Fancy', are still the themes of his discourse, but all in illustration of their peculiarities a quarter of a century back. He has not an anecdote less than twenty years old. To the rising generation he will (if his memory last) be as valuable a companion as he must soon become to his old acquaintances (if theirs does not fail) somewhat of a bore. . . . But it looks as if he had found out his failing, for instead of

remaining stationary as of old in this scene of his seven years' residence [Ostend], he now frequently shifts his quarters, and fluctuates between Paris and London, but not exactly in accordance with Brummel's definition of *his* abode in Calais, which meant remaining there at all times, *ex necessitate rei*.

Davies is greatly improved in his habits of life. One may now meet him at dinner without seeing him consume indiscriminately the contents of every bottle of wine within his reach. In the evening he is really capable of 'discourse of reason,' while in my morning walks on the *Digue* – that finest of sea-side promenades – I constantly meet him as early as seven or eight o'clock, and have then some pleasant snatches of chat with him. He is nevertheless greatly broken, and looking ten years older than his age, which cannot I should think exceed fifty [he was fifty-three]. But from his cheerful temper, good constitution, the absence of care, and the reformation in his way of life, he has a fair prospect of reaching a good round old age, and of being for many years to come sought after as a most accomplished diner-out.

A year later, in August 1837, Grattan met Scrope Davies at Ostend again. Scrope had just come from Paris, where he had seen Tom Moore and his son, 'the younger but somewhat taller Tommy'. He told Grattan that Moore was still 'plump and rosy and unbroken, but that "Tommy Secundus looks by no means poetical".' Moore's son was a wastrel who ended his days in the French Foreign Legion. On this occasion Davies annoyed Grattan by once again showing how closed his mind was to anything which had happened after the date of his exile:

The first thing Davies asked me was whether I had read the 'Physiologie du Goût'. I answered no; but on his strong recommendation I meant to read it – and I in return asked him if he had seen 'Charles Lamb's Letters', (a copy of which had been lent to me a couple of days previously by Tom Hood, who is here at present), and which I had been running through with great delight. Davies smiled a supercilious negative, and merely asked 'was that the man who wrote something in a magazine?' which I thought a most unbecoming slight to the memory of 'Elia', the exquisite essayist, the most genuine of critics, the friend of Coleridge, Southey, and Wordsworth. Had Charles Lamb rejoiced in the title of 'Honourable' before his name or 'Baronet' after it, Scrope Davies would have been the ready retailer of his quaintness, the echo of his quiddities.

Notwithstanding the unpleasant impression made by this incident, Grattan was becoming ever fonder of Scrope Davies, who in his turn felt driven to confess to his friend the true nature of his biographical collections, and to seek his advice. On 13 October 1837 Grattan wrote:

Nothing of its kind appears stranger to me than my increasing intimacy with Scrope Davies, after so many years of cold acquaintanceship. I find him greatly improved; he may possibly have the same opinion of me; or perhaps the mere force of habit is doing its work on both of us.

On my way to England about six weeks ago I met him by accident on the quay at Calais. He revived a subject which he had mentioned to me in this town [Ostend] some weeks before, and which I before alluded to, and he wished me much to make Dunkerque my way back, that I might see him in his bachelor's residence there and talk it over quietly. I could not manage that, but I entered cordially into the project he has so much at heart, for putting into form the scattered materials (which turn out to be just what I anticipated) for the book he is so desirous of completing. While in London last month I spoke to Murray on the subject, and I informed Davies, by letter, of his readiness to negotiate about it, as soon as a sufficient specimen of the work was forwarded to him for examination. This letter brought the following reply:

Dunkerque, October 4, 1837

Dear Grattan, — I feel much obliged to you for the trouble you have taken respecting me and mine. It is my intention to see you at Ostend early next week, and on the conclusions I may come to from a conversation personal (one in person is worth a thousand in letters) will depend the 'ubi' of my residence this winter. My papers are in a sort of chaos without form and void, and I have need of some master spirit to breathe life and order into the rude and undigested mass of aliment. One thing is certain, I can never put a finishing hand to any work I take in hand, unless I have free access to a library for reference, such a library too as is only found in cities. My own little collection of books I have gone over and over again – they are all good, but we may be satiated even with what is good. They are all 'pièces de résistance', like a round of beef, which to a man who lives alone as I do is without end (as indeed most rounds are except those of the Fancy); but I cannot live now as I did at Eton, without change of food. Then again in a city I fear lest I should be disturbed by the charm of society – in fact I wish to unite two things incompatible in themselves, the resources of society and the security of solitude. Although I am not, if I chance to be without company one of those who are (to use an expression of a charming writer of the days of Charles I.) 'like a becalmed ship and never move but by the wind of other men's breath, and have no oars of their own to steer withal' (which by the bye is a very exact portrait of vanity). Although I say I am not one of them, yet I cannot say I am one of those few persons on whom solitude can be well fitted and sit right, and of whom the same author thus speaks. 'They must have enough knowledge of the world to see the vanity of it, and enough virtue to despise all vanity; if the mind be possessed with any lust or passions, a man had better be in a fair than in a wood alone. They may, like petty thieves, cheat us and pick our pockets in the midst of company; but like robbers they are sure to strip and bind or murder us when they catch us alone. This is but to retreat from men and to fall into the hands of devils.' Can you tell me the author whom I have quoted? On my interview with you depends my winter sojourn. Till then adieu! . . .

How is it that you have energy enough, in the very thick (a favourite word of Sheridan's) of society, to make solitude your general rule, and now and then only

> 'To thy bent mind some relaxation give,
> And steal one day out of thy life to live'.

while I, like a blockhead, invert that system, and embrace as the general rule what ought to be the exception.

Commend me to Mrs Grattan. I shall bring some of my papers with me. God bless you.

> Yours ever,
> Scrope Davies

True to his promise, Davies arrived here three days ago; and after due consultation and a partial inspection on my part of his fragments, he set out again for Dunkerque this morning, to *set to* in earnest at the composition of some consecutive chapters of his work, which he is to forward or bring with him to Brussels as soon as I am settled in my winter quarters there. The only observation I have to make further is that when he told me, years ago, that he had completed his intended volume all but the *last* chapter, it was really the *first* he should have said, for there is nothing like such a division or distribution of matter to be seen in his manuscript pages, which are very few in number and totally unconnected. But something may come out of the chaos by and by.

Unfortunately for posterity, Scrope changed his plan. He never went to see Grattan in Brussels, and as far as the latter could make out the chapters were never written. Scrope was nevertheless happy to take an interest in the literary endeavours of others. Thomas Raikes asked him to look over the MS. of his *City of the Czars*, an account of St Petersburg, published in 1838. Scrope replied:

Dunkerque, December 13th 1837

My dear Raikes,

Gibbon, in his Journal, denounces the custom of submitting literary labours before publication to friends. 'Some,' says he, 'praise from politeness; others criticize from vanity.' He is right, perhaps. Still, I should much like to peruse your manuscript; not that my comments could improve the work, but the work might improve me; for I am deplorably ignorant about Russian statistics.

How can you suppose that I am more able than yourself to supply you with quotations? I have very few classical books here, and no classical acquaintance; while my memory is as treacherous as a black-lead pencil. Bob Bligh, when travelling with the Marquis of Ely through the Highlands, turned the Marquis out of his own carriage, because he did not know who was the mother of Queen Elizabeth. In vain might he look for a travelling companion here. Do you recollect a story of Tom Stepney's (a man far underrated, in point of humour, by you and your Oatlands friends,)[8] about his

8 Oatlands was the country house of the Duke and Duchess of York. Many dandies, including Brummell, were devoted to the Duchess.

countrymen, the.Welsh? On the restoration of Charles II a form of prayer and thanksgiving was sent down into Wales, to be read in all churches and chapels. 'This is all very well, perhaps, for Charles II,' said the Welsh, 'but what is become of Charles I?' Of Cromwell they had never heard a syllable. What I have, that I send thee.

The conduct of our ministers reminds me of a scene I once witnessed in the market place of Calais.[9] A number of old women were encouraged and hallooed on by a gang of ragged ruffians to seize the corn which was pitched in the market. The silly old creatures did this to the heart's content of their rascal abettors, who immediately ran off, and escaped with the plunder before the police interfered, and sent the offenders to prison. Thus, in this equitable division, the rogues got all the prey and the old women all the punishment.

You are quite right. Burdett did not bring himself, as it is said, to a temporary poverty by moneys spent at the Westminster election, but at the Middlesex contests with Mainwaring and the Ministers.

Commend me to your daughter, to whom I was introduced once, and saw no more — just beheld and lost — admired and mourned.

Two months later Scrope Davies wrote once more to Raikes, this time on the subject of one of his favourite pursuits:

Dunkerque. February, 1838.

Dear Raikes,

I pray you to seek [Ball Hughes], and to throw down before him my glove of defiance at tennis. About the middle of next month I hope to meet him, and I expect he will not refuse to engage me on equal terms. I am out of practice, having nothing here relating to tennis, save one ball in a drawer, and a street yclept 'Rue du Jeu de Paume' where a tennis-court once stood. The influenza has added half fifteen to my years, and has taken away from my play half thirty;[10] yet I empower and authorize you to hurl my defiance at his

9 A reference to Palmerston's foreign policy, probably as it concerned the war between Carlists and Legitimists in Spain.

10 A play on the method of giving handicaps at Royal Tennis.

head. I dare him to the combat, which shall be à l'outrance.

Juvenal, in his 14th satire seems to say that no man was too old, and no child too young, to shake the dice-box:

> 'Si damnosa senem juvat alea, ludit at haeres
> Ballutus, parvoque eadem movet arma fritillo.'

Suetonius, in his Life of Augustus, describes him as inordinately fond of play; and Claudius was so addicted to gaming, that he played while taking his rides in his chariot, and wrote a book on the subject of play. Hence Seneca, in his Apotheosis of Claudius, assigns to him as his occupation in hell, to play eternally at dice, with a box that had no bottom . . .

So much for the royal gamblers, of whom the greatest, perhaps, that ever existed, was the late Emperor Napoleon. He was all for double or quits, and threw in some dozen mains, and, finally, was of course ruined.

Tell me what [Ball Hughes] says to my challenge, and I will endeavour to send you a more worthy letter than I have here scrawled. Commend me to your daughter, and say that when I come to Paris, I will show her a French translation of 'Manfred', of which I possess the copyright, and which, should she declare it to possess such merit, as I am informed it does, I intend to publish, together with some other writings about which I have no alarm.

Unhappily the influenza struck again, and Scrope's match had to be postponed. On 14 March he wrote from Dunkirk again:

My dear Raikes,

Your agreeable letter found me in bed, suffering from a second attack of 'grippe', which has left me more dead than alive. Swift, on some occasion of illness, says, 'Thank God, I may now say with Horace, 'Non omnis moriar,'[11] for I am half dead already'.

There are two modes of getting rich — one by increasing your income, the other by diminishing your expenditure. It is Swift, also, who observes, that the accomodating your wants to your means is like cutting off your feet to avoid the expense of shoes.[12]

11 Not all of me shall die. Horace, of course, was referring to his poetry.

12 This witticism is also found in one of Scrope's notebooks in which he jotted down 'good things' for production at a later date.

Exile

One thing I have discovered, but somewhat too late in life, that a man can live on very little; and that philosophic happiness is perhaps preferable to civil, or vulgar, happiness (as Burke terms it): the former consists in wanting but little, the latter in wanting a great deal; and both, in possessing what we want. To you, the recollection of what has been seems more dear than the present. 'Quantum minus est', (as Shenstone says of his niece,) 'cum reliquis versari quam tui meminisse'. In Caliph Vathek is to be found the same sentiment. In Byron frequently this idea occurs; and at the head of one of his minor poems he has printed Shenstone's epitaph.

On Saturday night it is my intention to be in Paris; not to sleep, that I never can after a journey. How is it that, when, some nights 'twixt sleep and waking, I hear the chimes, the music appears unearthly?

'Sweet, as from blest voices uttering joy.'

I must finish the lines, the inspired lines, of Milton —

'Heaven rung with jubilee; and loud hosannas filled/
The eternal regions.'

No such poetry now!

When you ask me to partake of poor John King's favourite dish, a leg of mutton, pray do not ask above two persons. I really now have no impudence for a dinner party. 'Not fewer than the Graces, and not more than the Muses,' is a saying attributed to Lord Chesterfield: it is as old as Aulus Gellius. Swift says, 'a large number spoils company'. It is so; conversation is not general. They form parties of intellectual écarté, instead of playing a round game. During a space of nearly six months, I have never but once drank more than one bottle of weak Bordeaux per diem'. This I solemnly declare: I have surprised myself.

The French translation of 'Manfred' is already packed up in my trunk, and I must request your daughter's sincere and just opinion on its merits. In taste, we lie far behind the other sex. 'The hand of little employment hath the daintier sense.'

I pray you take an early opportunity of telling B[all] H[ughes] I mean soon to meet him in the arena at tennis. One of the markers told me that if he would exert himself he would beat me: I think otherwise. Tell me what he says. Commend me to the future critic of the French 'Manfred'.

Exile

Edward Hughes Ball Hughes, the celebrated 'Golden Ball', was a dandy who had dissipated a huge fortune, married a Spanish dancer, and been obliged to take up his abode at St Germain near Paris. According to Captain Gronow 'Scrope found the former gay young man very much improved in mind by adversity, and was wont to say, 'He is no longer "Golden Ball"; but since the gilt is off, he rolls on much more smoothly than he did.' It is interesting to see that Scrope had in his possession a French version of Byron's *Manfred*, of which he owned the copyright. If we are to believe Grattan, Scrope was by no means master of French, so for that reason, as well as his normal indolence, it seems unlikely that he was the translator. There are no indications as to how he came by this literary property.

A tennis match between the two ageing dandies did eventually come off, for Raikes records having watched one on 23 March 1840. The result, however, remains unknown. On 24 September of that year Scrope wrote to Raikes from the Hôtel d'Angleterre at Abbeville on a topic that united them in interest, Russian politics:

My dear Raikes,

In perusing a volume of Burke, which I have with me, I find this passage: 'Doctrines limited in their present application, and wide in their general principal, are never meant to be confined to what they at first pretend' — Burke's Appeal.

Under this passage I found written in pencil by me in 1828: 'Russia exemplifies this, 1828.' What Russia then was, she now is — save that she is more powerful than she was, and will be very shortly infinitely more powerful than she is.

I am on my way to St Germain, where I mean to pass four or five days, before taking an apartment in Paris — easy journeys suit me best. I shall be at Dieppe on Monday next, where I propose passing two or three days. Then I shall go to Rouen. The table d'hote at Rouen is admirable. There are objections to all tables d'hote but fewer to that at Rouen than to any I ever knew. There are rarely any English to be seen there; and besides, as Paris is France, so at this hotel, the table d'hote is the kitchen. Each and every dish, at a private dinner, is a rechauffe. Why should you not drop down the river, and pass two or three days at Rouen? I wish you would send me a line to the Hotel Royal at Dieppe, saying you will do so.

I met yesterday a Russian employe, whom I well know and

212

therefore cannot trust. He assured me Russia would be 'loyale'. But I always look at the dial, if I can, when I hear a clock strike; and in this instance I could plainly perceive, by a suppressed smile, how the countenance gave the lie to the tongue.[13]

On 15 August 1849, Grattan was astonished to run into Scrope Davies in Boulogne-sur-Mer. By this time Scrope was a neat little old gentleman of sixty-six, and Grattan found him much improved:

Can it be close on twelve years since I last saw Scrope Davies at Ostend? And is it really him whom I once more fell in with yesterday, in the *Rue de L'Écu* in this town, on his way to a table d'hote dinner at three o'clock; and again, in another part of the same street an hour later, on his return from his early repast, having, as he assured me, taken after it 'half a glass of brandy and water' – looking so old and bent, but so spruce, so neatly-dressed, so gentlemanlike in air, so lively and fresh in conversation, and in all respects so much improved in appearance and manner to what he was when I first met him in Brussels two-and-twenty years ago?

Yes, there is no doubt of it. Davies still lives, still flourishes according to his fashion, has still his wits (if not his wit) about him, and is thus likely to fulfil my prognostication dated so long back, and even now borne out as far as mere time is concerned. But he tells me that he is really and truly no longer a diner-out; that he is by no means well in health as I might imagine from his looks, and that he has lately taken to walking in his sleep, having on one occasion awoke, finding himself on the banks of a river – but I could not help remarking there was no fear of his going into the water unless it was mixed half-and-half with wine.

As he goes to Paris to his present lodgings, Rue Miromenil No. 2, this very day, I have no means of putting to the test his old qualities as a convivial companion, or talking over my wanderings in the New World and various parts of the old, since my return from America in 1846.[14]

13 In 1839 Great Britain, France, Russia, Austria and Prussia agreed to settle the conflict between Mehemet Ali of Egypt and the Sultan of Turkey. Palmerston was afraid of an alliance between Mehemet and Russia, while Russia hoped to divide Great Britain and France. The matter was settled in 1841, but during 1840 there was danger of a war between Britain and France.

14 From 1839 to 1846 Grattan was British Consul in Massachusetts.

Exile

We had half an hour's rambling talk about former acquaintances, and associates, dead and living or hovering between the world and the grave; — Lord and Lady Holland at Kensington, Lady Blessington at Paris, Brooke Richmond in this very town, Kit Hughes at Baltimore, Tom Moore at Sloperton, and others. Davies himself is evidently proud of his reformed and economical habits. He laid a creditably boastful emphasis on that 'half glass of brandy' as his after-dinner potation; and in the same breath assured me that he lived on eighty pounds a year. I praised his philosophy, and we parted — without any allusion to his Life of Byron — I promising to call on him when I next went to Paris; and he quoting a portion of one of our far-back conversations (which I had entirely forgotten) on the subject of Charles Lamb, whom he said he would never forgive for having in one of his criticisms (which I had made him read) talked of Ophelia's 'scraps' of songs, instead of 'snatches,' the true Shaksperian word.

Grattan's memoir reveals that by that date Scrope had moved to Paris, to the 'English quarter' in the Faubourg St Honoré, near to the British Embassy. A picture of his closing years is given by Gronow:

> Scrope Davies bore with perfect resignation the loss of the wealth he had once possessed; and though his annual income was very limited, he made no complaint of poverty. He daily sat himself down on a bench in the garden of the Tuileries, where he received those whose acquaintance he desired, and then returned to his study where he wrote notes upon the men of his day, which have unfortunately disappeared: that they existed there can be no doubt, as he occasionally read extracts from his diary to those in whom he placed confidence.

Whether the 'notes upon the men of his day' amounted by this time to anything more than the 'scattered materials' which Grattan had seen in 1837 is open to doubt — nevertheless, the notes alone would be worth having if by some happy chance they had survived somewhere, perhaps in a bank, perhaps in a lawyer's office. The fact that they had disappeared by the time that Gronow was writing — he died at Paris in 1865 — must, however, inspire us with no great hope. Nevertheless, Gronow is frequently unreliable, as is evidenced by an incident which he tells of Scrope. According to Gronow

Having heard that Brummell had obtained a consulship when Lord Melbourne came into office, Scrope went over to London and had an interview with the noble Lord; but he told his friends, 'Lamb looked so sheepish when I was ushered into his presence, that I asked him for nothing; indeed there were so many nibbling at his grass, that I felt I ought not to jump over the fence into the meadow upon which such animals were feeding'.

The problem with this tale is that Brummell was appointed Consul at Caen on 10 September 1830, the death of his old enemy George IV on 26 June having made the appointment possible, whereas the ministry in which Melbourne was Home Secretary and Palmerston Foreign Secretary did not come into office until November. Brummell's consulate was suppressed at his own recommendation in 1832, and Melbourne did not become Prime Minister, in which office he would be rather better placed to award consulships than as Home Secretary, until 1834. The story, with its elaborate tissue of puns, looks suspiciously like one of Scrope's 'good things', and no doubt Gronow the gossip was a victim hard to resist.

In the last year of his life Scrope twice revisited the scenes of long past and happier days. On Sunday 6 July 1851 Hobhouse wrote in the diary which he still kept, though there were no longer any χαμαιτυπαι to enliven its pages:

N.B. on Saturday the 28th of June going out of my house at $\frac{1}{2}$ p 11 in the forenoon I was accosted by an old man, shrivelled and bent, who, in a feeble voice, asked me if I knew him. I told him I did not. He said, 'Scrope Davies'. I was much shocked to see the robust active lively companion of my youth shrunk to such a remnant of himself but I had not seen him since he parted from me when I was in Newgate in 1819. I asked him to come into my house – or walk with me – he could not do either, but said he would call on me on the following Friday. He did come on Tuesday last – early – but I was not up – so I have not seen him – He is still obliged to live abroad, and continues to retain his King's Fellowship. He will not want it long.

In the thirty-one years since they met last Scrope Davies had merely existed. Hobhouse had risen from Newgate Gaol to a house in Berkeley Square, to an estate at Erle Stoke in Wiltshire, to Cabinet rank. He had dwindled from a Radical to one of the more conservative members of the Whig establishment, and in consequence had lost his seat at Westminster. He had represented Nottingham, where he, the reformer, was accused of electoral malpractice, and had opposed the reduction of working hours for children in the lace trade. As President of the Board of Control for India he had been blamed for the disastrous Afghan war. As Secretary at War he had failed to abolish flogging in the Army. At length, when his office was wanted for the purpose of tempting Sir James Graham into the Government he had, just four months before seeing the ancient Scrope, been raised to the peerage in the Gothic title of Baron Broughton of Broughton de Gyfford. Two lives – which had been the better spent?

At the end of May 1852 Edward Hawtrey, Head Master of Eton, wrote to Francis Hodgson, whom he was to succeed as Provost later that same year:

> I am sure you will be sorry to hear that our old friend, Scrope Davies, was found dead in his bed at Paris a few days since. He was a most agreeable and kind-hearted person, and I shall not soon forget the pleasant hours I have passed with him. He seemed quite broken down when I had a glimpse of him a few months since at Eton. I hardly knew him again, and should not have done so had he not mentioned his name.

What strange sensations must not Scrope have felt at seeing his old friend and fellow Colleger Head Master of the school – a Head Master, moreover, who had, with the active assistance of Hodgson, devoted eighteen years to sweeping away the Eton they had known. Long Chamber was abolished, Montem was suppressed, the number of the boys had doubled, and Scholars actually had to compete for their places. The decayed and disreputable institutions of the late Georgian world had been able to produce the men who were to reform them.

It had been during the night of May 23/24, at his lodgings in the rue Duras, that Scrope's life had come to its end. The *Gentleman's Magazine* informs us that

> For some time his constitution had evinced marks of decay. On the day previous to his dissolution he complained of cold, and retired early to his bed. He was found on the following morning lifeless upon the ground; it was evident that he had got up in the night, and had been seized by something approaching to apoplexy. It was imagined that he possessed some curious documents relating to

216

Lord Byron; but they have not been found, nor the ring which the noble lord sent on his death-bed by his valet Fletcher, and upon which Davies placed much value.

It is a comfort to learn from Grattan that Scrope 'finished his career in those Paris lodgings (where I never called as I had meant to do) . . . obscurely, but not quite deserted, or with any ignominious circumstances of discomfort'. He was buried in the cemetery at Montmartre. The plot was provided by one John Lyon, presumably a member of the British community in Paris.

Scrope had managed his exile better than had Brummell, who even in France had been imprisoned for debt, and had died prematurely senile in an asylum at Caen. He had been luckier in having an assured income, but he had at least learned to live within it. So ended the existence of one who had risen entirely by his own talents to a high position in social, political, sporting and University circles, a man of intelligence and wit who refused to be solemn about his beliefs, a friend who was loyal but never servile, whose kindness was a legend, a generous winner and a resigned loser, one doomed from the beginning by the fatal love of gambling, but who nonetheless contrived to stay afloat for over fifteen years, and who when he sank, did so with dignity and without repining. All of these amiable characteristics, however, would never have sufficed to rescue his memory from obscurity had they not combined with other qualities not so easily definable to win him the lasting devotion of possibly the greatest poet, and certainly the most fascinating individual of his age. Aimless as much of Scrope's existence no doubt was, many years of it were shared with a genius who from it could distil lines in which more of truth is revealed with less of solemnity than anywhere else in poetry. Byron's art, the 'spoiler's art', witty, wry and disabused, was formed and nourished in a milieu to which Scrope Davies made an important contribution, a milieu into which the contents of his trunk, after one hundred and fifty-six years, have provided us with a spy-hole, narrow perhaps, but for all that vivid and revealing.

A Selection of Letters and Mss found
in the Scrope Davies Trunk

Lord Byron	31 July 1810
Lord Byron	31 July 1811
Lord Byron	2 September 1811
Samuel D. Davies	31 August 1814
Samuel D. Davies	18 October 1815
Scrope Davies (draft)	13 March 1816
Percy Bysshe Shelley (sonnets)	1816
Lady Frances Webster	1818/1819
Thomas Moore	15 February 1819

Patras, Morea
31 July 1810

My dear Davies,

Lord Sligo[1], who travelled with me a few days ago from Athens to
Corinth, informs me that previous to his departure he saw you in London. —
Though I do not think you have used me very well in not writing after my
very frequent requests to that effect, I shall not give you an opportunity of
recriminating, but fill this sheet to remind you of my existence and assure
you of my regard, which you may accept without scruple, as, God knows, it
is no very valuable present. — As I do suppose that before this time my agents
have released you from every responsibility, I shall say nothing on that head,
excepting, that if they have not, it is proper I should know it immediately,
that I may return for that purpose. — Since I left England, I have rambled
through Portugal, the South of Spain, touched at Sardinia, Sicily and Malta,

1 Lord Sligo, who had succeeded his father as 2nd Marquess the preceding year, had been at
Cambridge with Scrope and Byron, at which time he was still known by his courtesy title of Lord
Altamont. His yacht was not only 'innavigable' but was to bring him into a peck of trouble. On
16 December 1812 he was convicted at the Old Bailey of having seduced some seamen from
H.M.'s ships in the Mediterranean to sail her back to England. He was fined £5,000 and
sentenced to four months in Newgate Prison.

been in the most interesting parts of Turkey in Europe, seen the Troad and Ephesus, Smyrna, &c in Asia, *swam* on the 3ᵈ. of May from Sestos to Abydos,[2] and finally sojourned at Constantinople, where I saw the Sultan and visited the interior of the Mosques, went into the Black Sea, and got rid of Hobhouse. I determined after one years purgatory to part with that amiable soul, for though I like him, and always shall, though I give him almost as much credit for his good qualities as he does himself, there is a something in his manner &c in short he will never be anything but the 'Sow's Ear'. – I am also perfectly aware that I have nothing to recommend me as a Companion, which is an additional reason for voyaging alone. – Besides, I feel happier, I feel free, 'I can go and I can fly' 'freely to the Green Earths end' and at present I believe myself to be as comfortable as I ever shall be, and certainly as I ever have been. – My apparatus for *'flying'* consists of a Tartar, two Albanian soldiers, a Dragoman, and Fletcher[3], besides sundry sumpter horses, a Tent, beds and Canteen. – I have moreover a young Greek in my suite for the purpose of keeping up and increasing my knowledge of the modern dialect, in which I can swear fluently and talk tolerably. – I am almost a Denizen of Athens, residing there principally when not on the highway. – My next movement from hence is to visit the Pacha at Tripolitza, and so on to headquarters. – Hobhouse will arrive in England before this, to him I refer you for all marvels, he is bursting to communicate, hear him for pity's sake. – He is also in search of tidings after that bitter 'miscellany', of which we hear nothing, Seaton to be sure compared him in a letter to Dryden, and somebody else (a Welch physician I believe) to Pope, and this is all that Hobby has yet got by his book. –

I see by the papers 15th May my Satire[4] is in a third Edition, if I cared much about the matter, I should say this was poor work, but at present the Thermometer is 125!! and I keep myself as cool as possible. – In these parts is my Lord of Sligo with a most innavigable ship, which pertinaciously rejects the addresses of Libs, Notus, and Auster, talking of ships induces me to inform you that in November last, we were in peril by sea in a Galliot of the Pacha of Albania, masts by the board, sails split, captain crying, crew below, wind blowing, Fletcher groaning, Hobhouse despairing, and myself with

---

2 In Greek myth Leander was supposed to have swum nightly across the Hellespont from Abydos to visit his beloved Hero in Sestos. Eventually he drowned, and Hero threw herself into the sea. Byron was very proud of his feat, though the distance was only about a mile, on account of the strong currents and the classical associations.
3 Byron's valet.
4 *English Bards and Scotch Reviewers*.

my upper garments ready thrown open, to swim to a spar in case of accidents; but it pleased the Gods to land us safe on the coast of Suli.

My plans are very uncertain, I may return soon, or perhaps not for another year. — Whenever I do come back it will please me to see you in good plight. I think of you frequently, and whenever Hobhouse unlawfully passed off any of your *good things* as his own, I immediately asserted your claim in all cabins of Ships of war, at tables of Admirals and Generals, Consuls and Ambassadors, so that he has not pilfered a single pun with impunity. I tell you with great sincerity that I know no person, whom I shall meet with more cordiality.

Address to me at Malta, whence my letters are forwarded to the Levant. — When I was in Malta last, I fell in love with a married woman,[5] and challenged an officer,[6] but the Lady was chaste, and the gentleman explanatory, and thus I broke no commandments. — I desire to be remembered to no one, I have no friends any where, and my acquaintances are I do suppose either incarcerated or made immortal in the Peninsula of Spain. — I lost five guineas by the demise of H. Parker.[7] — Believe me yours most truly

Byron

P.S.
I believe I have already described my suite, six and myself, as Mr Wordsworth has it 'we are seven' — Tell Mr E. Ellice that Adair has a letter for him from me to be left at Brookes's. — Adio! I place my name in modern Greek on the direction of this letter for your edification.[8] —

5 Mrs Constance Spencer Smith, a lady who led a most adventurous life, being imprisoned by Napoleon for her part in a conspiracy, rescued by the Marquis de Salro and subsequently shipwrecked.
6 Captain Cary, aide-de-camp to the Civil and Military Commissioner, General Oakes.
7 Harry Parker, 3rd son of Admiral Sir Hyde Parker, killed at the battle of Talavera.
8 Addressed to: Scrope Berdmore Davies Esqr
            Cocoa Tree
            St James's Street
            London
  μπαιρων Spelt thus Byron's name would in modern Greek be pronounced 'Byron'. The Greeks, however, have adopted his name in its English spelling as a forename, and consequently pronounce it 'Veeron'.

Letters and Mss

Reddish's Hotel
St. James's Street
31 July 1811

My dear Matthews[1],

    I have this day been informed that you are at Cambridge where you have possibly heard that I have been some fourteen days in England. — Of these, two were passed with Cam[2] of the Cornish Corps, who is exiled to Ireland with his Miners, of course I grieve, & so will you.—

    The rest of my time has been spent on business & in acquiring a Gonorrhea, which I regret as I was only just cured of a severe one contracted in Greece, of all places!

    Such things we know are neither rich nor rare
    But wonder how the Devil they got *there*. —

If you bend your steps hitherward, I shall be happy to see you before I leave town for Notts, I am going down to Newstead & afterwards to Rochdale for the purpose of arranging my affairs, in spring I shall probably return to the East, being sick of your climate already. — I have to thank you for a long & entertaining epistle which saved my life in an Ague at Malta; — your pugilistic qualifications have made you of marvellous celebrity in that department as I hear from Jackson and other deep mouthed Thebans, I meant to have attended lectures myself, but this Clap has laid an Embargo on all exertion. — Believe me

Yrs. very truly
Byron

1 This letter to Charles Skinner Matthews was found by Scrope Davies among Matthews' effects after his death by drowning on 3 August 1811.
2 John Cam Hobhouse.

Letters and Mss

Newstead Abbey
2 September 1811

My dear Davies,

I should have thought by this time that the Dragon of Harrowgate had as little chance of containing you as the Dragon of Wantley, & under that supposition I sent you a letter forwarded here by *Tom Stepney*[1] or Tom Thumb or Thomas d'Aquinas or some other uncouth correspondent, without adding a word of mine own. – I am detained here by the Ins. no – the In*d*olence of 'Office' (an Attorney's) & the 'Law's' or rather the Lawyer's 'delay' for my worldly Director will not come before 14th & I must be patient, for I like *fair* means as well as any body when *foul* are not likely to be so useful as they always are agreeable. – I shall attend to your hint in the Postscript, but what can I do? you might as well preach moderation to the mad or maudlin, as caution to an embarrassed man. – You know my situation, indeed you have a right to know it, you know too how completely I am in trammels, & all the advantage I am ever likely to derive from that property, is the sad satisfaction of knowing it to be lucrative, & never being able to make it so. – If my affairs are not in some order very soon I have made up my mind to the step I shall take, what that is, I think you will guess, & all things considered it would not be the worst. – I will not live to be the Shuttlecock of Scoundrels. – In the meantime I *hope* & *laugh* in Spite of Johnny Stickles.[2] –

I mean to accept your Invitation to Cambridge. – I am also invited by Bold Webster,[3] who is reconciled with as little reason as he was angry; I am invited by a friend in Lancashire, I am invited by you, & (now for an Omega) I am invited by *Wm Bankes*[4] to '*One of my places in Wales*'!!! but which of all these places this Deponent knoweth not, do you think Lewellyn ever invited any body to one of *his* places in such a manner? one would think Corfe Castle had perched itself upon Penmanmawr. – I have heard of purse = pride & birth = pride & now we have Place = pride. –Good Even. –I won't detain you from your Rubbers.

Yrs ever
Byron

1 Sir Thomas Stepney, 8th Bart.
2 See page 143, footnote 18.
3 James Wedderburn Webster, the husband of Lady Frances.
4 A Trinity College friend, described by Byron as 'the father of all mischiefs'. His family seat was at Kingston Lacy near the ruins of Corfe Castle, and he was also heir to the property in Flintshire of his great-uncle Sir William Wynne. He was to become a great traveller in the East.

Letters and Mss

[A letter from Samuel Decimus Davies to his mother giving an account of the burning of Washington by British troops in 1814. The letter conveys admirably the writer's boyish enthusiasm and pride which are given further immediacy by the additions scrawled both at its head: 'I have sent you a Rough Copy. Write this over again. A Letter Wrote on the Ground first Part on a table' and at its end: 'the Brig Sails. Excuse this Yankee Paper.']

H.M.S. Albion Chesapeak Bay
North America
31 August 1814

Dear David [written over Mother]

It is now the first convenience I have had for this 3 Months of sending Letters to England. I have most excellent opportunity now. The Recruit Brig Sails today strait for England with our 2nd Lieutenant Mr Scott with Private Dispatches from Admiral Cockburn[1] lately made Rear Admiral of the Red of our taking the City of Washington. I was at the Battle myself. I flatter my Kidneys I will give you an account of the Particulars of the Battle but most likely you will here a more exact account in the News Paper than I can tell you. There were 18 Troop Ships Arrived here about 3 Weeks ago Some from England & Bourdeaux besides 9 or 10 Frigates & Two 74 Tounnant Sir Alexander Cockrun[2] Commander in Chief on this Coast & the other Adm¹ Malkham[3] Junior Admiral to Cockburn both from Bermuda. They brought out the 4th Kings Own Regiment 85th 44 and 21 from Bourdeaux & two Marine Batallions from England in all above 5000 Men. Under the Command of Major General Ross.[4] We landed the Army at a place on the 20th of this Month called Benadict[5] about 64 English Miles from Washington. Besides a Navel Brigade from the Tuonnant of 200 Sailors Under the Command of 1 Lt & 3 MidshipMen & 91 Sailors from the Albion under the Command of Lt Cowan MidshipMen Barrs & me. We Marched the 21 at 4 in the Evening & Halted at 12 O clock that Night. It rained and Thundered in a

1 Admiral Sir George Cockburn, sent to harass the American coast 1812–1815.
2 Sir Alexander Cochrane, vice-admiral at Bermuda, and Commander-in-Chief of the expedition.
3 Admiral Sir Pulteney Malcolm.
4 Major-General Robert Ross after service in the Peninsula was instructed in 1814 'to effect a diversion on the coasts of the United States of America in favour of the army employed in the defence of Upper and Lower Canada'. On 12 September he was killed in an attack on Baltimore.
5 Benedict, Maryland, on the Patuxent River. The aim was to attack a flotilla of American gunboats under Commodore Joshua Barney which had run for cover in the river.

dreadfull manner. We were all very Wet In the Open Fields all Night. We all marched next Morning at Day light The Band playing here the Conquering Heroes Come. We Halted about 12 O clock in the Day at place called Nottingham & Marched again at 4 & never halted till next day at 5 O clock were we Arrived at a place called Marborough about 34 Miles from Washington a very Handsom Little Town about 1 hour before we Arrived there were 6000 American Soldiers but they all run in the Woods & in their hurry left their Nap Sacks full of things behind them. We had some fun here down by the Sea Side. All the Boats of the Ships had pulled up to Attack Commodore Barneys Gun Boats which were 14 in Number they all had their Yankee Ensigns & Commodore Barneys Broad Pedant [pennant] Flying. About an hour before our Boats got up with them they Blowed them all up but one, by chance We saved her. We took the Commodores Barge & Gig, the Admiral & Boats Crews Landed & Chased the Dam Rascals two of them were very near Shooting the Adm¹, we took them Presioners & they prove to be two of his Barge Men that were in the Implacable Real EnglishMen they will be hung when the Expedition is over. The General Sent fore Cockburn & sed he thought it would be Impossible to take Washington with such few Men. The Commander in Chief sent word that he thought it would be Impossible & like wise Adm¹ Malkham. Adm¹ Cockburn said he would go, that nothing was Impossible in the Soldiers that he had from France & Spain & that he would go himself & either Conquer or Die We gave 3 Cheers & the Adm¹ & Mr. Scott is Aiddecamp & 40 more Seamen under the Command of L¹ Lewis joined us we Marched that Night & the 25th we Engaged the Enemy in the Heat of the day on our March, the Enemy had a strong Possession at the Top of a High Hill with 8000 Men 20 Pieces of Cannon Long 24 [?ie] 12 & 12 besides 500 Sailors belonging to Commodore Barney the 85 Regiment were in Front they Marched right up the Hill the Enemy had their Guns Pointed right down on them in the Valley they fired very Sharp indeed for 1 hour & ½ till 8 hundred of our Brave fellows mounted the Hill then they run as if the Devil had them, Capsised their Guns & took to the Woods⁶. We soon all mounted the Hill & took Possession of every thing, the dam rascals had fired at us out of the Wood the Sailors got the Field Pieces up & Scattered the Woods like Hail Stones. I had the Pleasure of Killing a Dam Rascal who shot a MidshipMan belonging to the Tounnant through the Face he made the first

6 The Americans were drawn up on a hill behind the East Branch of the Potomac River, opposite the village of Bladensburg. The steadiness of the British regular troops, together with their Congreve rockets, dismayed the American militia who, lacking leadership, broke ranks and fled.

Blow at me with his Sword at my Head I parried it of like a Sailor with my
Cutlass & then it was my turn so I run him through the Guts & killed him, he
as deprived me of the use of my Middle Finger on my left hand by cutting the
Sinues. We took Commodore Barney he had a shot go through both his
Thighs. 6 of the 85 & 9 of the 21ˢᵗ Droped down dead mounting the Hill
with Fatigue the Ground was covered with Dead & Wounded on both sides.
I have no occasion to tell you the Number as the Newspaper will tell you
that. We sent a Flag of Truce after the Battle into Washington to know
wether the Town had Surrendered or not on Entering the Dam rascals Fired
out of a most Elegant House & hollowed out here comes the English Bugers
they shot the Generals Aiddecamps Horse from under him killed a Corporal
wounded a Private & shot the Trumpeters Horse. The Soldiers & Sailors all
Entered the Town it was quite Dark at Night & I & 4 Sailors burnt this
House with Everything in it by order of Cockburn next day he sent for me &
4 Sailors to Burn the Congress & Sennet House we soon Burnt them the
Banks Gaols Docks Yards Rope Walks 44 Gun Frigate 28 Gun Sloop of War
& Spiked 100 Pieces of Cannon Burnt the Frame of a 74 & the Presidents
House. The General Had 3 Horses shot from under him in the Battle & our
Admˡ had his stirrup shot away by a Musket Ball without any injury to him
or his Horse. We Marched that same Night we were surrounded by 20000
Soldiers but they would not engage us the Dam rascals. I am just halted & am
so Fatigued that I am hardly able to write.

I remain Ever Your
Affectionate Son
Samuel D. Davies

[A letter from Samuel Decimus Davies to Scrope Davies telling of
Napoleon's voyage to exile in St Helena.]

H.M.S. Northumberland
Off Sᵗ Helena at Anchor
18 October 1815

Dear Scrope,

The Redpole Man of War Brig Sails for England in two or three days with
Dispatches announcing the arrival of Bonaparte & his suit at Sᵗ Helena. I am
now going to give you an account of our Voyage which has been rather long
considering, 10 weeks. Napoleon & the whole of his suit were in good spirits
all the Voyage. I have no occasion to describe Bonapartes person to you as
your friend Lord Lowther will do that. The moment he heard I was a Brother
of yours he asked Captain Ross to introduce me to him which was performed

with the greatest pleasure he told me you were in Brighton & asked me how David liked the Ordnance I told him very well that was the last word I spoke to him. Napoleon told Mr Littleton if Whitbread had been alive he would have remained in England. He walks the Deck at 7 every night with Count Las Cases & Bertrand[1] dines 5 in the Evening Breakfasts at 10 – goes in the Cabin all day & plays at Chess & Vantune Night the same, all he wins he leaves on the table for his servants he won 300 dollars of the Admiral[2] one night at Vantune Sunday is the same as any other day the day we crossed the Equinoctial line shaving was allowed according to the Rules of the service to those who had not crossed it before Captain Ross was the first on the list Lieutenants next French Men next Midship Men & servants the last we crossed it on the 23d of September Neptune hailed the ship about 8 in the Morning the Captain answered him he told him he should be on board at 10 he came Aft with about 40 of his Tribe sounding horns & Trumpets all painted Red & Blue drawn along by four Black fellows as Sea horses on a Cannonade slide the moment he came aft he asked the Admiral what sort of weather he had, where he was from & that he understood Napoleon Bonaparte & some of his Suit were on board. the next was if they had crossed those waters before the Admiral said no nor even the Captain of the ship *he* was interduced to him by the Admiral off they went with the Captain hove about 3 Buckets of water over him & let him off next was Lt Waren he was Tar'd & Shaved with an iron scraper till all the skin was off his face the next on the list was Nap he could not be seen General Bertrand Gourgoux Montholon Count Las Cases Ladies & Children the Admiral said he would shave the Ladies himself the Generals were just sprinkelled & the Children Nap offered the Ships company 100 Napoleons the Admiral would not allow them to accept it the Generals & Ladies laughed very much to see us Shaved such Scrapin Tar Oil & every thing that could be got was shoved into our mouths such a ducking I never had but I enjoyed the fun afterwards. When we came to an anchor which was the 15th of this month Nap came on deck Viewed the Rocks shook his head & walked into the Cabin again he came out about an hour afterwards Viewed the Rocks with his Spy Glass for about two hours & then told the Admiral it was impossible to make his escape the

1 Napoleon was accompanied to St. Helena by a suite consisting of Count and Countess Bertrand with three children, Count and Countess Montholon and a child, Count de Las Cases and his son, General Baron Gourgaud, and various servants.

2 Sir George Cockburn, who had commanded Samuel Decimus in the burning of Washington, was charged with seeing Napoleon safely conveyed to St. Helena. He remained there until June 1816 when he was relieved by Sir Pulteney Malcolm. The Northumberland then returned to England.

Ladies said they would rather remain on board than go on such a Rocky Island I belong to Captain Ross' Barge have the Command of her we landed the whole of FrenchMen last night they were very sorry to leave the ship Lady Bertrand is a Delightful Woman she shook hands with me when I landed her & said she was very much obliged to the MidshipMen for behaving so well to her children they were fine Children I have four Italian Double Napoleons for you which b[e]longed to Nap Silk Handkerchiefs are very cheap [lacuna] If you wish me to buy you some I will with the greatest pleasure Dear Scrope write to me the first opportunity.

  God Bless & protect you

I remain Ever
Your Affectionate
Brother
Samuel D Davies

PS Lord Charles Summersets
wife is dead.[3]

Excuse the writing   Nothing to eat
duty calls I must obey.   except ships provision

3 Lord Charles Somerset, 2nd son of the 5th Duke of Beaufort, was Governor of the Cape of Good Hope.

[Draft of a letter from Scrope Davies to Robert Wilmot, making clear his position in the negotiations for a financial settlement between Lord and Lady Byron:]

[13 March 1816]

  Mr. Davies recollects Lord Byron (on Thursday last) to have expressed himself as obliged to enter into a negotiation with Lady Byron, in consequence of his (Lord B.) having made a promise to that effect in a letter to Lady Byron some time since.
  Mr. Davies recollects Lord Byron to have declared at the same time that circumstances had arisen, subsequent to the period at which Lord Byron wrote the above letter, which rendered it impossible that Lord Byron should enter into any negotiation whatsoever till Lady Byron had made a declaration to a certain point.

Mr. Davies did not hear Lord Byron assent, nor does Mr. Davies believe that Lord Byron did assent to any principle of separation, previous to the appearance of Lady Byron's Declaration on Saturday last.

Mr. Davies took no share in, nor does he recollect the subject-matter of any discussions which might have taken place between Lord Byron and Mr. Wilmot on the arrangement of pecuniary terms. Mr. Davies has ever avoided such conversation, assigning his ignorance on that subject as the cause of such conduct. Mr. Wilmot may probably recollect Mr. Davies frequently to have expressed himself to that effect.

Mr. Davies recollects no specific proposition made by Lord Byron to Lady Byron on the subject of pecuniary terms, Mr. Davies having purposely avoided in all cases any discussion which appeared likely to take such a turn.

Mr. Davies declares that the only part taken by Mr. D. in this transaction was the impressing upon Lord Byron's mind the necessity of Lady Byron's Declaration preceding all negotiations.

Does not Mr. Wilmot recollect Mr. Davies to have declared thus much? — and does Mr. Wilmot recollect Mr. Davies at any time to have uttered one word on the subject of pecuniary terms, but to declare his (Mr. D's) utter ignorance on the head?

Mr. Davies has in conversation with Lord Byron cautioned him in the manner expressed in Mr. Davies's communication of yesterday.

Mr. Davies recollects Mr. Wilmot and Mr. Hobhouse to have shaken hands — a 'move' not unseasonable surely at the commencement of a negotiation, not that Mr. Davies is prepared to prove that Mr. Wilmot ought not to have considered it a proof of its conclusion — Mr. Davies not knowing what may have passed between Mr. Wilmot and Mr. Hobhouse previous to Mr. Davies's arrival.

[Two sonnets by Percy Bysshe Shelley; 1816. The two sonnets, unknown until the discovery of Scrope Davies's trunk, appear to be part of Shelley's reaction to the poetry and personality of Byron. In the first the poet says that his thoughts, like lutes under the influence of a lady's voice, have responded to the voices of nature, and yielded a music which he would think unique to himself, did he not see that, in response to the same themes, others have sung even more beautifully. In the second sonnet Shelley attacks heartless, cruel, mocking laughter — to merry laughter he had no objection. Again it is very possible that Byron who believed himself to have been hounded from England,

the butt of caricature and gossip, may have inspired the poem. It is
noticeable, however, that in both sonnets Shelley asserts his own right
to be considered a votary of Nature and her associated powers.]

Upon the wandering winds that through the sky
Still speed or slumber, on the waves of Ocean,
The forest depths that when the storm is nigh
Toss their grey pines with an inconstant motion,
The breath of evening that awakes no sound
But sends its spirit into all, the hush
Which, nurse of thought, old midnight pours around
A world whose pulse then beats not, o'er the gush
Of dawn, and whate'er else is musical
My thoughts have swept until they have resigned
Like lutes inforced by the divinest thrall
Of some sweet lady's voice that which my mind
(Did not superior grace in others shewn
Forbid such pride) would dream were all its own.

To Laugher

Thy friends were never mine thou heartless fiend:[1]
Silence and solitude and calm and storm,
Hope, before whose veiled shrine all spirits bend
In worship, and the rainbow vested form
Of conscience, that within thy hollow heart
Can find no throne — the love of such great powers
Which has requited mine in many hours
Of loneliness, thou ne'er hast felt; depart!
Thous canst not bear the moon's great eye, thou fearest
A fair child clothed in smiles — aught that is high
Or good or beautiful. — Thy voice is dearest
To those who mock at truth and Innocency.
I, now alone, weep without shame to see
How many broken hearts lie bare to thee.

1 Possibly a slip of the pen for 'friend'.

Letters and Mss

[Part of two letters written by Lady Frances Webster to Scrope Davies; 1818/1819.]

I have nothing to say —tis past- tis done- the bitter Cup has been long held to my lips- I have tasted it- but tis now- now- ah! now I am to drink its poisoned Draught—the gates of misery are opened wide to receive me— Destruction sits enthroned— Come fast— come sure & throw thine arms round me— I am ready to die— come Death— Oh! I have long been indifferent to my fate— and I have to thank your kind liberation for making me more so— 'Our will cannot alter our feelings' —and mine will burn an unconsumed fire— you cannot quench it— but it will never reach you more— here it will burn— Eternal— its progress is sure— & would it were more quick— I will not complain. I will not reproach you— No! I will persuade myself you are right— 'twas my own fault— I cherished the fatal spark— & gently fan'd it till it burst into an Eternal flame— Oh God! what shall I do— forget you do you say— smile & forget you! — there is madness— madness— fever in the thought— . . .

Adieu! if you will go— let me bless you first be happy— happier than me you must be— Oh God! Oh God! Oh God! Heaven bless you— you have preserved me from ye agonies of guilt— my Child may now look upon me without a blush— Remember my life is in yr hands— Farewell I am going— I know not where— I shall go [to] the Theatre— & when my Carriage is dismissed—I shall leave ye house & go— God knows where— I know where you dine Yes! & I will see you— tho' unseen I will! I am calm for ye moment I will dismiss my Carriage & pretend anything— anything— so as I see you but unseen— Yes! I shall do something— Oh! I tremble for myself—

Take yr letters which I loved next to my heart's God— take them— you have my life— but the last Never!! I will wear it on my heart— till it Crumbles to Nothing— & If my life goes first— there it will remain— you cannot fear then, in Death I cannot harm you— In Death I shall be yours— mention it no more— Never shall you have it— God bless you. I give you my hair— torn from my head by that which shall drink my life— if you do not preserve yours— I am firm— a demon's firmness has this day ta'en possession of me & now I feel a mad fool— & my mind is big with ye idea of seeing you tonight— I will walk— nobody will see me— & return to ye Play— Adieu— I can no more—

I cannot resist the desire I feel stirring within me to communicate with you once more, especially as it may be my fate never again to have the opportunity of doing so —Between the hours of two and three to morrow I may perhaps be what the chymists call, 'decomposed' — If such should be my lot, remember me with affection for I have loved you to madness — if I should survive then, I pray you, destroy this letter — My mind is quite calm nor can anything make it otherwise — Of all the pangs which I shall feel, that of separating from you will be the greatest — There is at this moment a Demon urging me on, and I cannot resist — But where will this end? If there be existence in another world, and if our Spirits may revisit these scenes mine shall most assuredly do so. Dear Creature adieu — I have destroyed all your letters — The time approaches and I am resolved — Farewell — I am giddy giddy even to Death — it is — the hand that now writes this will soon be cold — It is done — Conceal this letter as you value your soul's health — as you dread the vengeance of an angry Spirit — All is deadly — Farewell — farewell — your hair is in my bosom — When you see Byron tell him that you heard from me in my last hour — but tell no one else —

[Lady Frances, the daughter of the first Earl of Mountnorris, was married at the age of seventeen in 1810 to James Wedderburn Webster, a somewhat asinine friend of Scrope and Byron. In 1813 she had a brush with Byron but he, as he put it, 'spared her'. Her name was linked with that of the Duke of Wellington in 1815, while her affair with Scrope Davies occupied the winter of 1818/1819. Her marriage ended in separation, and she died in 1837. Twenty-one of her letters were found in Scrope's trunk. A melodramatic touch entirely consistent with the style of the love-letters is the fact that they lack any salutation or signature which might betray the guilty pair. It has been stated that Byron wrote his poem 'When we two parted In silence and tears' in response to the news that on 16 February 1816 James Wedderburn Webster was awarded £2,000 damages against one Baldwin proprietor of the *St James's Chronicle*, who had alleged in his issue for 5 August 1815 that Lady Frances had been the mistress of the Duke of Wellington. The presence in the British Library, however, of a MS. of the poem in the hand of Lady Byron with corrections by Byron (Add. MS. 31038) would appear to make this unlikely since the Byrons had parted, never to see each other again, on the 15th of January. There had been plenty of rumours during the preceding summer — the P.S. of a letter written to Scrope by Robert Milnes on 28 July 1815 reads 'Lady F Webster you may have heard was at Paris — the avowed mistress of the D of Wellington' — and in September of the same year Webster even wrote to Byron on the subject. It would appear therefore that the account given by Miss Frances Williams Wynn in her *Diaries of a Lady of Quality*, 1864, may have an element of truth in it, except in so far as the date is concerned. Lady Frances and the Duke did not meet until shortly before the battle of Waterloo, and Byron's interest in her had passed by the beginning of 1814. Miss Williams Wynn wrote:

In England, we are apt to exclaim with Byron, in his suppressed lines:

> Then fare thee well, Fanny, thus doubly undone,
> Thou frail to the many, and false to the one.
> Thou art past all recalling, e'en would I recall,
> For the woman so fallen for ever must fall.

These lines about which frequent enquiry has been made, were given me by Scrope Davies. They originally formed the conclusion of a copy of verses addressed by Lord Byron to Lady Frances W(edderburn) W(ebster) to whom he was (in his manner) devotedly attached until (early 1815) she threw him over for the Duke of Wellington, then in the full blaze of his Peninsular glory. 'Byron', said Davies, 'Came one morning to my lodgings in St. James's Street, in a towering passion, and standing by the fire, broke out, 'D—— all women, and d—— that woman in particular.' 'He tore from his watch-ribbon a seal she had given him, and dashed it into the grate. As soon as he left the room, I picked it up, and here it is.' He showed it to me, and allowed me to take an impression of it, which I have still. It was a large seal, representing a ship in full sail, a star in the distance, with the motto, '*Si je la perds, je suis perdu.*' Two or three days afterwards his Lordship presented himself again with a copy of verses addressed to his fickle fair one, from which Davies with some difficulty induced him to omit the four concluding lines.

Lady Frances has a double claim to immortality for at least one letter from the hero of Waterloo was addressed to her from the battle-field. Scrope Davies, who took the credit of being high in her favour, told me her peculiar mode of manifesting preference, which I suppress.

Thomas Moore met Lady Frances during the period of her affair with Scrope Davies. In his diary entry for 5 January 1819 he recorded that the conversation was chiefly about Byron

whom she talked of, as if nothing had happened — and (if I may believe Scrope Davies) nothing ever did — but B. certainly gave me to think otherwise, and her letters (which I saw) showed, at least, that she was (or fancied herself) much in love with him . . . I should pronounce her cold-blooded & vain to an excess — & I believe her great ambition is to attract people of celebrity — if so, she must have been gratified — as the first Poet & first Captain of the age have been among her lovers — the latter liaison was, at all events, not altogether spiritual — at least the character of the man makes such platonism not very probable — her manner to me very flattering & the eyes played off most skillfully — but this is evidently her habit — the fishing always going on, whether whales or sprats are to be caught—]

[A letter from Thomas Moore to Scrope Davies, 1819.]

> Sloperton Cottage, Devizes
> 15 February 1819

My dear Davis — I was very unlucky not to see you, when I was in town, though I called at your lodgings, two or three times — 'mais vous êtes tout *esprit*', et, par consequent, *invisible*'. You see the Memorial[1] is announced and that it is taken off Jackson's[2] shoulders (though strong enough to bear a much heavier thing than, I trust, this will be) & removed to Crib's[2] — I have more need of your *silence* about it now than ever — as I do not think I have succeeded very well in the attempt — indeed, I was a good deal interrupted in it, and taken oft from the *slang* to the *sentimental* (having had some Songs to write for my musical Publisher) which disturbed my imagination (alias, Fancy) exceedingly — I don't mind people guessing or saying it is mine — for *that* they are sure to do — but I don't wish to have them say so from *authority*, & I have even gone to the trouble of having my Ms. transcribed, before it goes to the Printer, in order to enable me to go through the *forms* of denial — There is one learned question which I wish to propound to you, & which is (next to my re-injunction of secrecy) the chief object of this letter — viz. Which is Caleb Baldwin's[2] *nose* or Bill Gibbons's[2] the *redder*? My own private opinion is that Jack Scroggins's[2] is equal to either in rubicundity, but 'I pause for a reply'. And, as it is of some importance to me to know your opinion upon this case 'De Nasis' *immediately*, I shall expect your answer by return of post.

> Yours, my dear Davis, very truly
> Thomas Moore —

1 See page 169.
2 All well known pugilists.

Sources

GENERAL

The most important original source for this book has been the Scrope Davies Papers, now Loan 70 in the Department of Manuscripts at the British Library. Next in importance have been the letters and journals of Scrope's two closest friends, Byron and Hobhouse. In the case of the former I have used Leslie A. Marchand's new edition, except for those letters from Byron to Scrope himself found in the trunk, and hitherto unknown. Letters from Byron to Scrope from other sources are noted as such. All letters from Hobhouse to Scrope, except where otherwise stated, were found in the trunk. Hobhouse's letters to Byron are taken, with one exception, from the proof sheets of an abandoned edition now shelf-marked C.131. k.2. in the Department of Printed Books, British Library. Scrope's letters to Byron, with two exceptions duly noted, are in the archives of John Murray. Hobhouse's diaries were edited by his daughter in a heavily excerpted form. I have used the originals which are mostly in the British Library, with a few in the New York Public Library. Since those in the British Library were incorporated at different times it is complicated to find which volume a particular entry may be in. I accordingly give here a table of dates and volumes:

8 July – 26 Dec. 1809 British Library Additional MS. 56527
27 Dec. 1809–19 Oct. 1810 British Library Additional MS. 56529
20 Oct. 1810 – 19 Jan. 1813 British Library Additional MS. 56530
20 Jan. – 7 Sept. 1813 British Library Additional MS. 56532
7 Sept. – 29 Nov. 1813 British Library Additional MS. 56533
30 Nov. 1813 – 2 Jan. 1814 British Library Additional MS. 56535
3 Jan. – 1 July 1814 New York Public Library
1 July 1814 – 29 Mar. 1815 British Library Additional MS. 47232
29 Mar. 1815 – 5 April 1816 New York Public Library
5 April – 21 July 1816 British Library Additional MS. 47232
22 July – 22 Sept. 1816 British Library Additional MS. 56536
22 Sept. – 5 Nov. 1816 British Library Additional MS. 56537
5 Nov. 1816 – 12 Jan. 1817 British Library Additional MS. 56538
12 Jan. – 31 Jan. 1817 British Library Additional MS. 56539
21 May – 29 July 1817 British Library Additional MS. 47233

Sources

29 July 1817 – 14 Feb. 1818 British Library Additional MS.47234
15 Feb. – 11 Sept. 1818 British Library Additional MS.47235
11 Sept. 1818 – 30 Jan. 1820 British Library Additional MS.56540

In addition I have made use of the following sources:

Chapter 1
Scrope's family: material supplied by Martin Davies Esq.
Samuel Decimus Davies: Public Record Office Adm. 102/440 Naval Hospital Jamaica, Musters 1821–4.
Eton: H.C. Maxwell Lyte, *A History of Eton College*, 1911; H.E.C. Stapylton, *The Eton School Lists 1791–1850*, 2nd ed., 1864, pp. 1–9, 29–37; Eton College Minute Book, entry for 18 Mar. 1661; [W.H. Tucker], *Eton of Old*, 1892, p. 28; A.W. Kinglake, *Eothen*, chapter xviii; [H.C. Blake], *Reminiscences of an Etonian*, 1831; F. Lillywhite's *Cricket Scores*, i, 1862, pp. 261, 276, 291; Eton College, *Montem Lists, from 1773 to 1832, inclusive*, 1835.

Chapter 2
Byron on making friends with Hobhouse and Matthews: letter to John Murray, 19 Nov. 1820.
Augusta Leigh on Douglas Kinnaird: Malcolm Elwin, *Lord Byron's Family*, 1975, p.193.
Hobhouse on Kinnaird: diary entry for 12 July 1819.
Scrope esteemed a 'ripe scholar': Captain R.H. Gronow, *Celebrities of London and Paris*, 1865, p.117.
Byron on Matthews, Scrope etc.: letter to Robert Dallas, 7 Sept. 1811.
Byron's letter to Scrope mentioning suicide: Scrope Davies Papers, Vol.1, ff. 8–9b.
Scrope's letter to Byron mentioning suicide: letter of [?May] 1817. John Murray Archives.
Byron on Hobhouse as 'guide philosopher and friend': letter to Lady Melbourne, 24 May 1813.
Hobhouse drunk on piquet: diary entry for 11 April 1811.
Byron calls Scrope 'our Yorick': letter to Hobhouse, 16 May 1816.
Byron on *'us youth'*: letter to Hobhouse, 4 Aug. 1819.
Hobhouse and Bessy Rawdon: diary entry for 14 June 1814.
Hobhouse and prostitutes: diary entries for 12 Jan., 5 & 7 Feb. 1811.
Hobhouse's share of joint letter with Byron to Matthews, 22 June 1809: British Library Add. MS.47226, ff.6, 6b, 7b.

Sources

Hobhouse finds Scrope in bed with girl: diary entry for 11 April 1818.

Matthews and Boatswain's monument: letter of Byron to John Murray, 9 Nov. 1820.

Chapter 3

Robert Joy bill: Scrope Davies Papers, Vol.4, f.48.

Scrope a 'first-rate calculator': Gronow, *op. cit*.

Hobhouse's letter on Byron's gambling: John Murray Archives.

Byron, Scrope and Hobhouse at Brighton: Frances Williams Wynn, *Diaries of a Lady of Quality*, 1864.

Byron's letter to Hobhouse inviting him and Scrope to Geneva: 1 May 1816.

Byron's conversation in exile: Edward Trelawny, *Records of Shelley, Byron and the Author*, 1858.

Scrope's generosity: Hobhouse's diary for 2 Jan. 1820.

Brummell's final collapse: Kathleen Campbell, *Beau Brummell*, 1948, pp.120–121.

Coach-builder's bill: Scrope Davies Papers, Vol.3, ff.145*, 145**.

Scrope's reputation at Cambridge: Hobhouse's diary for 3 July 1814.

Scrope's rooms at King's: *Etoniana*, No. 34, 31 July 1923, p.542.

Cambridge in Scrope's day: D.A. Winstanley, *Unreformed Cambridge*, 1935.

Racing: Edward and James Weatherby, *The Racing Calendar*, 1810–1819; James Rice, *History of the British Turf*, 1879.

Examples of Scrope's bets: Scrope Davies Papers, Vol.21.

Scrope and Hobhouse's tour of the Highlands: Scrope Davies Papers, Vol.18.

Manton's bill: Scrope Davies Papers, Vol.3, ff.87, 88.

Byron on killing Major Cartwright with Manton's pistols: letters to Kinnaird and Hobhouse, 19 and 20 Aug. 1819.

Byron on Scrope's challenge to Lord Foley: letter to Thomas Moore, 22 Aug. 1813.

Byron on Cambridge: letter of 26 Oct. 1807.

Byron on gambling: 'Detached Thoughts' 33 (*Letters and Journals,* vol.ix).

Scrope's tennis account: Scrope Davies Papers, Vol.16.

Draft proposals for a tennis club: Scrope Davies Papers, Vol.2, f.171.

Hobhouse on obscurity of Scrope's affairs: letter to Byron, 5 June 1818.

Scrope's win of £6065: Hobhouse's diary for 11 June 1814.

Scrope 'steeped in poverty': letter to Byron of Sept. 1817 (Clark Library, University of California, Los Angeles).

Scrope's partial recovery: Hobhouse's diary for 5 Feb. 1818.

Sources

Byron and the Massingberds: Doris Langley Moore, *Lord Byron Accounts Rendered*, 1974, pp.153–163.

Hanson's letter to Byron: British Library, Egerton MS.2611, ff.130–1.

Byron on C.S. Matthews: letter to John Murray, 19 Nov. 1820.

Byron's letter to Scrope of 26 March 1814: William L. Clements Library, University of Michigan.

Chapter 4

Except where otherwise specified Hobhouse's account of the proceedings is taken from his diary. The text of Augusta's letters is taken from Malcolm Elwin, *Lord Byron's Wife*, 1962 and *Lord Byron's Family*, 1975.

Rumours as reason for Byron refusing separation: J.C. Hobhouse, *Contemporary Account of the Separation of Lord and Lady Byron etc.*, 1870.

Byron's anger at appeal to his mercenary instincts: *ibid*.

Hobhouse's appeal to Annabella: *ibid*.

Wilmot's letter to Byron: J.C. Hobhouse, *Recollections of a long life*, 1909, 1911, Vol.2, Appendix F (p.361).

Leigh Hunt on Scrope and Hobhouse: *Lord Byron and some of his contemporaries*, 1828, p.5.

Polidori's journal: *The Diary of Dr John William Polidori 1816*, edited W.M. Rossetti, 1911.

Polidori's letter to Hobhouse: *ibid*., p.213.

The Hollanders and the glacier: Mary Godwin's journal for 23 July 1816.

John Murray letters to Byron: John Murray Archive.

Scrope Davies's letter to John Murray of 25 Oct. 1816: John Murray Archive.

Chapter 5

Minutes of the Rota: British Library, Additional MS.36457, ff.3–4b.

Sir Robert Wilson: Michael Glover, *A Very Slippery Fellow*, 1978.

Sir Francis Burdett: M.W. Patterson, *Sir Francis Burdett*, 1931.

Westminster Committee: R.J. White, *Waterloo to Peterloo*, 1957; Graham Wallas, *The Life of Francis Place*, 1898.

Bickersteth's letter on the break-up of the Rota: British Library, Additional MS.36457, f.285.

Wilson's resignation from the Rota: British Library Additional MS.36457, ff.185, 186.

Holland House Dinner Books: British Library, Additional MSS.51950–51957.

Sources

Kinnaird's letter to Hobhouse of 4 Aug. 1818: British Library, Additional MS.36457, f.19.

Burdett's letter to Hobhouse of 10 Aug. 1818: British Library, Additional MS.36457, f.87.

Bruce's letter to Hobhouse of 19 Aug. 1818: British Library, Additional MS.47226, ff.30–31.

Thomas Moore: *Memoirs, Journals and Correspondence of Thomas Moore*, ed. Lord John Russell, 1853, vol.II, pp.157–159, 228–238.

Westminster Election of 1819: J.C. Hobhouse, *An authentic narrative of the events of the Westminster Election*, 1819. When compared with Hobhouse's diaries the narrative appears to be less authentic in some places than in others.

Scrope's quarrel with Hobhouse: Scrope's letter to Hobhouse, British Library Additional MS.36457, f.408; Kinnaird's letter to Scrope, Additional MS.47224, f.6; Hobhouse's letter to Scrope, Additional MS.36457, f.409.

Scrope's letter to Hobhouse of 26 Oct. 1819: British Library, Additional MS.47226, f.50.

End of Burdett's friendship with Scrope: British Library, Additional MS.36457, ff.378, 398.

Scrope's letter to Edmund Byng: MS. in possession of Mr. Cole, Enfield.

Chapter 6

John Murray's letter to Byron, 15 Aug. 1820: John Murray Archive.

Byron's belief that Scrope had been in Pisa: Thomas Medwin, *Conversations of Lord Byron*, 1824, p.68.

Scrope's letters to Augusta Leigh on Byron's death: British Library, Additional MS.31037, ff.65, 86.

Scrope's letter to Hodgson, 1828: J.T. Hodgson, *Memoir of the Rev. Francis Hodgson*, B.D., 1878.

Thomas Raikes's journal: *A Portion of the Journal kept by T. Raikes Esq., from 1831 to 1847*, 1856, 57.

Scrope's letter to John Murray, 1836: John Murray Archive.

Catalogue of the
Scrope Davies Papers

Miscellaneous papers and correspondence of Scrope Berdmore Davies, as deposited by him in 1820 with Messrs. Ransom, Morland and Co., bankers, and placed on indefinite loan at the Department of Manuscripts, British Library, by their successors, Barclays Bank Ltd; 1798–1852. The loose papers have been arranged and bound into volumes. The names of all the writers of the letters bound in volumes 1 and 2 will be found in the index following this description. Twenty-three volumes, arranged as follows:

Volume 1 (ff.136) Letters, mostly to Scrope Davies, as follows:
  (a) Letters from Lord Byron, 1809–1819. ff.1–35b.
  (b) Letters relating to Lord Byron's separation from his wife, 1816. ff.36–43b.
  (c) Letters from the Hon. Augusta Leigh, 1819, n.d. ff.44–50b.
  (d) Letters relating to Lord Byron, from various correspondents, 1809–1817, n.d. ff.51–67b.
  (e) Letters from Lady Frances Webster, 1817–1819.
  (f) Family letters, mostly from Samuel Decimus Davies, brother, 1798–1819.

Volume 2 (ff.173) General Correspondence, 1802–1819, arranged chronologically.

Volume 3 (ff.248) Letters from bankers and moneylenders, bills and receipts, 1808–1819, arranged chronologically.

Volume 4 (ff.252) Letters from bankers and moneylenders, bills and receipts, as found impaled on four spikes, 1799–1817, arranged chronologically.
  (a) Spike 1, 1799–1812. ff.1–114.
  (b) Spike 2, 1807–1813, n.d. ff.115–145.
  (c) Spike 3, 1807–1813. ff.146–206.
  (d) Spike 4, 1807–1817. ff.207–252.

Catalogue of the Papers

Volume 5 (ff.25) Bills and receipts from Eton College, and tradesmen in the town on account of Scrope Davies and his younger brother Thomas, 1796–1802.

Volume 6 *Childe Harold*, by Lord Byron; 1816. *Autograph* fair copy, with revisions and additions, of Canto III, written in a red morocco bound notebook. This MS. is what Byron called the 'first copy' from his draft, and it served as the copy-text for two transcripts, one, dated 16 June, and lacking some of the late additions, in the hand of Mary Godwin (now in the Sterling Library, London University), the other, dated 4 July, in the hand of Claire Clairmont (now in the possession of Mr. Murray). The latter was that taken back to England by Shelley. The present MS. was dated by Byron in several places. On the first page (f.2) he wrote 'Begun at Sea', and above this 'Copied in Ghent. April 28th 1816' (this presumably refers to the first sixteen stanzas). The original ending (stanza 114 in the editions) is signed and dated 'Sechairon – Geneva. – June 8th 1816'. (f.51b). Then follow the stanzas to his daughter, dated 'June 9th 1816', above which Byron has written 'I know not whether to make these part or no as yet.' (ff.52–53b). Two long passages written later are carefully sewn in. The first of these, stanzas 92–98 as printed, bears the note 'The storms to which these lines refer – occurred on the 13th of June 1816 at midnight – I have seen among the Acroceraunian Mountains of Chimari – several more terrible – but none more beautiful –' (ff.43–44b). The second, stanzas 99–104 as printed, was written after Byron's voyage round the Lake of Geneva with Shelley (ff.45–46b). Two additional stanzas (87, followed by 33) were added at the end (ff. 54, 54b), with instructions to the copyist as to their proper place of insertion. The MS. is inscribed in Scrope Davies' hand 'This M.S. was given by Lord Byron to Scrope Davies at Geneva September 2d 1816.' (f.1).

Quarto; ff.57.

Volume 7 *The Prisoner of Chillon*, by Lord Byron: 1816. Fair copy in the hand of Mary Godwin, with extensive emendations and additions by Byron, written in a notebook with marbled orange, black and blue paper covers. This MS. also appears to be the 'first copy'. The draft is at Yale, and the 'second copy' in the possession of Mr Murray. The MS. is dated at the beginning 'June 30th 1816' and signed and dated at the end 'Byron July 2d 1816'. It is inscribed 'Scrope Davies' inside the back cover (f.14).

Octavo; ff.14.

Catalogue of the Papers

Volume 8 'Hymn to Intellectual Beauty', 'Mont Blanc' and two sonnets, one beginning 'Upon the wandering winds that through the sky' and the other entitled 'To Laughter', by Percy Bysshe Shelley: 1816. *Autograph* fair copy in the case of 'Mont Blanc', fair copies in the hand of Mary Godwin in the case of the other poems, all written in a notebook with marbled orange, black and blue paper covers. Of the two sonnets this is the only MS. Drafts of the other two poems survive in Bodleian MS. Shelley adds. e, 16. The text as found in the present MS. differs considerably from that first printed in the *Examiner* for 19 Jan. 1817 in the case of the 'Hymn' and in *History of a Six Weeks Tour*, 1817, in the case of 'Mont Blanc'. A correction almost certainly in Shelley's hand in line 5 of 'Hymn' suggests that he looked over Mary's transcripts before copying out 'Mont Blanc' himself.

   Octavo; ff. 7

Volume 9 (ff. 56) School and College Exercises, Academic papers, Commonplaces mostly in the hand of Scrope Davies etc.; n.d. (watermarks 1799–1817). Among the papers are *copies* of 'To E–', 'The Cornelian' and 'On the Death of a Young Lady, Cousin to the Author, and very Dear to Him' by Lord Byron, written on two conjoined leaves watermarked 1813.

Volume 10 (ff. 20) Legal Documents, 1807–1819, n.d.

Volume 11 Deed of covenant for securing an annuity of £50 granted by Thomas Davies and Scrope Berdmore Davies to Sarah Oldis: 24 June 1807. The signatures of Scrope and Thomas have been cut out of the document.

   One membrane.

Volume 12 *Goldsmith's Almanack* for 1811, containing betting notes etc. in the hand of Scrope Davies.

   Duodecimo; ff. 29.

Volume 13 Cellar Book, also containing commonplaces and accounts, in the hand of Scrope Davies: 1811, 1812.

   Octavo; ff. 21.

Volume 14 Commonplace-book with entries in the hand of Scrope Davies contained in a red morocco case: *ca* 1814.

   Duodecimo; ff. 9.

Volume 15 Accounts kept by Philip Rippin, Scrope Davies's groom, with a
note by Scrope Davies: June – July 1814.
   Octavo; ff.3.

Volume 16 Scrope Davies's account with R. Matt, tennis professional,
including the sums won by Davies in bets with other gentlemen: 1818.
   Octavo; ff.6.

Volume 17 Record of Scrope Davies's account with Messrs Biddulph Cocks's
and Ridge's, bankers: 1813–1815. An entry on 26 March 1814 records
the repayment by Byron of the loan which Scrope Davies had originally
guaranteed and subsequently taken over himself.
   Octavo; ff.8.

Volume 18 Accounts and journal kept by Scrope Davies while on a tour of the
Highlands with John Cam Hobhouse in 1806.
   Octavo; ff.24.

Volume 19 Records of bets etc.: watermark 1813.
   Duodecimo; ff.4.

Volume 20 Records of bets: 1816.
   Duodecimo; ff.27.

Volume 21 Notebook employed for accounts, commonplaces and records of
bets: 1809–1812.
   Octavo; ff.33.

Volume 22 *An Extract from the Case of the Obligation on the Electors of Eton College
to supply All Vacancies in that Society With those who are or have been Fellows of
King's College, Cambridge, so long as Persons properly qualified are to be had
within that Description*, 1771, by Thomas Ashton D.D. The volume is
inscribed by the author.
   Folio; pp.xii + 45.

Volume 23 (ff.79) Miscellaneous *printed* material; 1806 or later – 1852, n.d.

A small trunk, 55 × 32 × 24cm., with a brass plate on the lid bearing the
inscription '*Mr Scrope Davies*.' It was in this trunk that the papers were

Catalogue of the Papers

found, together with a pair of kid gloves and four spikes on which some of the papers were impaled. The latter items are preserved with the trunk. On the lid are the remains of a wax seal bearing the arms of Douglas Kinnaird, in whose bank Scrope Davies deposited the trunk. Inside the trunk is the label of J & W Lowndes, Military and Camp Equipage Warehouse, No 18 Haymarket.

Index of Correspondents

Alvanley, *Baron. v.* Arden (William).

Arden (William), *2nd Baron Alvanley.* Letters to Scrope Davies, 1814, n.d. Vol. 2, ff. 13, 140.

Argyll, *Duke of. v.* Campbell (George William).

Berdmore (Scrope), *Warden of Merton College, Oxford, uncle of Scrope Davies.* Letter to Scrope Davies, 1814. Vol. 1, f. 117.

Bickersteth (Henry), *1st Baron Langdale* 1836. Letter to Scrope Davies, n.d. Vol.2, f. 144.

Bilson-Legge (Henry Stawell), *2nd Baron Stawell.* Letter to Scrope Davies, n.d. Vol.2, f. 166.

Bonaparte (Napoleon), *Emperor of the French.* Watercolour of, on board H.M.S. Northumberland, 1815. Vol.1, f. 124.

Bridport, *Baron. v.* Hood (Samuel).

Bruce (Patrick Craufurd). Letters to Scrope Davies, 1818. Vol.2, ff. 81, 83.

Bunbury (*Sir* Thomas Charles), *6th Bart., M.P.* Letter to Scrope Davies, 1817. Vol.2, f. 45.

Burdett (*Sir* Francis), *5th Bart., M.P.* Letters to Scrope Davies, 1817, 1818, n.d. Vol.2, ff. 39, 41, 56, 63, 64b, 85, 92, 146.

Burdett (Sophia), *wife of the preceding.* Letter to Scrope Davies, n.d. Vol.2, f. 148.

Bury (Catherine Maria), *1st Countess of Charleville.* Invitation to Scrope Davies, 1817. Vol. 2, f. 30.

Byng (*Hon.* Edmund), *second son of 5th Viscount Torrington.* Letter to Scrope Davies, [?1819]. Vol.2, f. 123.

Byron (George Gordon), *6th Baron Byron; poet.* Letters to Scrope Davies, 1809–1819. Vol.1, ff. 1–6b, 8–35b.
– Letter to C.S. Matthews, 1811. Vol.1, f. 7.
– Letter to R.J. Wilmot, 1816. *Draft* in the hand of Scrope Davies. Vol.1, f. 41.

Campbell (George William), *6th Duke of Argyll.* Letter to Scrope Davies, n.d. Vol.2, ff. 2*, 7, 9.

Caumont (*Comte* Auguste-Marie de). Letters to Scrope Davies, 1812, 1814. Vol.2, ff. 2, 7, 9.

Charleville, *Countess of. v.* Bury (Catherine Maria).

Charlton (E. Lechmere), *of Ludford, Salop.* Letters to Scrope Davies, 1818. Vol.2, ff. 77, 79.

Colborne (Nicholas William Ridley –), *1st Baron Colborne* 1839. Letter to Scrope Davies, 1816. Vol.1, f. 42.

Crabtree (Richard). Letter to Scrope Davies, 1818. Vol.2, f. 47.

Davies (Margaretta De L'Angle), *sister of Scrope Davies.* Letter to Scrope Davies, 1819. Vol.1, f. 135.

Davies (*Rev.* Richard), *father of Scrope Davies.* Letter to Dr. Samuel Berdmore, 1798. Vol.1, f. 115.

Davies (Samuel Decimus), *midshipman; brother of Scrope Davies.* Letter to his mother, 1814. Vol.1, f. 119.
– Letters to Scrope Davies, 1815 –1819. Vol.1, ff. 121, 129–134b.
– Banker's draft signed by at St. Helena, 1816. Vol.1, f. 128

Davies (Scrope Berdmore). Letters to R.J. Wilmot, 1816. Vol.1, ff. 37, 42b.

244

Index of Correspondents

– Letter to Sir Francis Burdett, 1818. Vol.2, f. 64.

– Letter to Sir Robert Wilson, 1819. *Copy*. Vol.2, f. 133.

– Letter to – Bligh, n.d. Vol.2, f. 149.

Davy (Martin), *Master of Caius College, Cambridge*. Letters to Scrope Davies, 1818, 1819, n.d. Vol.2, ff 54. 115, 136, 150.

Douglas (J.) Letter to Scrope Davies, 1813 or 1819. Vol.2, f. 113.

Drury (Henry Joseph Thomas), *Master of the Lower School at Harrow*. Letter to Scrope Davies, 1817. Vol.2, f. 35.

Elphinstone (*Hon*. Margaret Mercer), *Comtesse de Flahaut* 1817, *Baroness Keith* 1823, *Baroness Nairne* 1837. Letter to Scrope Davies, 1817. Vol.1, f. 62.

Franklin (William Temple), *grandson of Benjamin Franklin*. Letter to Sir Robert Wilson, 1818. Vol.2, f. 52.

Hanson (Charles), *son of the following*. Letter to Scrope Davies, 1817. Vol.1, f. 65.

Hanson (John), *attorney to Lord Byron*. Letters to Scrope Davies, 1811, 1812, 1817. Vol.1, ff. 53, 57, 65.

Harley (*Lady* Charlotte Mary), *daughter of 5th Earl of Oxford*. Letter to Scrope Davies, n.d. Vol.2, f. 152.

Harley (Jane Elizabeth), *Countess of Oxford*. Letters to Scrope Davies, 1818. Vol.2, ff. 86, 93.

Harwood (———), *widow of Sir Busick Harwood*. Letter to C.H. Townshend, 1818. Vol.2, f.61.

Hibbert (John), *of Bray Wick, Berkshire*. Letters to Scrope Davies, 1819. Vol.2, 107, 127.

Hobhouse (John Cam), *politician; 1st Baron Broughton de Gyfford* 1851. Letters to Scrope Davies, 1807–1818. Vol.1, ff. 51, 58, 60; Vol.2, ff. 3, 68, 95; Vol.4, f. 207b.

Hodgley (J———), *Chairman of the*

United Reform Committees of the Out Ward of St. George & St. Margaret & St. John, Westminster. Letter to Scrope Davies, 1819. Vol.2, f. 99.

Holland, *Baron. v*. Vassall Fox.

Hood (Samuel), *2nd Baron Bridport*. Letter to Scrope Davies, n.d. Vol.1, f. 66.

Howard (*Hon*. William), *second son of 5th Earl of Carlisle*. Letter to Scrope Davies, n.d. Vol.2, f. 154.

Jones (Edward), *of King's College, Cambridge*. Letter to Scrope Davies, 1802. Vol.2, f. 1.

Leigh (*Hon*. Augusta Mary), *half-sister of Lord Byron*. Letters to Scrope Davies, 1819, n.d. Vol.1, ff. 44–50b.

Leycester (George), *of King's College, Cambridge*. Letter to Scrope Davies, 1818. Vol.2, f. 90.

Mantell (Edward Reginald), *of Emmanuel College, Cambridge*. Letter to R.P. Milnes, 1818. Vol.2, f. 67.

Matthews (Arthur), *of Brase Nose College, Oxford; brother of Charles Skinner Matthews*. Letters to Scrope Davies, 1817, 1818. Vol.2, ff. 32, 59.

Meyler (Richard), *MP; 'Dick the Dandy-killer'*. Letter to Scrope Davies, 1817. Vol.2, f. 43.

Milner (Isaac), *President of Queens' College, Cambridge*. Letters to Scrope Davies, ' n.d. Vol.2, ff. 156, 158.

Milnes (Richard Rodes), *brother of the following*. Letters to Scrope Davies, 1819. Vol.2, ff. 117, 119, 121, 129, 131, 134.

Milnes (Robert Pemberton), *MP; father of the 1st Baron Houghton*. Letters to Scrope Davies, 1815, 1818, n.d. Vol.2, ff. 22, 65, 75, 161.

—— Letter to Richard Rodes Milnes, n.d. Vol.2, f. 159.

Montagu (*Lord* Frederick), *second son of the 4th Duke of Manchester*. Letter to Scrope Davies, 1819. Vol.2, f. 125.

Index of Correspondents

Moore (Thomas), *poet*. Letter to Scrope Davies, 1819. Vol.2, f. 101.

Nangle (Matthew H.), *formerly headmaster of St. Patrick's School, Westminster*. Letter to Scrope Davies, 1819. Vol.2, f. 138.

Newman (John), *of Newmarket*. Letter to Scrope Davies, 1817. Vol.2, f. 37.

Osborne (*Lord* Sidney Godolphin), *3rd son of the 5th Duke of Leeds*. Letter to Scrope Davies, n.d. Vol.2, f. 163.

Oxford, *Countess of. v*. Harley (Jane Elizabeth).

Parr (Samuel), *pedagogue; the 'Whig Dr. Johnson'*. Letters to Scrope Davies, 1814. Vol.2, ff. 15, 17.

Perceval (Spencer), *son of the Prime Minister*. Letters to Scrope Davies, 1814, 1817. Vol.1, f. 55; Vol.2, f. 28.

Percy (R.), *secretary of the Westminster Committee*. Letters to Scrope Davies, 1818. Vol.2, ff. 71, 73.

Perren (John), *servant to Viscount Lowther*. Letter to ——— Bonnett, stable-keeper, of Farm St. Mews, 1815. Vol.2, f. 20.

Pole-Tylney-Long-Wellesley (William), *4th Earl of Mornington*, 1845. Invitation on behalf of himself and his wife to Scrope Davies, 1817. Vol.2, f. 34.

Pugh (*Rev*. William), *of Trinity College, Cambridge*. Letter to Scrope Davies, n.d. Vol.2, f. 165.

Pugilistic Club. Invitation to Scrope Davies, 1816. Vol.2, f. 26.

Rennell (Thomas), *of King's College, Cambridge*. Letter to Scrope Davies, 1814. Vol.2, f. 11.

Roberts (J.), *secretary of the St. James's, Westminster, Parochial Reform Committee*. Invitation to Scrope Davies, 1819. Vol.2, f. 105.

St. Helena, *Island of*. Coastal profile, 1815. Vol.1, f. 123.

– Views and plan of Longwood House, 1816. Vol.1, ff. 125–127.

Sebastiani (*Comte* Horace Francois Bastien de), *French Marshal*. Letter to Scrope Davies, [?1815]. Vol.2, f. 24.

Stepney (Catherine), *novelist, wife of Sir Thomas Stepney, 8th Bart*. Letters to Scrope Davies, 1818, n.d. Vol.2, ff. 86, 168.

Stewart (*Lt.-Gen. Sir* William), *KB, GCB* 1815. Letter to Viscount Hood, 1814. Vol.2, f. 5.

Trevelyan (Raleigh), *of Netherwitton, Northumberland; miscellaneous writer*. Letters to Scrope Davies, 1814, 1818, 1819. Vol.2, ff. 19, 97, 103.

Turton (Thomas), *of St. Catherine's College, Cambridge; bishop of Ely* 1845. Letter to Scrope Davies, n.d. Vol.2, f. 169.

Vassall Fox (Henry Richard), *3rd Baron Holland*. Invitation, on behalf of himself and his wife, to Scrope Davies, 1818. Vol.2, f. 58.

Weatherby (J.), [*? the publisher of the Racing Calendar*]. Letter to John Hibbert, 1819. Vol.2, f. 109.

Webster (*Lady* Frances), *wife of James Wedderburn Webster*. Letters to Scrope Davies, 1818–1819. Vol.1, ff. 68–114.

Wellesley (Arthur), *1st Duke of Wellington*. Uncompleted *printed* invitation from, 1815. Vol.2, f. 25.

Wellington, *Duke of. v*. Wellesley (Arthur).

Wilmot *afterwards* Wilmot-Horton (Robert John), *3rd Bart* 1834. Letter to Scrope Davies, 1816. Vol.1, f. 39.

Wilson (*Maj-Gen. Sir* Robert Thomas), *General* 1841. Letter to W.T. Franklin, 1818. *Copy*. Vol.2, f. 48.

General Index

*Individuals are indexed under the names by which
they were best known to Scrope Davies.*

Alvanley, William Arden, 2nd Baron
(1789–1849), 53, 65, 69; letter to SBD,
73

Apperley, Charles James, 'Nimrod'
(1779–1843), 202

Arden, William, *see* Alvanley, Baron

Bankes, William John (1787–1855)
traveller, 32, 222

banks: Barclays, 2–7 *passim*; Biddulph, Cocks
Ridge and Co., 73, 96; Eaton and
Hammond, 56, 71, 73; James Esdaile and
Co., 73–74, 92; Hammersley, 76;
Hoare's, 94, 95; George, Caesar, Charles
and Edmund Hopkinson, 73; John
Mortlock and Sons, 73–4; Ransom and
Morland, 4, 5, 30, 73, and Byron, 5, 30,
Douglas Kinnaird a partner, 5, 30, 73

Barbey D'Aurevilly, Jules Amédée
(1808–1889): *Of Dandyism and of George
Brummell* (1845), 50, 51, 53

Barclays Bank, 1 Pall Mall East, *see* banks

Barnard, Edward (1717–1781) Provost of
Eton, 18

Becher, Rev. John Thomas (1770–1848),
letter from Byron, 46–7

Bentham, Jeremy (1748–1832) philosophical
reformer, 155, 156, 157

Berdmore, Rev. Samuel (c. 1676–1743)
SBD's great-grandfather, 11

Berdmore, Rev. Dr. Scrope (1709–1770)
SBD's grandfather, 11

Berdmore, Rev. Dr. Scrope, the younger
(1744–1814) SBD's uncle, Warden of
Merton College, Oxford, 12–13, 26

betting *see* sports and pastimes

Betty, William Henry West (1791–1874)
actor 'The Young Roscius', 91

Bickersteth, Henry, later 1st Baron Langdale
(1783–1851), 152, 154, 156, 170, 179,
180

Biddulph, Cocks Ridge and Co., bankers,
London, *see* banks

Birch and Hanson, solicitors, *see* Hanson,
John

Birch, John, solicitor, 76

Bolton, Samuel, solicitor, draws up Byron's
will 1811, 87

Bonaparte, Napoleon, Emperor of the
French: SBD's attitude to, 121, 144, 149,
210; dethroned 1814, 151; voyage to St
Helena, 2, 12, 225–7; drawings of, and of
Longwood House, St Helena, 4, plates 2a,
2b

boxing *see* sports and pastimes

Brighton, SBD, Byron and Hobhouse at,
47–9, 55

'British Forum', debating society, SBD
frequents, 45

Brooks's *see* clubs

Brougham, Henry Peter, later 1st Baron
Brougham and Vaux (1778–1868), 180;
hostility to Byron, 64, 140, 166, 170, 188

Bruce, Michael (1787–1861), 35, 158, 160,
165, plate 10; letter to Hobhouse about
dinner in honour of Major Cartwright,
167; proposes Hobhouse as candidate for
Westminster, 171; marriage, 167

Brummell, George Bryan, 'Beau'
(1778–1840), 20, 21, 29, 50, 51; clubs,
65; and SBD, 1, 52; involvement of SBD
in his financial affairs, 52–3; SBD's joke
about stolen by Byron, 32; SBD and
Hobhouse visit in exile, 121, 145; in exile,
4, 192, 199, 205, 215, 217

Burdett, Sir Francis (1770–1844), Bt.,
M.P., radical reformer, 9, 141, 148, 171,
178; clubs, Brooks's, 150, Hampden,
148, Rota, 152, Union, 65; family, 166;
gout, 158; politics, 147, 150, 152, 153,
155, 156, 159–62, 171, 178–9, 184–5,
187, 209, election and chairing 1818,
162–5, 168, and dinner in honour of Major
Cartwright, 167; SBD's friendship with,
56, 141, 143; SBD's quarrel with,
189–90; SBD with 1818, 10, 166, 167,

168–9; Hobhouse and Kinnaird with 1818, 10, 166–7, 168–9; Hobhouse with 1819, 187; and Countess of Oxford, 147–8, 168, 178

Burdett, Susannah (d. 1886): and SBD, 169; and Hobhouse, 166

Byron, Anne Isabella, Lady, 'Annabella' (1792–1860) wife of the poet: and Bryon, engagement to, 98, marriage to, 98–9, separation crisis, 100–17, Byron's opinion of in 1817, 140, 177; opinion of Byron's friends, 98–9; and J. Hobhouse, 107–8; letters from Augusta Leigh, 98, 100–1, 102, 131–2, 134, 135; letter to Augusta Leigh, 102, meeting with, 107; letters to her mother, 106, 116; SBD hears strange reports of 1829, 195

Byron, Catherine (1765–1811) mother of the poet, 74, 75, 83–4

Byron, George Anson, 7th Baron (1789–1868) cousin of the poet, 87, 100, 101, 103, 104

Byron, George Gordon, 6th Baron (1788–1824) poet: accused of atheism, 98, 175; letter to J. Becher, 46–7; biographies, 195–6, 203–4, 206–8; and Bonaparte, 121, 144, 149; boxing, 52, 66, 96; at Brighton, 47–9, 55; and H. Brougham, 64, 140, 166, 170, 188; and G. Brummell, 32, 50; and F. Burdett, 147; and Cambridge, 29, 30, 43, 64, 87–8, 98, 152; attacks Castlereagh, 175, 177; at Cheltenham, 56, 91; on J. Claridge, 34; H. Clarke attacks, 47; clubs, 66, 150; letter to R. Dallas, 32, 33–4; as dandy, 49–50; and SBD, supposed to be writing Byron's biography, 203–4, 206–8, at Brighton with, 47–9, 55, visits at Cambridge, 87–8, 98, caricature of Byron by, 39, plate 4, owned Byron's chair, 196, at Cheltenham with, 56, 91, Byron gives MS. of *Childe Harold*, Canto III, 125, 129–31, opinion of *Don Juan*, Canto I, 174–7, preferred each other as second in duels, 63, on SBD's exile, 192, 193–4, financial involvement with, 74–83, 89–96, friendship, 1, 5, 8, 9, 29–42, 43, 46, 76–8, 120, 135, 173, visits Byron at Geneva, 120–9, letters from, 33, 41, 42, 47, 55, 64, 69, 76–7, 78–9, 82, 83–4, 85–6, 86, 91, 92, 93, 138–9, 140–2, 142–3, 171–2, letters to,

33, 34, 39, 41, 55, 79–80, 84, 86–7, 89, 93, 94–5, 95, 103, 136–8, 139–40, 164–5, 173, 176–7, 218–20, 222, SBD offers Byron's letters to Augusta Leigh, 194, first meeting, 31, exchange miniatures, 2, 66, 194, plate 6, at Newstead, 86, Byron's opinion of, 9, 32, 33, 35, 46, 49, 55, 63, 64, 80, 84, 88, 89, 103, 129, 130, 137, 153, 154, 165, 173, 176, 192, 193, his opinion of Byron, 41, *Parisina* dedicated to, 8, 42, *The Prisoner of Chillon*, takes MS. to J. Murray, 129–31, quarrels, 31, 94–5, his advice respected by Byron, 32, given Byron's rings by Augusta Leigh, 194–5, part in separation crisis, 9, 99, 103–17, 227–8, in Byron's Will, 87; death, 194; drinking, 36, 43–5, 47, 48, 96, 100, 111, 117, 118, 119, 120, 132, 138, 151, 153, 184; letter to H. Drury, 36; duelling, 62–4, 140, 188; and J. Edleston, 38–9; financial affairs, bank accounts, *see subject heading* banks, and SBD, 74–83, 89–91, 91–6, in debt, 74–83, 87, 97, 99, 102, and Mrs Massingberd, 74–5, 78, 79, 81, 90, 94; gambling *see subject heading* sports and pastimes; and J. Hobhouse, letters from, 38, 39, 46, 71, 120, 122, 156, 160, 163, 166, 169, 174–6, 183, 187, 193, letters to, 12, 33, 34, 35, 40, 45, 46, 49, 63, 82–3, 87, 120, 123, 141, 153, 154, 164–5, 173, 176, 183, 185, 192, 193, friendship with, 29–31, 34, 41, 47–9, 90, 94, 98–9, 100–1, 164–5, 173, 188, Byron's opinion of, 33, 34, 35, 154, 164–5, 173, Byron's *Siege of Corinth* dedicated to, 41–2, visits Byron at Geneva, 120–9, tours Greece with, 34, 36, 41, 76, tours Italy with, 135–43; and F. Hodgson, 33, 86, 139, 193–4; and D. Kinnaird, 5, 30, 175, 176, 192, letters to, 40, 49–50, 63, 93–4, 130, 161, 173, 185, 188, Byron's opinion of, 39–40, and separation crisis, 99, 103, 105, 111, 116, 117, 119, 120; and Caroline Lamb, 38, 97, 105, 132; and Augusta Leigh, 74, 97, 105, 135, 152, 172, 173, 'Epistle' to, 124, 132–5, letters to, 123–4, 125, 135, 140, offered Byron's letters by SBD, 194, and Byron's marriage and separation, 98, 100–16, gives Byron's rings to SBD, 194, 'Stanzas' to, 124, 132–5; marriage and separation, 98–117, 140, 149, 177, 195; and C.S. Matthews, 29–31, 33–4, 36, 42, 83–6, 221; and Lady Milbanke, 185; mistresses, 46–8, 119, 123, 132, 135, 137, 188 *see also* Caroline Lamb, Augusta Leigh, Lady Oxford, Frances Webster; and Thomas Moore, 64, 135, 139; and his mother, 74, 75, 83–4; and J. Murray, 39, 86, 98, 124, 129, 130, 131, 133, 137, 176, 177, 194, 202; Newstead Abbey, 86, 87, 89, 90–1, 94, 97, 139, 142; and Lady Oxford, 38, 92, 148; and Margaret Parker, 39; politics, 121, 144, 146–8, 152–4, 161, 165, 173, 175, 183–5; and Elizabeth Rawdon, 35, 91; Rochdale, 77, 81, 86, 139; sexual activities *see subject heading* sex; and P.B. Shelley, 123–4; and R. Southey, 175–6; suicide, 33, 48–9, 87, 104, 116, 139; swimming *see subject heading* sports and pastimes; E. Trelawny on, 49, 198–9; and Lady Frances Webster, 38; Will, 76, 80, 81, 87; and R. Wilmot, 103, 107–15; Works *see individual titles*

Cartwright, Major John (1740–1824) political reformer, 148, 155, 156, 160, 184, plate 10; dinner in honour of 1818, 167–8, 169; challenges Hobhouse to a duel, 63; and Westminster election 1819, 181, 182

Castlereagh, Robert Stewart, Viscount, later 2nd Marquis of Londonderry (1769–1822) statesman: attacked by Byron in *Don Juan*, 175–7

Charlotte Sophia, Queen of England (1744–1818): at Eton, 24, 25; death, 172–3

Cheltenham: SBD at with Byron, 56, 91

Childe Harold's Pilgrimage, by Byron, Cantos I, II, 75, Canto III, 4, 7, 38, 121, 123, 124, 125, 129, 130–1, 133, 190, Canto IV, 32

Clairmont, Clara Mary Jane 'Claire' (1798–1879), 123, 124, 126, 134

Clarendon Coffee-House *see* coffee-houses

Claridge, John Thomas (1782–1868), Byron contrasts with SBD, 34

Clarke, Hewson (1787–1832?) writer: attacks on Byron, 47

Claughton, Thomas: attempts to buy Newstead, 90, 91, 92–3, 94, 95, 98

clubs, 80; Brooks's, 65, 66, 120, 150, 162, 178, 190, plate 8b; Cocoa Tree, 66, 78, 80, 95, 96, 103, 151, 152; Hampden, 148, 153; Jockey Club, 56, 60, 67; Pugilistic Club, 67; Rota, 152–3, 155–6, 179, 183; Rackets, 80; tennis club, proposals for foundation of, 67, 68–9; Union, 65, 71, 72, 80, 117, 120, 190; Watiers, 65, 71, 72, 100, 103, 111, 201; Whig, at Cambridge, 146; White's, 53, 65, 66, 201

Cocoa Tree *see* clubs

coffee-houses: Clarendon, 117; Robert Joy's, 43; George's, 110; Holme's, 186; Piazza, 52, 109, 152, 162, 181; St James's 67, 115, 192, 193; Stevens's, 63

Colborne, Nicholas William Ridley, later 1st Baron (1779–1854), 113, 114

Coleridge, Samuel Taylor (1772–1834) poet: Hobhouse belittles, 175–6

Conversations of Lord Byron (1824), by Thomas Medwin, 194

Courtney, William Prideaux (1845–1913): *Eight Friends of the Great* (1910), 8

Coutts, Thomas (1735–1822) banker, 147

cricket *see* sports and pastimes

Crockford, William (1775–1844) of the gambling club, 56, 59

Dallas, Robert Charles (1754–1824) miscellaneous writer: letter from Byron, 32, 33–4

dandies, 13, 20–2, 27–8, 37, 42, 43–74 *passim*, 122, 170, 183, 201, 212

Davies, John (1779–1835) eldest brother of SBD, 1

Davies, Rev. Richard (1747–1825) father of SBD, 11, 13, 15, 20, 26, 190; miniature of, 2

Davies, Samuel Decimus (1797–1824) youngest brother of SBD, 11–12, 223–7; receives allowance from SBD, 12, 70; SBD tries to help career, 191; sends home drawings of Napoleon, 4; portrait of, 2

Davies, Scrope Berdmore (1782–1852):
I. Chronology
    1782: born at Horsley, Glos., 11
    1794–1802: at Eton, 14–28
    1802: admitted to King's College, Cambridge, 27
    1805(?): makes friends with J. Hobhouse, 31
    1806: tours Scotland with J. Hobhouse,

31, 60–1

1807: makes friends with Byron, 31

1808: in London and Brighton with Byron 43–5, 47–9; guarantees loan for Byron, 74–5, 89–90, 93–4

1809: Byron goes abroad leaving SBD responsible for much of his debt, 74–82

1811: Byron returns, 83; C.S. Matthews drowned, 83–6

1812: at Cheltenham with Byron, 56, 91

1813: challenges Lord Foley to a duel, 64

1814: Byron discharges his debt to SBD, 93–6; SBD encourages J. Hobhouse to seek election as M.P. for Cambridge University, 150–2

1816: with Byron during separation crisis, 100–19, 227–8; travels to Geneva with J. Hobhouse to visit Byron, 56, 120–9, 190; conveys Byron's MSS. to J. Murray, 129–31; assists Murray in defeating an imposter, 130–1; advises Augusta Leigh over publication of Byron's 'Stanzas to Augusta', 132–5

1818: chosen a member of the 'Rota', 152–4; helps Burdett and Kinnaird fight the election in Westminster, 154–62; visits Burdett at Ramsbury, 166–9; meets Thomas Moore, 168–9

1819: helps J. Hobhouse fight by-election at Westminster, 170–3, 178–82; advises suppression of Don Juan, Canto I, 174–7; involved in attempted betting coup, 57–60; in increasing financial trouble, 185–9

1820: 2 Jan., bids farewell to J. Hobhouse prior to fleeing from his creditors, 189–91

1824: writes to Augusta Leigh from Ostende on the death of Byron, 194–6

1827: meets T.C. Grattan in Brussels, 196–8

1828: writes to F. Hodgson from Ostende, 199–200

1835: meets T. Raikes in Paris, 201–2

1836: writes to J. Murray from Paris thanking for the gift of Byron's *Works*, 202–3

1837: meets Thomas Moore in Paris, 205; meets T. Grattan in Ostende, 205–6, and Calais, 206; writes from

Dunkirk about proposed memoirs, 206-8

1838: writes from Dunkirk to T. Raikes, 209–12

1840: writes to T. Raikes from Abbeville, 212–13

1849: meets T. Grattan in Boulogne, 213–14

1851: meets J. Hobhouse in London, 215;

1852: 23/24 May, dies in Paris, 216–17

II. PERSONAL CHARACTERISTICS

Appearance and manners, 32, 33, 51, 66–7, 196–9, 204–5, 213, 216; betting *see subject heading* sports and pastimes; enthusiasm for Bonaparte, 121, 144, 149, 210; boxing *see subject heading* sports and pastimes; clubs *see subject heading*; cricket, 22–3; as dandy, 20–22, 49–50, 51–4, 55, 88; drunkenness, 13, 23, 43, 47, 48–9, 83, 87–8, 96, 98, 109, 117, 119, 120, 153, 192, 196–7, 201–2, 205, 211, 213, 214; duelling, 63–4, 169, 179–80, 190; family, 1, 2, 11, 12, 190, 191; finances, 13, 15–23, 26, 27, 31, 51, 52–4, 57, 60, 64–5, 69–74, 88, 117, 120, 143, 151, 185–6, 188–91, 210–11, 214, 217, guarantee and loan to Byron, 74–83, 87, 89–96; gambling, 39, 43, 46, 53, 88, 103, 117, 120, 146, 151, hazard, 45–6; generosity, 53–4, 55, 190; horse racing *see subject heading*; Fellow of King's College, Cambridge, 23, 27, 46, 54–5, 71, 143, 151, 192; lodgings, 69–70; marriage and celibacy, 39, 82–3, 169; memoirs, 1, 203–4, 206–8, 214, 216–7; miniature of, 2, 66, caption to plate 6; politics, 9–10, 52, 65, 144–6, 149, 150–173 *passim*, 178–184 *passim*, 192, 198, 200, 202, 209, 212–13; sexual activities *see subject heading* sex; shooting *see subject heading* sports and pastimes; sports and pastimes *see subject heading*, 33, 48–9, 87, 139; swimming *see subject heading* sports and pastimes; tennis *see subject heading* sports and pastimes; discovery of his trunk, 2, 3–7, plate 1

Davies, Rev. Thomas (1785–1840) brother of

General Index

SBD, 1; a rogue, 11, 190; at Eton, 13, 15, 17, 26; at Oxford, 11, 26

Don Juan, by Byron, 50, 183, Canto I, 174–7, Canto XI, 50, 185

drinking, 43–5, 96, 98, 100–1, 109, 117, 118, 119, 153, 197, 205, 211, 213; at Cambridge, 55, 64, 87–8; at Eton, 15, 23

Drury, Henry (1778–1841) assistant master at Harrow: letter from Byron, 36; letter to SBD, 138

Drury, William (1792–1878) chaplain of the English Chapel, Brussels, 200

Drury Lane Theatre, 30, 100, 111, 119

Eaton and Hammond, bankers at Newmarket, *see* banks

Edinburgh Review, 47, 157

Edleston, John (1790–1811) chorister at Trinity College, Cambridge: SBD had copies of Byron's poems to, 38–9

Ellice, Edward (1781–1863) politician, 175, 177

Elphinstone, Margaret Mercer, Comtesse de Flahaut, Baroness Keith, Baroness Nairne (1788–1867), 124, 132–5

'Epistle to Augusta', by Byron, 124, 132–5

Esdaile, Sir James and Co., bankers, *see* banks

Eton College, 12, 13, 216; ceremonies, Electiontide, 18–19, 23, 25, Montem, 24–6, plate 3, ripping, 27; cricket, 22–3; condition of the Scholars, 13–15; SBD, bills from the College and tradesmen, 15–23, influence on, 27, 28, 54

Examiner, 127, 151

Fox, Charles James (1749–1806) statesman, 65, 144, 145, 179

Fox, Elizabeth Vassall *see* Holland, Lady

Fox, Henry Richard Vassall *see* Holland, Baron

Fugitive Pieces, by Byron, 39

gambling *see* sports and pastimes

Geneva, SBD visits Byron at, 120–9; plays tennis at, 67, 129

George III (1738–1820) King of England; his love of Eton, 15, 24, 25; death, 193

George's Coffee-House *see* coffee-houses

Godwin, Mary Wollstonecraft (1797–1851) later wife of P.B. Shelley, 123, 124, 126, 195

Gore, Catherine Grace Frances (1799–1861) novelist and dramatist: *Cecil; or, the adventures of a coxcomb* (1841), 51

Grattan, Thomas Colley (1792–1864) writer and journalist: *Beaten Paths and those who trod them* (1862) gives account of SBD in exile, 8, 196–9, 204–8, 213–14, 217

Gronow, Captain Rees Howell (1794–1865): *Reminiscences* (1888) gives account of SBD, 8, 41, 51, 53–4; SBD in exile, 212, 214–15

Guiccioli, Teresa, Countess (1800–1873), 188

Hammersley, bankers, *see* banks

Hampden Club *see* clubs

Hanson, John, solicitor: and Byron, 76, 77, 79, 80, 81, 82, 83, 86, 87, 90, 91, 92–3, 94; and Byron's separation, 106, 108, 111–13, 116; letter to SBD 1811, 83; and J. Hobhouse, 170

Harley, Lady Anne (b. 1803), 169

Harley, Jane Elizabeth, *see* Oxford, Countess of

Harley, Lady Jane (b. 1796), 148, 152

Harrington, Sarah, 'dame' at Eton, 17, 20

Harrogate, SBD at, 55, 86

Hawtrey, Edward Craven (1789–1862) Head Master and Provost of Eton: informs F. Hodgson of SBD's death, 216

Heath, George (1747–1822) Head Master of Eton, 17

Hints from Horace, by Byron, 39, 143

History of a Six Weeks Tour (1817) by Mary and P.B. Shelley, 127

Hoare's bank *see* banks

Hobhouse, John Cam, later 1st Lord Broughton de Gyfford (1786–1869), 7–8, 30, 34, 41–2, 215–16; abroad, 34, 36, 76, 120–9, 135, 136, 137, 140, 150; enthusiasm for Bonaparte, 144, 149, 151; at Brighton with Byron and SBD, 47–9; brother, 168–9; and M. Bruce, 167, 171; visits Brummell in exile 121, 145; and F. Burdett, 166, 187; and S. Burdett, 166; and Byron, 29–31, 34, 41, 47–9, 90, 94, 98–9, 100–1, 164–5, 173, 188, letters from, 12, 33, 34, 35, 40, 45, 46, 49, 63, 82–3, 87, 120, 123, 141, 153, 154, 164–5, 173, 176, 183, 185, 192, 193, letters to, 38, 39, 46, 71, 120, 122, 156, 160, 163, 166, 169, 174–6, 183, 187, 193, views on Byron, 29, Byron's views on, 33, 34, 35, 154, 164–5, 173, on

General Index

journey to Greece with, 34, 36, 41, 76,
219, on journey to Italy with, 135–43.
quarrels with, 164, separation crisis,
99–117 *passim*, opinion of *Don Juan*,
174–6, and Byron's Will, 87; clubs, 152;
belittles S.T. Coleridge, 175–6; and SBD,
caricature of Hobhouse by, 39, plate 4,
bids farewell, 189, financial affairs, 31,
71–2, 185–6, 188–90, letters from, 71–2,
85, 179, letters to, 80, 85, 136, 157–8,
180, meets in London 1851, 215, opinion
of, 31, 39, 53, 55, 71, 88, 185, 190, 193,
215, SBD's opinion of Hobhouse, 42, 141,
142, quarrels, 48–9, 179–80, rivalry for
Byron's friendship, 31, 41–2, stays with,
in Cambridge, 151, in London, 69, 103,
tours Scotland with, 31, 60–1, tour to
Switzerland with, 56, 120–9, 190;
duelling, 63, 113, 115; father, 145, 156,
186; financial affairs, 76, 90; and Harley
family, 147–8; and D. Kinnaird, 30, 40,
120, 150, 152, 156, 171, 189;
imprisonment, 150, 186–90, 192–3; and
Augusta Leigh, 99, 100–1, 108, 116; and
C.S. Matthews, 29–31, 33, 36–7, 42, 84,
85; ostracised, 166, 170; and F. Place,
170, 178, 180–1, 182; and J. Polidori,
117, 118, 120, 128; politics, 144–9, 154,
184–95, 215–16; attempts to enter
Parliament and electioneering 1814,
150–2, 1818, 154–65, 1819, 170–3,
177–83, and Major Cartwright, 63,
167–8, 169, father a hindrance, 145, 156,
182, imprisoned for breach of privilege,
186–9, 193, 'Peterloo', 184–5; sexual
activities *see subject heading* sex; works,
*Historical Illustrations of the Fourth Canto of
Childe Harold* (1818), 137, *Narrative of the
separation of Lord and Lady Byron*, 99,
pamphlets, 151, 156, 186–7

Hodgson, Francis (1781–1852) Provost of
Eton: on SBD and Byron, 33; letters, from
Byron, 86, 193–4, to Byron, 139, from
SBD, 199, 200, from E. Hawtrey, 216
from Augusta Leigh, 107, 116

Holland, Elizabeth Vassall Fox, Lady
(1770–1845): cuts Hobhouse, 162

Holland, Henry Richard Vassall Fox, 3rd
Baron (1773–1840), 4, 214; and Byron,
147, 172; mediator in Byron's separation,
106; and SBD, 149, 172; Holland House
Whigs, 153, 159, 174; and Bonaparte,

149; falls out with Westminster
Reformers, 159, 162, 166, 170, 174
Holme's Coffee-House *see* coffee-houses
Holmes, James (1777–1860) painter and
miniaturist: tells story of SBD, 66–7; takes
miniatures of SBD and Byron, 2, plate 6,
194
Hopkinson, George, Caesar, Charles and
Edmund, bankers, *see* banks
horse racing *see* sports and pastimes
Horton, Sir Robert John Wilmot — *see* Wilmot
hotels: Batt's, 69; Limmer's, 69;
d'Angleterre, Abbeville, 212; Royal,
Dieppe, 212
Houghton, Richard Monckton Milnes, 1st
Baron (1809–1885), 57
Hours of Idleness, by Byron, 29, 47
Hughes, Edward Hughes Ball 'Golden Ball'
(d. 1863), 209–12
Hughes, Kit, U.S. Minister at Brussels, 198,
214
Hunt, Henry 'Orator' (1773–1835) radical
politician, 155, 156, 158, 160, 171, 180,
184, plate 10; Byron's views on, 185
Hunt, James Henry Leigh (1784–1859),
116–17, 127; editor of the *Examiner*, 151
'Hymn to Intellectual Beauty', by P.B.
Shelley, 4, 123, 126–7

Jockey Club *see* clubs
Jones, Edward, junior, Fellow of King's
College, Cambridge: resignation allows
SBD to go up to King's, 27
Robert Joy's Coffee-House *see* coffee-houses
Joyce, Michael, *My Friend H* (1948), 8

Keate, John (1773–1852) Head Master of
Eton, 17–18
Keith, Baroness *see* Elphinstone, Margaret
Mercer
Keppel, Maria, Douglas Kinnaird's mistress,
39–40
King's College, Cambridge: annual visit of
Provost to Eton, 18–19; choice of Scholars
for, from among Scholars of Eton, 23–4;
Scholarships and Fellowships at, 13–14;
SBD admitted to, 27; SBD's duties as
Fellow, 54–5, 71, 143, 192; SBD and
Hobhouse dine in Hall, 151; claims SBD's
papers, 6
Kinnaird, Douglas James William

(1788–1830) banker, 5, 30, 40, 139; and F. Burdett, 10, 166–7, 168–9; and Byron, 5, 30, 39–40, 173, 192, on *Don Juan*, 175, 176, financial advisor, 93–4, 139, 142, 183, letters from, 40, 49–50, 63, 93–4, 130, 161, 173, 185, 188, and separation crisis, 99, 103, 105, 111, 116, 117, 119, 120, visits in Venice, 141; clubs, 120, 152, 190; and SBD, 160, 179–80, 189, 192, SBD on, 143; and Drury Lane Theatre, 30, 119; and J. Hobhouse, 40, 120, 156, 171, 189, opinion of, 152, Hobhouse's opinion of Kinnaird, 30, rivalry, 150, 152; mistress, Maria Keppel, 39–40; Augusta Leigh's opinion of, 30; politics, 144–5, 149, 152, 154, 156–60, 161, 170–1, chairs dinner for Major Cartwright, 167–9, and Bishop's Castle, 30, 150, 183, M.P., 150, 156, 183, and Westminster, 156–60, 170–1, 178–83; partner in Ransom and Morland, 5, 30, 73; at Trinity College, Cambridge, 30

Lalla Rookh, by Thomas Moore, 138, 139, 142
Lamb, Lady Caroline (1785–1828), 150; and Byron, 38, 97; spreads rumours about Byron, 105, 132; and SBD, 38; canvasses against Hobhouse in Westminster 1819, 182
Lamb, Charles (1775–1834) essayist: SBD belittles, 205–6, 214
Lamb, Hon. George (1784–1834) politician and writer, 105; quarrels with SBD, 181; opposes Hobhouse in Westminster election 1819, 181–2
Lamb, Hon. William *see* Melbourne, Viscount
Langdale, Baron *see* Bickersteth, Henry
'To Laughter', by P.B. Shelley, 7
Leigh, Augusta (1783–1851) Byron's half-sister, 38, 100, 124, 132–5; and Byron, 74, 97, 152, 172, 173, letters to, 132, 185, letters from, 97, 123–4, 125, 135, 140, with the Byrons at Piccadilly Terrace, 98, in separation crisis, 100–16 *passim*, ostracised, 116, *Epistle to Augusta*, 124, 132–5, gives Byron's rings to SBD, 194, offered Byron's letters by SBD, 194; and Lady Byron, letters to, 100–1, 102, 131–2, 134, 135, letter from, 102, meeting with, 107; and SBD, 97, 131–5,

138, 185, letters from, 194–5; and Hobhouse, 99, 100–1, 108, 116; and F. Hodgson, letters to, 107, 116; and D. Kinnaird, 30; and J. Murray, 132–5; and R. Wilmot, letters to, 107, 111
Londonderry, 2nd Marquis *see* Castlereagh, Viscount
Luddites, 146–7
Lushington, Stephen (1782–1873) Civilian, 101, 106, 107, 109, 110
Lyon, John, provides plot for SBD's grave in Paris, 217

Manfred, by Byron, 131, 133, 137, 139, 142, 210–12
Manton, Joseph (1766?–1835) gunsmith, 62–3, 71
Massingberd, Mrs. (d. 1812), 74–5, 78, 79, 81, 90, 94
Matthews, Charles Skinner (1782–1811): boxing, 86, 221; Byron on, 32, 33–4, 86; friendship with Byron and Hobhouse, 29–31, 33–4, 36–7, 42, 83–6, 221; and SBD, 31, 83–6; drowned, 9, 83–6; on Hobhouse, 42; homosexuality, 36; politics, 144, 146; caricature portrait of, by SBD, 79, plate 4; at Trinity College, Cambridge, 29
Maxwell, Sir Murray (1775–1831) Captain R.N.: stands for Westminster 1818, 158–162, plate 10; SBD makes jokes about, 160–1; stands for Westminster 1819, 171, 174; withdraws, 178
Medwin, Thomas (1788–1869), said to be writing biography of Byron, 195
Melbourne, Elizabeth, Viscountess (d. 1818) wife of 1st Viscount, 98, 105
Melbourne, William Lamb, 2nd Viscount (1779–1848) statesman and prime minister, 215
Meyler, Richard (1792–1818) M.P.: and Brummell's downfall, 53; Lord Alvanley's views on, 53
Milbanke, Anne Isabella *see* Byron, Lady
Milbanke, Judith, Hon. Lady (1751–1822) mother of Lady Byron: and her daughter's separation, 101; letters from Annabella, 106, 116; Byron on, 185; letter from Mrs. Clermont, 109
Milbanke, Sir Ralph, Bart. (1747–1825) father of Lady Byron, 102–3; letter to Byron, 101–2, letter from Byron, 102

General Index

Milnes, Richard Monckton *see* Houghton, Baron

Milnes, Richard Rodes (1785–1835): letters to SBD re betting coup 1819, 57–60

Milnes, Robert Pemberton (1784–1858) M.P., 57; letter to SBD, 231

Moers, Ellen: *The Dandy* (1960), 51

money-lenders, 75; Thomas and Riley, 76, 89, 90

'Mont Blanc', by P.B. Shelley, 4, 123, 126–8

Moore, Doris Langley, *The Late Lord Byron* (1961), 8

Moore, Thomas (1779–1852) poet, 124, 138, 175, 214; letters from Byron, 64, 135; stays with F. Burdett, 10, 168–9; meets SBD at F. Burdett's, 168–9, SBD helps with his *Tom Crib's Memorial to Congress*, 169, 233, letter to SBD, 233, SBD meets in Paris, 205; on Lady F. Webster, 232–3

Mortlock, John, and Sons, bankers at Cambridge *see* banks

Murray, John (1778–1843) publisher, 118, 121, 125, 130–1, 133, 134, 157, 173; letters from Byron, 39, 86, 98, 124, 129, 130, 133, 176, 177, letters to Byron, 131, 137; SBD's opinion of his conduct towards Byron in 1816, 202, offers SBD a copy of Byron's *Works*, 202, letters from SBD, 134, 202, and SBD's proposed memoirs, 203–4, 206; letter to Augusta Leigh, 134

Nairne, Baroness *see* Elphinstone, Margaret Mercer

Napoleon *see* Bonaparte, Napoleon

Newmarket *see* sports and pastimes, horse racing

Newstead Abbey, Byron's house and estate *see* Byron, Lord

Noel, Judith, Hon. Lady *see* Milbanke

Noel, Sir Ralph, Bart. *see* Milbanke

Noel-Long, Edward (1788–1809) friend of Byron, 29

Norton, Solomon, 52, 109

Oxford, Jane Elizabeth, Countess of (1772–1824), 150; and H. Bickersteth, 152; and F. Burdett, 147; and Byron, 92, 97, 148; and SBD, 38, 56, 149, 168; and J. Hobhouse, 147–8, 168, 178; politics, 147–8, 178, 179

Palmerston, Henry John Temple, 3rd Viscount (1784–1865) statesman, 150–2, 209, 213, 215

Parisina, by Byron, 8, 41–2

Parker, Margaret (d. 1802) cousin of Byron, 39

Parr, Samuel (1747–1825) 'The Whig Dr. Johnson': correspondence with SBD, 31

Perceval, Lady, 47

Perceval, Hon. Spencer (1762–1812) statesman, 145

Perceval, Spencer (1795–1859) son of the preceding: note to SBD, 88

Piazza Coffee-House *see* coffee-houses

Place, Francis (1771–1854) radical reformer, 153, 155, 157, 158, 159, 161, 170, 171, 187; supports D. Kinnaird, 170; his 'Report of the General Meeting of the Committee' damages Hobhouse 1819, 178, 180–1, 182; Byron on, 165

Polidori, Dr. John William (1795–1821) physician and author, 117, 118, 120, 123, 128, 132, 136–7, 139; letter to Hobhouse, 120

politics: Byron in House of Lords, 146–8; electioneering, 154, 157–62, 171–3, 178–82; 'genteel reformers', 155, 158, 159, 178, 183, 184; Hampden Club, 148, 153; 'Peterloo' massacre 1819, 184–5; 'philosophical' radicals, 155; radical reformers, 52, 144, 147, 148, 149, 150, 152–5, 159, 162, 165, 167–9, 171, 178, 179, 181–3, 184, 186–7; 'Rota' Club, 152–3, 155–6, 179, 183; Tories, 144, 145, 147, 155, 158–9, 160–2, 171, 178, 182, 200; Westminster Committee (of reformers), 153, 155, 157–8, 159, 160, 164, 171, 178, 181, 183, 184; Whigs, 65, 142, 144–6, 147, 149, 150, 153–5, 157–62 *passim*, 166, 169–70, 171, 174, 178, 181–2, 183, 184–5, 186, 209, 212–13, Whig Club at Cambridge, 146

Ponsonby, Colonel Sir Frederic Cavendish (1783–1837): plays tennis with SBD, 68

The Prisoner of Chillon, by Byron, 38, 123, 124, 126, 130, 133

Pugilistic Club *see* clubs

Quennell, Peter: *Byron, the Years of Fame* (1935), 8

Rackets Club *see* clubs

General Index

radical reform *see* politics

Raikes, Thomas 'Apollo' (1777–1848) dandy and diarist, 146; *Diary* (1856 and 1857) gives account of SBD in exile, including letters, 201–2, 208–13

Rawdon, Elizabeth Anne (1793–1874), 35, 91, 149

Riley and Thomas *see* money-lenders

Rogers, Samuel (1763–1855), poet, 117

Romilly, Sir Samuel (1757–1818) law reformer, 103, 111, 157, 159–62; death, 170, 171

Rota Club *see* clubs

St. James's Coffee-House *see* coffee-houses

The Satirist, 47

Sawbridge, Colonel: makes loan to Byron, 76, 81, 94, 96

Scrope, Martha, great-grandmother of SBD, 11

Segati, Marianna, mistress of Byron, 135

sex: sexual activities of Byron and his friends, 35–40; Byron, homosexuality, 36–7, 38, 97, 105, mistresses, 38, 46–8, 135, 137, 188, rumours re sodomy and incest, 103, 105, 108, 109, 119, 132, whoring, 43, 45, 46–8, 49; SBD, takes up Byron's discarded mistresses, 38, 168, 199, not homosexual, 9, 38–9, in love, 169, contemplates marriage, 82–3, whoring, 37–8, 45, 49, 51, suffering from infernal —, 142; J. Hobhouse, *mauvaise honte,* 35, whoring, 36, 'frightful suspicions', 97; D. Kinnaird, fidelity to his mistress, 39–40, 'frightful suspicions', 97; C.S. Matthews, homosexuality, 36–7; Lady Oxford, 147, 148, 150; sexual *mores* of upper classes, 150

Shelley, Mary *see* Godwin

Shelley, Percy Bysshe (1792–1822) poet: friendship with Byron, 49, 123, 124, 125; returns to England with Byron's MSS. 1816, 124, 133; and Byron's 'Epistle to Augusta', 134; notebook found in SBD's trunk, 3, 4, 126–8; poems, 'Hymn to Intellectual Beauty', 'Mont Blanc', 'To Laughter' and 'Upon the wandering winds', 123, 126–8, 228–9

Sheridan, Richard Brinsley (1751–1816), 121, 150, 197; clubs, Union, 65

shooting *see* sports and pastimes

Siege of Corinth, by Byron, 41

Sligo, 2nd Marquis of, 218

Southey, Robert (1774–1843) poet: attacked by Byron in *Don Juan,* 175–6

sports and pastimes: betting, 56, 57–8, on cricket, 22, hazard, 46, horses, 56–60, 117, tennis, 67–8, SBD as bookmaker, 57; boxing, 52, 66–7, 108, 138, and Byron, 96, clubs, 67, and SBD, 52, 66–7, and Matthews, 86, 221; cricket, 22–3; duelling, 62–4, 113, 115, 138, 140, 169, 188; gambling, 15, 27, 39, 43, 45–6, 48, 57, 64–6, 71, 88, 103, 117, 120, 146, 151, 190, 191, hazard, 45–6, 56, 64, macao, 71; horse-racing, 56–60, 70, 117, 122, Newmarket, 54, 56–7, 71, 73, 80, 91, 117, 122, 191; shooting, 60–3; swimming, 18, 48, 86; tennis, 67–70, 129, 209–12

'Stanzas to Augusta', by Byron, 132–5

Stevens's Coffee-House *see* coffee-houses

Stewart, Robert *see* Castlereagh, Viscount

suicide: and Byron, 33, 48, 49, 79; and SBD, 33, 79

swimming *see* sports and pastimes

Switzerland: SBD and Hobhouse visit, 56, 122–5, 128–9

Tavistock, Francis, Marquis of, later 7th Duke of Bedford (1788–1861), 159, 162, 170

tennis, real, *see* sports and pastimes

tennis club *see* clubs

Temple, Henry John *see* Palmerston, Viscount

Thomas, William: *The Philosophic Radicals: Nine Studies in Theory and Practice, 1817—1841* (1979), 10

Thomas and Riley *see* money-lenders

Tompkyns, John (d. 1849): Captain of Montem at Eton 1802, 25

Trelawny, Edward John (1792–1881) adventurer: on Byron, 49

Trinity College, Cambridge, 29–30

Tuthill, Sir George Leman (1772–1835) physician, 201

Union Club *see* clubs

Villiers, Mrs George, friend of Lady Byron, 133, 134, 135

Voltaire, François Marie Arouet de (1694–1778): appearance described to SBD and Hobhouse, 124

Walker, Adam (1731?–1821) lecturer in Natural Philosophy, 18

Washington, Capital of the U.S.A.: account of burning by British troops, 12, 223–5

Watiers *see* clubs

Webster, Lady Frances Caroline Wedderburn (1793–1837): and Byron, 38, 231–2; and SBD, 38, 199, 230–2, letters from, 38, 230–1; and Thomas Moore, 232–3; portrait, plate 7

Webster, Sir James Wedderburn, 137, 199, 222

Whigs *see* politics

White's *see* clubs

Wilmot, later Wilmot-Horton, Robert John, 3rd Bart. 1834 (1784–1841) cousin of Byron, 103; mediator in Byron separation crisis, 107, 108, 109, 110–15, letter to Byron, 111–12, letter from Byron, 113; letters to SBD and Hobhouse, 112–13, letters from SBD, 114–15, 227–8; letters for Augusta Leigh, 107, 111

Wilson, Sir Robert Thomas (1777–1849) soldier and politician, 152, 153–4, 156, 158, 160, 162, 195, 200

Wordsworth, William (1770–1850) poet: Hobhouse belittles, 175–6

Wynn, Frances Williams – (d. 1857), 47, 231–2; *Diaries of a Lady of Quality* (1864), 47, 231–2

Poetical Works

Lord Byron

George Gordon, Lord Byron, was one of the dominant influences
on the Romantic movement. His poetry has delighted subsequent
generations, as it delighted and scandalized his own, with its
persistent attacks on 'cant political, religious and moral', its energy,
and its lyrical beauty.

OPUS

Romantics, Rebels and Reactionaries

English Literature and its Background 1760–1830

Marilyn Butler

This book takes a fresh look at one of the most fertile periods in English literature, an age which produced writers such as Blake, Keats, Coleridge, Byron, Scott and Jane Austen.

'Learned and toughly factual survey of the English Romantics. Dr Butler is brilliantly acute ... at restoring to literary works the subdued political ticks and rumblings which the alarmed ears of their first readers would have picked up.' John Carey in the *Sunday Times*.

THE WORLD'S CLASSICS

Vathek

William Beckford

Edited with an introduction by Roger Lonsdale

Vathek, originally written in French, remains one of the strangest of eighteenth-century novels. Grotesque comedy alternates with evocative beauty in the story of the ruthless Caliph Vathek's journey to damnation. Pervading the whole of the novel is a strong element of self-indulgent personal fantasy on the part of Beckford himself, youthful millionaire, dreamer, and eventually social outcast. Byron, Poe, Mallarmé, and Swinburne are but a few of the literary figures who have admired *Vathek*'s imaginative power.

THE WORLD'S CLASSICS

Selected Letters of Sydney Smith

Edited by Nowell C. Smith

With an introduction by Auberon Waugh

The wit and charm of Sydney Smith runs throughout his letters as he comments on the people and events of his day with an eye for both the tiny detail at home and more general affairs. Himself a clergyman, he was ever ready to poke fun at the Church, in the nicest possible way. Those who took themselves too seriously were also subjects for his scorn. But he was not merely amusing – his outspokenness on literary, political and religious affairs betrayed a rare moral courage, which went alongside the warmth and generosity he showed in his daily life.

'No man writing in English combined wit and common sense in more nicely balanced proportions than Sydney Smith. . . . Auberon Waugh brings affection as well as insight to his introduction, and the whole book is one by no means to be missed.' David Williams in *Punch*.

OXFORD PAPERBACKS

The Wynne Diaries

The Adventures of Two Young Sisters in Napoleonic Europe

Edited by Anne Fremantle

New introduction by Christopher Hibbert

The diaries of Betsey and Eugenia Wynne provide one of the most detailed and vivid accounts we have of the Napoleonic era, as well as a delightfully amusing picture of the lives of two young women. The rich, rather unconventional Wynne family spent its time travelling in Europe with a large retinue of servants. The girls' diaries record the family's progress, their own romantic secrets, and later, when Betsey marries a captain in Nelson's navy, impressions of some of the Admiral's great sea-battles.

'The Wynne family, and especially the sister diarists, Betsey and Eugenia, are very good acquaintances to make.' Marghanita Laski in *Country Life*.